DATE DUE

THE
GNOSTIC
JUNG

and the Seven Sermons
to the Dead

Cover design by *Jane Evans*
Photograph of Jung by *Cartier-Bresson*

The Gnostic Jung

and the Seven Sermons to the Dead

Stephan A. Hoeller

This publication made possible with the assistance of the Kern Foundation

The Theosophical Publishing House
Wheaton, Ill. U.S.A.
Madras, India/London, England

 Printed on Recyclable Paper

Published by the Theosophical Publishing House, a depart-
ment of the Theosophical Society in America.

Library of Congress Cataloging in Publication Data
Hoeller, Stephan A.
    The gnostic Jung and The Seven Sermons to the dead.
    "A Quest book."
    "A Quest original."
    Includes bibliographical references and index.
    1. Jung, C.G. (Carl Gustav), 1875-1961. VII sermones ad
mortuos. 2. Occult sciences—Miscellanea. 3.
Gnosticism—Miscellanea. I. Title.
BF1999.J863H63   1982   299'93   82-50220
ISBN 0-8356-0573-6
ISBN 0-8356-0568-X (pbk.)

Printed in the United States of America

To Kristofer, a true son of Hermes, who
brought the medium of the Conjunction to
many, including the author.

Contents

Preface

The substance of the commentaries on the *Seven Sermons to the Dead* was delivered by the author in a class in the psychology of religion at the Institute for the Study of Religion East and West of the University of California at Los Angeles in the Spring Quarter of 1977. The Prologue, "Premonition of an Inescapable World of Shadows," was originally published in *Psychological Perspectives* (of the C.G. Jung Institute, Los Angeles) Spring issue, 1982.

The author is profoundly grateful to the following facilitators of this book:

The Academy of Creative Education, and its president, Dr. James C. Ingerbretsen, whose grant of funds made the writing possible.

The Ourobouros Circle of Beverly Hills, California, and its generous host and hostess, Mr. and Mrs. Arthur Malvin.

Irene Malvin, for specially creating and donating her drawing of Abraxas for this work.

Professor John Algeo who, while reading the manuscript, enriched its quality with valuable suggestions.

Prologue

Premonition of an Inescapable World of Shadows

The year was 1949. A deep covering of snow obscured the outline of the splendid baroque buildings in the old city of Innsbruck. The venerable capital of the land of the Tyrol seemed depopulated by the grim force of the Alpine Winter. The wide avenue named after the Empress Maria Theresia, beloved matriarch of a long-vanished united states of Eastern Europe, was empty of its afternoon strollers, who had fled the elements to find shelter where they could. Shelter, especially of the heated variety, was in poor supply to be sure. The scarcity of heating materials left most public and many private buildings without heat. Even the historic chambers of Innsbruck's famous university housed shivering masses of heavily clad students huddled around professors whose learning was exceeded only by their discomfort. Greengrocers dispiritedly offered their all-too-small store of frostbitten vegetables for sale, while the Moroccan Spahis and Senegalese infantrymen of the French occupational army vociferously cursed the day when their generals decided to station them in this land of snow and ice. Happy indeed was the man, the woman, or the child who found it possible to repair to a heated room on a day like this.

On a small side street of the inner city, two hatted, overcoated and scarved figures were speedily betaking themselves to just such a place of blessedness in the shape of the public reading room maintained for the intellectual enrichment—and incidentally, or not so incidentally, for the physical comfort—of the population by the Information Service of the United States of America. There, in the midst of books and periodicals printed in several languages, all bearing the ideals of the richest and most generous of the four occupational powers, weary and cold refugees from the Tyrolean winter gathered with great frequency. The two figures here referred to were refugees, not only from the elements, but from other, more enduring forms of adversity as well. They were refugees from their nearby homeland, Hungary, who had come to reside, even though temporarily, in the sister country, the Austrian imperial homeland of the many peoples of Eastern Europe. The elder of the two compatriots was of singularly impressive appearance and of equally impressive credentials in the fields of learning, religion and public life. Professor J. was a priest of the Roman Catholic Church, and until recently a member of the Jesuit Order, which he relinquished with the official approval of the church, while retaining his priestly status. For many years he was known as one of the outstanding luminaries of the academic world of his country and the youngest professor ever to hold a seat at a Hungarian university. He was the author of numerous learned books on philosophy, and a recognized expert on Existentialism, personally acquainted with Heidegger, Jaspers, and Jean Paul Sartre. In 1945 his name was one of several nominated for the leading archbishopric of Hungary, which entailed the leadership of the church of the entire nation, but he was by-passed in favor of the heroic and tragic prelate, Cardinal Mindszenty, whose imprisonment scandalized the entire world a few brief years later. At this time Professor J. was living in quiet semi-retirement in Austria, an austere and mysterious figure, known to but a few of his countrymen and having personal contact with even fewer. One of the elect whom he conversed with regularly was his present companion on his wintry walk, a young and precocious student of philosophy with aspirations toward entering the priesthood. This young man—none other than the writer of the present treatise—had strangely arrested the attention of the reclusive professor who seemed to be amused by his great attraction to religion, coupled with unconventional thinking and youthful flamboyance. "I like you, my young Baron," he said on their first meeting; "In an earlier age you might have become a real heretic and would have been burned by the Dominicans!" These promising opening remarks led to a friendship, punctuated by almost daily meetings at the reading room of the American library, and on rare occasions of momentary prosperity at a nearby cafe, over Turkish coffee and French cognac.

"We may have a treat for you this afternoon," the professor said to his companion. "A strange book is on its way to us that will assuredly interest you."

"A strange book? Of what content and authorship?"

"I am told it concerns your old friends, the Gnostic heretics, whom you never cease to rave about—and moreover it was written by another man whom you are interested in, the redoubtable Dr. Jung."

"The Swiss psychologist, who lives across the mountains from here, and who is reputed to be a regular wizard in the good old tradition of witches and alchemists?" the young man asked, not without some excitement.

"The very same. The 'Hexenmeister' [warlock] of Zurich himself."

The intriguing news thus having been announced by the professor, the two frostbitten travelers entered the reading room, and after shedding their snow-covered overgarments, settled comfortably down to a large and suitably deserted table in the far end of the room. The Austrian girl librarian reverently curtsied to the "Hochwurdiger Herr" (Reverend Gentleman) in her accustomed fashion, while depositing several publications of the professor's usual reading material before him. The two companions enveloped themselves in an etheric cloud of quiet and scholarly comfort, greatly augmented by the pleasant warmth of the room, so generously heated by the funds of the Marshall Plan. An hour passed.

The opening of the door and the excited whispers of the librarian heralded the arrival of the expected bearer of heretical and psychological wonders, who—according to Professor J.—was to join them in their present shelter. They were approached by a small, rather unprepossessing individual whose two unusual characteristics, a bulky briefcase of enormous size and a clerical collar projecting from his shabby black overcoat, soon revealed him to be none other than Father Z., an itinerant Hungarian priest, whose calling involved frequent traveling in the countries of Austria, Switzerland and Italy.

The visitor approached the table quietly and solemnly bowed to the professor.

"Laudetur Jesus Christus," (Praise be to Jesus Christ) he said in the traditional manner of the Latin greeting of the monastic clergy of Hungary.

"In aeternum. Amen," (In all eternity. Amen.) the professor and his associate answered in the proper manner, while the visitor silently established himself in an empty seat at the table occupied by his compatriots. In hushed but discreetly audible tones, there now ensued a conversation of considerable length. The topic initially and understandably was of matters close at hand and dear to the anxious heart. The newest moves of the Communist dictatorship in Hungary were recounted; the most recent arrests of priests and nuns, the show-trials of members of the higher clergy, the capture and imprisonment of ill-fated friends and relatives. The whispered hopes of the exile community, the possible fall of the Russian-supported tyranny due to political pressures from Western nations, the hopes of the Vatican, the vacillations of politicians the world over, the plight of the numerous refugees in camps and other facilities all over Western Europe—these and other related matters were recounted and discussed to the accompaniment of furrowed brows and distressed glances. Finally, the urgencies having abated and anxious inquiries answered, it was time to attend to the long-awaited matter.

"My friend," the professor said, revealing a portentous deliberateness in his voice, "you had told me this morning of a small book by Doctor Jung. Have you brought it along?"

Father Z. slowly and carefully unlocked his briefcase and began to search in its amply filled recesses. After a few minutes he drew forth a smallish volume and deposited it on the table where both the professor and his young friend could view it with ease. The professor opened the volume and turned it at an angle where the light would illumine the pages in the most efficient manner. All three men looked with rapt attention. Before them reposed an expensively bound small book, printed in a highly decorative type on parchment-like artistic paper. The initial letters of the short chapters resembled nothing more than elaborate initials in medieval manuscripts, and the text on each page was enclosed by a frame, leaving margins of great width, whereon the page numbers were noted in Roman numerals. The text of the book was in German, as one could note at a glance on account of the old-fashioned Gothic German type, long since fallen into disuse. In spite of the German text, the book bore a Latin title, elaborately and artistically lettered on the front page. It read:

VII Sermones ad Mortuos

The author was identified in a line below the title as *Basilides,* and the place of writing as *Alexandria, the City Where East and West Meet.*

The young man flushed and drew himself up as though he had been struck. Laboriously and with bated breath, he asked the priest: "Professor J. told us, and you seemed to agree, that the book was written by Dr. Jung. Why is it then that it bears the name of Basilides, the famous Gnostic heretic of Alexandria in Egypt? Are you sure you have the correct book?"

"Yes, Baron, it is the right book, *The Seven Sermons to the Dead.* Let me quickly tell you its history, so that you will understand. It was written by Dr. Carl Jung in 1916 but was never published for the use of the public. This is a very rare copy from the edition printed privately by Jung for the use of some of his closest friends. In fact, this volume was given by Jung long ago to a doctor in Holland, who before his death gave it to an Italian prelate who was visiting the Dutch church and who was most interested in psychology. The old *monsignore,* who is now at the Vatican, gave it to me for very similar reasons. As you may have heard, Dr. Jung has a more than ordinary interest in the teachings of the old Gnostics, and so he used the name of Basilides as a *nom de plume* in this particular instance."*

"He is not the only one with a fascination for the Gnostics," smiled Professor J. "The young Baron is quite heretical himself. But let us look at the book further."

The text of the volume was most certainly as outlandish and fascinating as the title page promised. The first chapter, entitled "Sermo I," began with the ominous sentence in German:

> *Die toten kamen zurück von Jerusalem, wo sie nicht fanden, was sie suchten. Sie begehrten bei mir Einlass und verlangten bei mir Lehre und so lehrte ich sie:*

---

*See Appendix I, Translator's Note.

*Höret: ich beginne beim Nichts, das nichts ist
dasselbe wie die fülle. In der Unendlichkeit ist voll so
gut wie leer. Das Nichts ist leer und voll. Ihr konnt auch
ebenso gut etwas anderes vom Nichts sagen, z.b.es sei
weiss oder schwarz oder es sei nicht, oder es sei. Ein
unendliches und ewiges hat keine Eigenschaften, weil es
alle Eigenschaften hat . . .*

* * * * * * *

*The dead came back from Jerusalem, where they did
not find what they were seeking. They asked admittance
to me and demanded to be taught by me, and thus I
taught them:*

*Hear Ye: I begin with nothing. Nothing is the same as
fullness. In the endless state fullness is the same as emptiness. The Nothing is both empty and full. One may
just as well state some other thing about the Nothing,
namely, that it is white or that it is black or that it exists
or that it exists not. That which is endless and eternal
has no qualities because it has all qualities . . .*

They read on in the first chapter, or sermon, until the young
man addressed the professor: "What is all this obscurity? I
recognize the word *Pleroma,* the Plenum of which the old
Gnostics wrote, and a few other ideas which I have seen
expressed by the Fathers who wrote about, or rather against the
Gnostics. I cannot understand this so-called sermon at all!"

The professor replied at once: "It is a description of the
Absolute, the indescribable. No wonder Doctor Jung has a difficult time with it. Do you remember the mystical darkness intimated by Dionysius the Areopagite? Or the poetic vagueness of
the descriptions of Meister Eckhart? Jung was no doubt confronted with a task which these earlier mystics had also encountered. Read on!"

A page bearing the heading "Sermo III" arrested their attention next:

*The dead approached like mist out of the swamps and
they shouted: "Speak to us further about the highest
God."—Abraxas is the God whom it is difficult to*

*know. His power is the very greatest, because man does
not perceive it all. Man sees the* summmum bonum *of the
sun, and also the* infinum malum *of the devil, but
Abraxas, he does not see, for he is undefinable life
itself, which is the mother of good and evil alike.*

Professor J. interrupted the reading of the text. "Oh,
yes—Abraxas. The Gnostic universal ruler, whose head is like
that of a rooster. How much more colorful our holy pictures and
statues would be if we had retained some of these strange
Gnostic deities. Surely one gets tired even of the image of Our
Lord Jesus, especially here in Austria, where he is always
covered in gold leaf. But, never mind, Jung has really got
something with his description of the old rooster-god. I must say
this is impressive poetry, to say the least! Listen to this!"

And he read on, in a steady, though subdued voice:

*He is fullness, uniting itself with emptiness.
He is the sacred wedding;
He is love and the murder of love;
He is the Holy one and his betrayer.*

*He is the brightest light of day and the deepest night of
madness.*

*To see him means blindness;
To know him is sickness;
To worship him is death;
To fear him is wisdom;
Not to resist him means liberation.*

After a brief interval of silence, he once again began to read
aloud:

Such is the terrible Abraxas.

*He is the mightiest manifest being, and in him creation
becomes frightened of itself.*
*He is the revealed protest of creation against the
Pleroma and its nothingness.*
*He is the terror of the son, which he feels against his
mother.*
He is the love of the mother for her son.

He is the delight of Earth and the cruelty of Heaven.
Man becomes paralyzed before his face.
Before him there exist neither question nor answer.
He is the life of creation.
He is the activity of differentiation.
He is the love of man.
He is the speech of man.
He is both the radiance and the dark shadow of man.
He is deceitful reality.

"This Jung is truly a poet," the priestly bearer of large brief-cases and rare books interjected. "This passage is worthy of Goethe, or at least of our most philosophical Hungarian poet, Endre Ady, who called God a terrible shark."

"Shark or rooster, it is very much the same thing. God is terror and darkness just as much as he is love and light. How else can one explain Auschwitz, and the torture chambers in Siberia and in Budapest managed by Stalin and his servants?" Professor J. shook his head, his long white hair rearranging itself in untidy waves over his forehead.

"But are these dark and horrible deeds not the province of the devil, rather than of God?" Father Z. asked.

"Not at all, my friend. The Swiss doctor rightly says in this little book that there are countless gods and devils. And incidentally, what is a devil anyway? The church calls him a fallen angel, and so he is. But where did he fall from? From God's kingdom of greatness, or from the *Pleroma* or fullness, as it is called here. To fall means to descend, to come down from on high. So the devils are beings who have come down from God to the lowest of all levels of creation, called hell. Some think that the word *diabolos* really means *little god*. These little evil gods may indeed be responsible for instigating some errors, but the final responsibility for all good and evil must devolve on God. And this is precisely why Jung's Abraxas is a more accurate image of God than the one we hold, when we follow St. Thomas and our theologians, who say that evil is only an absence of good. The German and Russian death camps and their authors are not merely lacking in good; they *are evil*."

It was time for the youngest of the threesome to cautiously chide his elder: "It seems, Professor, that this time you are the one who speaks like a Gnostic heretic. Surely a God who is both evil and good at the same time would be a most unsatisfactory object of worship for the people."

"If under 'people' you mean the masses of believers, then you are of course correct. Still, your Gnostic friends of olden days would have said that the knowledge of God is more important than the worship of God, and in order to know God one must also know evil."

"I agree with you that this is what the Gnostics would have said, but what do *you* say, Professor?"

"I shall ask myself if what I would say is both wise and necessary. And so I will say nothing."

"Still spoken like a Jesuit," muttered Father Z., instantly regretting his impulsive statement.

"Be it as it may, Jesuits have been known to survive when most others succumb." The Professor turned his attention once more to the book.

The survey of the book was nearing its end. The last chapter offered itself to the gaze of the three readers. Entitled "Sermo VII" and bearing the page number XVII in Roman numerals, it began with a huge illuminated initial which was a Gothic letter *D*:

Des nachts aber kamen die Toten wieder mit kläglicher gebärde und sprachen: noch eines, wir vergassen davon zu reden, lehre uns vom Menschen . . .

* * * * * * *

At night the dead came back again and amidst complaining said: "One more thing we must know, because we had forgotten to discuss it: teach us concerning man."

—Man is a portal through which one enters from the outer world of the gods, demons and souls, into the inner world—from the greater world into the smaller world. Small and insignificant is man; one leaves him soon behind, and thus one enters once more into infinite space, into the microcosm, into the inner eternity.

*In immeasurable distance there glimmers a solitary star
on the highest point of heaven. This is the only God of
this lonely one. This is his world, his Pleroma, his
divinity.*

*In this world man is Abraxas, who gives birth to and
devours his own world.*
This star is man's God and goal.
It is his guiding divinity: in it man finds repose.

*To it goes the long journey of the soul after death; in it
shine all things which otherwise might keep man from
the greater world with the brilliance of a great light.*

To this One, man ought to pray.
Such a prayer increases the light of the star.
Such a prayer builds a bridge over death.
*It increases the life of the microcosm; when the outer
world grows cold, this star still shines.*

*There is nothing that can separate man from his own
God, if man can only turn his gaze away from the fiery
spectacle of Abraxas.*

*Man here, God there. Weakness and insignificance
here, eternal creative power there.*
*Here is but darkness and damp cold. There all is sun-
shine.*

*Upon hearing this the dead fell silent, and they rose up
like smoke rises over the fire of the shepherd, who
guards his flock by night.*

The text ended with four lines of barbarous words, entitled
"Anagramma," indicating ostensibly an attempt on the part of
Dr. Jung to disguise some secret and personal messsage, but
possibly also containing a magical sequence of Gnostic formulae
in the manner frequently found in late Egyptian sources.

The three readers glanced at each other in a uniformly significant fashion. A chill spirit of awe and amazement seemed to
have risen at the table. Even the owner of the book, whose
acquaintance with its contents extended over a number of years,
was visibly affected. No one spoke for several minutes.

The silence was broken by Professor J.: "Dr. Jung is a seer and a mystic after the fashion of the magicians of the Renaissance. I have known for some time that there is more to him than meets the academic eye. Unlike Freud, he is not fearful of the dark mysteries of the spirit. Among his friends and supporters are people of unconventional and peculiar affiliations and interests. I hear that one of his Italian pupils is a theosophist, while an English follower, who is also a doctor, became a devotee of a Russian wizard.* There must also be some contact between him and the group founded by the Austrian mystic Rudolf Steiner, whose headquarters is in Switzerland. It is known to most of us that Dr. Jung was fascinated by the phenomena of spiritism and that he got his doctorate by writing a thesis on occult phenomena. Some think that he is a spiritual pagan, while others accuse him of being biased in the direction of Christianity. This little book would set both of these opinions in the wrong, for it shows that he is a kind of Gnostic, which would take him out of the categories of pagan and Christian. I am certainly pleased to have perused this remarkable document, and I am thankful to you Father."

The mild-mannered priest barely had opportunity to acknowledge the professor's comments when their younger companion burst into the conversation with even more than his usual ardor: "And I am truly thankful beyond measure and beyond words also. I am greatly concerned, however, since I recall that you said to us that this book is quite unobtainable. I wish I could memorize its contents by heart so as to retain every word. If I ever encountered a book I should like to own, this is assuredly the one!"

"It may not be necessary to thus tax your memory, Baron, for I am not leaving Innsbruck until tomorrow night, and you may be able to copy these few pages without much difficulty by then. Just be so kind and return the book to me before five o'clock tomorrow. I am lodged at the Franciscan monastery, not far from here."

---

*See Roberto Assagioli in *The Unfinished Autobiography of Alice Bailey* (New York: Lucis Publishing Company, 1951) and Maurice Nicoll's *Psychological Commentaries on the Teachings of Gurdjieff and Ouspensky* (London: Vincent and Stewart, 1964).

He handed the book to his happy compatriot, who with trembling hand grasped it and carefully hid it in the inner pocket of his overcoat. "I will copy it tonight. You may have it as early as you wish, even before morning Mass."

Outside, the early darkness of winter had fallen. The reading room had become well-nigh empty of patrons, and the librarian was obviously preparing to close the doors. After polite expressions of good wishes, the three companions donned their coats and other protective clothing and exited from the premises. The winter evening received them in due fashion, and after a short walk together they dispersed to take up their individual journeys to their various quarters. A remarkable day had come to a close.

Not quite. One of the company was certainly not prepared to see his day come to a close. No knight of the round table could have carried the Holy Grail with greater reverence and burning desire than the Hungarian student carried that copy of Jung's *Seven Sermons to the Dead*. The cold and slow-moving street-car, the walk from the terminal to his quarters in an outlying district of the city, the frantic preparations involving the securing of adequate quantities of paper and of a sturdy fountain pen—these activities took on the nimbus of events on a journey to a place where a lifetime of toil and expectancy would be rewarded and crowned. The kitchen, hallowed locale of culinary alchemical operations, was speedily turned into a nocturnal scriptorium, and the enthusiastic scribe plunged with utmost dedication into one of the most magical activities of his young life.

Page upon page of carefully written script came to repose on the massive kitchen table, the prized possession of the aged landlady, who was wont to utilize it for innumerable useful tasks, from the matutinal brushing of her dog's fur to the preparation and serving of several daily meals and the ironing of clothing, to the frequent nocturnal card games, played with the medieval *Tarock* cards, a variant of the magical deck known as *Tarot*. Yet never had this venerable table witnessed greater diligence and more fervent devotion.

It was well past midnight when the task was completed. Soon it was time to rise once again and to rush to the monastery of the Franciscans, attending early Mass, and after the conclusion of the same handing the precious volume over to the somewhat groggy Father Z. in the door of the sacristy.

The work was finished, but the mystery had just begun. An inescapable world of shadows had entered the daylight world of ordinary life.

* * * * * * *

The time passed and the world changed, the *Seven Sermons* remained an object of wonder and interest to their one-time scribe. Thirteen years later, in distant California, the dead "came back" to their enthusiastic admirer once more. They did not come from Jerusalem but from Zürich, and they appeared in a book then just issued by the publishing house Rascher Verlag under the title *Erinnerungen Traume Gedanken* von C.G. Jung (*Memories, Dreams, Reflections* by C.G. Jung). A German prepublication copy having been presented to him by a Swiss friend, our protagonist quickly discovered that the appendix of this book contained the German text of the mysterious *Sermons*. The page introducing the *Sermons* contained an ominous foot-note: "To be published only in the German edition." Once again the enthusiasm of the scribe rose to a great pitch. The suggestion came to his mind with some force that the German text ought to be made available to many good people who read only English, but who should not be deprived of this experience for that reason. Now came another somewhat less romantic but still intriguing piece of work, which consisted of his translation of the text into English from the German original. This translation came to be privately printed and distributed to a select number of personal friends, very much like the original German edition had been distributed by Jung himself. By this time, of course, the wise old man of Zurich and Kusnack had departed from the stage of his earthly career. His personality, still subject to speculation and obscure gossip, had already emerged with far greater clarity than had been the case earlier. Jungian psychology was slowly gathering momentum outside of the German-speaking world, and its founder's unconventional spiritual interests were already in part documented by the appearance of his great works on alchemy, and by his Gnostic assault on conventional theology in his *Answer to Job*.

The translation of the *Seven Sermons* remained a private concern, however, and it remained as a text to be studied by a small number of persons whose interests were in the fields of Gnosticism and of the psychology of Jung. For some years it was the only such translation, and an unknown one at that. Another small piece of work was finished, but the mystery continued and the world of shadows grew longer.

* * * * * * *

Time passed again and the world changed even more than before. The 1960's and most of the 1970's passed, and with them came an era of turbulence and much spiritual creativity. The Viet Nam war was lost (the only war ever lost by the United States of America), but the war against trivial consciousness and the small-souledness of modern Western culture was almost won. The children's crusade of what some were pleased to call the Age of Aquarius, not unlike earlier crusades, temporarily liberated the Holy Sepulchre wherein the saving power of the spirit reposed. The wide-eyed children of the new age rolled away the stone and proclaimed that an ineffable greatness had risen. A rough but glorious beast, once foretold by the poet Yeats, slouched closer to Bethlehem to be born. The minstrels sang: "The times, they're a changing," and they did change. The wings of angels were in the air.

In these new times, Dr. Jung came ever more into his own. Though for long physically removed, his presence came to be felt increasingly year by year. The psychologists and psychiatrists continued to play the games of Freud and Skinner, delighting in the libido and in the mazes of neurotic rats, but the world of literature, mythology, poetry and of such culture as there still remained in an increasingly uneducated world became more and more aware of Jung. Jung had become more important than his therapy, more important even than his analytical psychology, and curiously enough, this circumstance seemed quite just and right.

Along with the rise of Jung and of other previously arcane figures and subjects, the world also saw a modest renaissance of interest in Gnosticism, the old spiritual discipline with which Jung associated himself in the *Seven Sermons*. Long-buried codices came to light in Egypt which arrested the attention of many scholars and of even more imaginative and creative lay persons. Words and names such as *Pleroma, Abraxas,* and *Basilides* were no longer totally foreign to a fair number of insightful and creative folk. The time of Jung and of the Gnostics had come. The time for the *Seven Sermons to the Dead* had come.

It was thus that the dead came back once more from Jerusalem and demanded attention. Thirty years had taken their toll among the agents of the original small drama, which was instrumental in establishing the link between the *Sermons* and the person who once devotedly copied them without any foreknowledge of their future use. The noble figure of Professor J. has departed the academy of earth. It was reported that his heart was broken by the disastrous failure of the patriotic uprising of his people in 1956, which he anxiously observed from his later place of exile in Munich in Bavaria. Father Z, the bearer of the book, had also died, very much like he lived, unobtrusively and modestly, a humble worker in an alien vineyard. The exile continued, mirroring perhaps that greater exile referred to by the ancient Gnostics—the exile of the lightsparks from the fullness of light. Far from the Tyrolean Alps where he first confronted them, the once-young scribe continued to be haunted by the dead and by the sermons delivered to them by Basilides the Wise. The encouragement of new companions in a new world had fanned the flame kindled on a wintry afternoon long ago and far away. And so three decades after the original events here recounted, the Gnosis of Dr. Jung, as enunciated in his *Seven Sermons*, is now made available to a larger circle.

In every age of human history there were individuals who were imbued with an especial quality of knowing, or Gnosis. Carl Jung was such a man. This knowing, as he repeatedly stated, could not be found in the available traditions of the science and religion of his day, or of any day. There was only one way open, one option left; Jung had to undergo the original experience. This experience of Gnosis, the *Urerfahrung* (archaic, or source-experience), as he called it, led him to the shadow world of Basilides and the questioning dead. Even while living in the bright daylight world of his earliest years, he never could escape a condition which he later described as a premonition of an inescapable world of shadows. This premonition is assuredly not a unique experience of Jung but is shared in common to a degree by all humanity. The gnostic nature of the human vocation is evidenced by the presence, in all persons, of a sense of this world of shadows. In spite of its non-rationality and improbability, the transcendent element of an inward Gnosis is indelibly inscribed in the human heart; all the trivialities of the everyday world due to inattention and consequent ignorance are unable to extinguish its remembrance. The denial of Gnosis only secretly affirms its power. As Meister Eckhart put it, "The more man blasphemes the more he praises God."

The state of forgetfulness of Gnosis always carries with it a troublesome sense of privation, which will not be stilled until its one true object—instead of the many false and counterfeit ones—has been found again. The ancient Gnostics, from whose shadowland Jung brought forth the *Seven Sermons,* often said that all the desires persons feel, all their attempts to gain excitement, happiness and love from this thing or that experience, are but signs of a never-failing homesickness for the *Pleroma,* the 'fullness of Being,' which is the soul's true homeland. Only those who have found the way home can show it to others. A man who missed his own way makes a poor guide. The egalitarian contention that holds that the uninformed can render service to the world as long as they are well intentioned is vitiated by this fact. In the long run, only *those who know* can offer useful service, for they are the ones who know the road by having walked it.

C.G. Jung was a healer of souls and a healer of the culture. A more efficient servant of humanity the world has seldom seen. This efficiency and wisdom was the result, not of heredity, environment, education, but of his having walked the road to the land of shadows where the secret knowledge of the soul dwells. To walk this road, and to find one's objective, means to go contrary to the world and to the notions of the reasonable and the probable. Jung once wrote that our picture of the world only tallies with reality when the improbable has a place in it. It is improbable that order will prevail against chaos and that meaning will win out over meaninglessness. Still, the improbable happens; it is possible and not beyond our reach. In a very real sense the improbable is the true vocation, the authentic destiny of the human being. This is the vocation that can be said to make us human, for we are less than human in proportion as we disregard it or ignore it. The trees and flowers, the birds and beasts who follow their destiny are superior to the human who betrays his.

The present prologue, now at an end, is in the nature of a personal statement. To its writer, the *Seven Sermons* and the manner in which he once discovered them, were and remained a grand symbol of a curious destiny, at once deeply personal and totally universal. Life was not, could not be the same after that magical moment in the cozy reading room in the cold and snowy city in the Alps. Like a volume of sacred scripture or a codex of transformative formulae of power, the transcribed words of the mysterious little book changed the course of a life. The safe harbor of orthodoxy had lost all its attractiveness, and with it the establishments of time-honored belief and tradition. The loss of conventional faith and loyalties might well have brought with it the signs of spiritual rootlessness, so characteristic of those who substitute thought for faith and search for tradition. How readily one may condemn oneself at such a time to the fate of the Flying Dutchman and sail the ocean of life endlessly to and fro, terrified by its gales and bewitched by its calms, while always seeking a harbor which is never found! Such could not be the fate of one who was touched by the spirit of Jung and of the Gnostics; such will not be the fate of anyone who enters the enchanted world of archetypal shadows armed with the sword of Gnosis. From a premonition, life created a realization and an experience. It is often thus; the realities, which at first are but an intriguing but distant vision, prove to be closer at hand than one dreamt. They are "closer than your jugular vein," as the Prophet of Islam expressed it, speaking with the terse eloquence of the desert. The inescapable world of shadows is present in everyone's room, as certainly as it was present in Jung's. The only pity is that for too many it remains forever invisible. To those, however, who in vision and dream, in the magic synchronicities of the daylight, or in the dark wizardry of sleep, have effectively contacted these shadows, they not only retain their visibility, but they become in very truth the wellsprings of existence itself. It was perhaps this imperative quality of the shadow world that Jung wished to express when he said to Laurens van der Post: "The dream is like a woman. It will have the last word as it had the first."

A prologue is defined as the first word. In another sense it also must be the last, for in it ought to be summed up the Alpha and Omega of the work which follows. Whether these lines succeed in accomplishing this is not for the writer to judge. All he can do is to nourish the hope that the reader will have received a premonition of the frame of mind or tone of spirit which served as the moving force of his work. Jung said that only a poet could begin to understand him, and so it may be fitting to conclude this with some lines from the poet A.E., another wanderer in the strange land of Gnosis:

> Out of a timeless world
> Shadows fall upon Time,
> From a beauty older than earth,
> A ladder the soul may climb.
> I climb by the phantom stair
> To a whiteness older than Time.

I

The Gnosis of C.G. Jung

A Science Born of Mystery

In this latter quarter of the twentieth century, few would deny the truth of the statement that depth psychology has proven to be one of the mightiest transforming forces of the culture of our era. Emerging from the dark alienation of consciousness that characterized the nineteenth century, the rediscovery of the unconscious mystery within the human mind has become very much like the biblical leaven that made an entire new world of the spirit rise before the eyes of past generations. The German philosopher Martin Heidegger spoke a great truth when he called the nineteenth century the darkest of all the centuries of the modern era; yet it was precisely at this time of the greatest obscuration of the light of the spirit that the two pioneering giants of the unconscious, Sigmund Freud and Carl Gustav Jung, were born, in 1856 and 1875 respectively.

Freud was a great discoverer, destined to unmask many things. Psychologists, as well as the public, are still slow to realize the debt of gratitude they owe him. A man of the old,

1

narrowly materialistic school of science, whom only practical exigencies drove from the biologist's laboratory into the healing arts, Freud could do no other than use the patterns of thought of his times. By a tragically ironic twist of fate, the very man whose discoveries ultimately shook the very foundations of scientific rationalism remained himself chained to rationalistic and reductionistic dogma, which he guarded and defended with desperate conviction. Like Moses, he could not enter the promised land toward which he led others, the task of the final conquest thus falling to a younger man, a new Joshua of the mind, whose name was Carl Gustav Jung.

Who was Jung and how did he accomplish the crowning task of psychic pioneering? What were the sources of his prophetic insight into the most secret recesses of the human soul? From whence did he derive his wisdom?

All through Jung's long life (July 26, 1875 to June 6, 1961) people were puzzled by the curiously esoteric and magical overtones of his work. Here was a phenomenon hitherto unheard of in the world of the intelligentsia since the era of the Enlightenment. Symbols and images of dark and ancient power were resuscitated from the dust of their millenial tombs. Heretics and alchemists, mystics and magicians, Taoist sages and Tibetan lamas lent the treasures of their arcane quests to the wizardry of the modern Swiss Hermes. Gone were the mundane, personalistic preoccupations of the earlier psychoanalysis with its childhood traumas and infantile vagaries, and the gods and heroes of old were no longer regarded as the glorified masks of childish lusts and terrors. Like Venus arising from the foam of the sea, or Athena springing from the brow of Zeus, the archetypes arose from the *prima materia* of the collective unconscious; the Gods once again walked with men. Above these primeval creative waters of the psyche moved the spirit of one man, the genius of Jung. Well could the learned wonder and the wise be astonished, for a new era of the mind had come.

To those informed regarding the arcane disciplines and theories of the alternative reality tradition, sometimes called the perennial philosophy, or *theosophia* (divine wisdom), it soon became clear that certain parallels existed between Jung's teachings and what to them was long known as the path of initiation. As the noted esoteric poet and diplomat, Miguel Serrano, observed in his seminal small work, *C.G. Jung and Hermann Hesse,* it was as though there were a second language underlying the first in all of Jung's works. The analyst came to be a hierophant of the mysteries, while the patient became a neophyte, or disciple. Sickness revealed itself as a divided or incomplete condition and health as a state of spiritual wholeness. Analytical psychology began to appear as a dialogue between the individual and the universe, without destroying the personality or the ego after the fashion of some Buddhist and Hindu theories.

The sources of Jung's work remained a subject of conjecture for many decades. During his lifetime Jung shrouded the origins of his discoveries in a mantle of caution that often bordered on Hermetic concealment. He said again and again that everything he wrote was based on empirical evidence, indicating that no matter how esoteric and mystical much of his work appeared, it always rested on experience in the psychological field. Most persons took this to mean that Jung treated many patients, that he also had access to the practical research of many of his junior colleagues, and that his books were no doubt the result of data gathered from these sources. Of course, there were rumors which declared that he was a most unconventional scientist indeed, and that he associated with astrologers and men of religion. It was also whispered that he, himself, had occult and weird experiences, saw ghosts and consulted oracles.

It was not until after Jung's death in 1961 and especially after the publication of his remarkable autobiographical fragments, entitled *Memories, Dreams and Reflections,* that a continuous stream of progressively more daring revelations began to pour forth from the pens of his disciples and from posthumously published notes and letters of Jung himself. From these sundry disclosures we learn that between 1912 and 1917 Jung underwent an intense period of experience which involved a tremendous flooding of his consciousness from within by forces which he called archetypal but which previous ages would have declared to be divine and demonic. A certain amount of information regarding these experiences Jung communicated in confidence to various of his associates, but undoubtedly he experienced much more than he ever disclosed, indeed more than ever will be disclosed. The great explorer often called this experience, or rather cycle of experiences, his *Nekyia,* using the term whereby Homer described the descent of Odysseus into the underworld.* At this time, so we are told, he withdrew from most external activities, with the exception of a modicum of his psychiatric practice. It is even reported that during this period he did not read any books, assuredly a great event in the life of such an avid student of every form of literature. Although he did not read, he wrote. His writing at this time consisted of the records of his strange, inner experiences which filled 1,330 handwritten pages, illustrated by his own hand. His handwriting at this time changed to one that was used in the fourteenth century; his paintings were painted with pigments which he himself made, after the fashion of the artists of bygone ages. He had some of the most beautiful paintings and scriptures bound in red leather and kept in a place of honor among his belongings; hence they became known as the *Red Book.* According to eye-witnesses, the writings of this period of his life fall into two distinct categories; some are bright and angelic, while others are dark and demonic in form and content. One is tempted to say that Jung, in the manner of other magicians, went through experiences belonging to the categories of Theurgic Invocation of gods and of Goetic Evocation of spirits and that he kept a "magical record" of each.

Fascinating as these facts about Jung's early transformation are in themselves, their true importance is only disclosed when we realize that there is evidence that much, if indeed not all, of his scientific work may be based on visionary revelations. The much-repeated adjective *empirical,* characterizing the sources of Jung's work, thus appears in an entirely new light. Jung's psychological science was indeed grounded in empirical elements, but these were not primarily of an external nature but consisted of the experiences and experiments he carried out in his own secret world, in the occult regions of his deepest unconscious. Of course, Jung is not "scientific" in the narrower sense of the word in use today in that he did not control

---

*See James Kirsch, "Remembering C.G. Jung, in *Psychological Perspectives*, Vol. 6, p. 57.

variables and conduct careful, repeatable experiments. His "science" consisted in developing a systematized body of knowledge derived from observation and study and discovery of principles and meaning behind the area of his studies, using scientific standards of objectivity. He (and Freud) have an acceptable modern-day scientific ally in phenomenology, whose proponents consider the various modes of human consciousness as their primary data and construct hypotheses, theories and explanations based on these.

It may be useful to remember that Freud carried out much of his research in a manner like that of Jung. The great Viennese doctor discovered the secrets of dreams by way of analyzing his own dreams, and indeed he remained, perhaps, the only psychoanalyst never to submit to analysis by anyone else, discounting a brief discussion of a few of his own dreams with Jung on their common American voyage. Jung was not alone in seeking the company of occultists and unconventional mystics, for Freud was an avid visitor of the haunts of soothsayers, and nourished an important friendship with a crank scientist named Wilhelm Fliess.* One is tempted to characterize Jung as a supremely rational anti-rationalist, while Freud could be called a very irrational rationalist. However, both were seeking the same thing: "More Light" (Goethe's famed *Mehr Licht*) concerning the mysteries of the psyche.

In 1917 at the conclusion of his great descent into his personal, spiritual underworld, Jung was faced with a portentous choice. He could have taken his revelations at face value, perhaps published them as some sort of off-beat religious tome, and thus joined the ranks of the great occult writers of his time like H.P. Blavatsky and Rudolf Steiner. Instead, Jung decided to remain within the field of his chosen scientific discipline, namely depth psychology, but not without utilizing the 1,330 pages of mysterious and archetypal revelatory material to enrich his scientific work. There is good reason to suspect that Jung, throughout his entire life, continued to draw on this record of secret lore and to incorporate elements of it in his numerous books as he deemed fit. There is incontrovertible evidence

---

*See Ernest Jones, *Life and Works of Sigmund Freud* (New York: Basic Books, Inc.).

available that he did this in the case of the first great work which
he authored after his personal transformation, namely his book
Psychological Types, published in 1921. While afflicted with
contagious whooping cough and thus isolated from his usual
patients, he dictated the manuscript for this work at an in-
credibly furious pace, completing the first 583 pages in six weeks
time. He subsequently confessed to the Dutch poet Roland Holst
that *Psychological Types* was written entirely on the basis of the
material contained in thirty pages of his *Red Book.**

As one might expect, Jung maintained a constant contact with
the mysterious sources that inspired his *Red Book* throughout
his life. He remained an inspired—some might say
haunted—revelator for the rest of his days. His scientific work
never represented a compartment of his existence that would or
could be separated from his mystical and prophetic life; the two
were intricately and inexorably interrelated. Jung the mystic
guided and inspired Jung the scientist, while the physician and
psychologist supplied balance and common sense to stabilize
and to render practical the messages of the archetypal gods and
demons. Thus was the epochal work of Carl Jung conceived and
executed. In both its content and intent, it was an example of the
precious principle of *coniunctio oppositorum,* the union of the
polarities that ever produces the elixir of ultimate meaning.

The *corpus* containing Jung's original experiences of the
unconscious from the period of his great transformation was
never made available to the public by him. The attitude of his
heirs appears to be, if anything, even more secretive in this
regard than Jung's had been. It appears at the time of the
writing of these words (1982) that any hope or expectation one
may nourish for the publication of this material is not likely to
be fulfilled for some time to come. Thus we are left with Jung's
scientific works and very little more. Still, in this category of
more we find at least one most remarkable document which tells
us a great deal about the sources of Jung's psychology. This is a
small work, hardly more than a diminutive monograph,
although the significance of its contents may easily elevate it to

---

*Reported by G. Quispel in a lecture at the first Panarion Conference of Jungian
scholars, at Los Angeles in 1975.

an item of major importance in the study of Jung's message and mission. The work we refer to is known as *The Seven Sermons to the Dead.*

Preaching to the Dead

Carl Jung permitted the publication of only one solitary fragment from the vast amount of archetypal material which he wrote under mysterious inspiration in the early part of his career. It was written in a short time sometime between December 15, 1916, and February 16, 1917. According to Jung's statement in his autobiographical fragments, it was written in three evenings.* The writing of this small book was heralded by weird events and was replete with phenomena of a parapsychological nature. First, several of Jung's children saw and felt ghostly entities in the house, while he himself felt an ominous atmosphere all around him. One of the children dreamt a religiously colored and somewhat menacing dream involving both an angel and a devil. Then—it was a Sunday afternoon—the front doorbell rang violently. The bell could actually be seen to move frantically, but no one visible was responsible for the act. A crowd of "spirits" seemed to fill the room, indeed the house, and no one could even breathe normally in the spook-infested hallway. Dr. Jung cried out in a shaky and troubled voice: "For God's sake, what in the world is this?" The reply came in a chorus of ghostly voices: "We have come back from Jerusalem where we found not what we sought." With these words the treatise, which is entitled in Latin *Septem Sermones ad Mortuos,* commences and then continues in German with the subtitle: "Seven exhortations to the dead, written by Basilides in Alexandria, the city where East and West meet."

Even a superficial reading of the treatise reveals that it is written in the manner of second century Gnosticism and uses largely the terminology of that era. The very subtitle reveals the name of the famous gnostic sage Basilides, who taught in Alexandria in Hellenistic Egypt around the years A.D. 125-140. To Basilides, in

---

*See C.G. Jung, *Memories, Dreams, Reflections,* Aniela Jaffé, ed. (New York, Random House, Inc., Pantheon Books).

fact, does Jung seem to attribute the authorship of the document itself, thus suggesting to some an element of mediumship and (or) automatic writing. In this regard it may be necessary to remember that for many centuries it was customary for authors of spiritually toned literature not to sign their own names to such works but to ascribe them poetically to someone whom they considered to occupy a position superior to their own. The celebrated *Zohar* of the Kabbalistic *corpus* is thus fictitiously attributed to Rabbi Shimon ben Jochai, its real author being unknown. It is more than likely that C. G. Jung utilized this time-honored exercise in poetic humility when using the name of Basilides as the author of the *Sermons*. Yet, the parapsychological element contained in the phenomena surrounding the writing of the treatise was freely acknowledged and emphasized by Jung, even to the extent of applying to it the words of Goethe in the second part of *Faust:* "It walks abroad, it's in the air!" One thing is certain: this is an unusual work, written under most unusual circumstances.

The importance of the *Seven Sermons* within the context of Jungian thought is an issue on which opinions differ. When Jung was questioned about it later in life, he grumbled, calling it a "youthful indiscretion." Some of his more conservative disciples, such as Aniela Jaffé, tend to perpetuate the myth of a "youthful indiscretion," while others feel differently. M. L. von Franz, a most important disciple indeed, affirmed that while Jung referred to *the publication* of the *Sermons* as a youthful folly, this by no means included the conceptions which they contained. A panel of Jungian scholars, assembled at the first Panarion conference in Los Angeles, California, in 1975, agreed that the *Seven Sermons* are nothing less than "the fount and origin" of Jung's work, and the C. G. Jung centenary exhibit, which toured the world at the time of his 100th birthday in 1975, showed the first page of the original edition of the *Sermons,* describing them as follows: "The 'Septem Sermones ad Mortuos' represent a summary of Jung's experiences with the images from the unconscious." Even more significantly, Jung himself went on record regarding the contents of the *Red Book* and the *Sermons,* stating that all his works, all his creative activity has come from these initial visions and dreams, and that everything that

he accomplished in later life was already contained in them.*
These are hardly words whereby one might refer to a mere
youthful indiscretion!

The small, poetic treatise was published privately by Jung for
the delectation of an inner circle of friends, the German text
soon being translated into English by H.G. Baynes. It was
included in the appendix of the original German edition of
Memories, Dreams and Reflections, published by Rascher
Verlag in Zurich in 1962, but omitted from the English edition
published simultaneously by Pantheon Books. This deliberate
omission can only be explained as a further evidence of the well-
known suspicion of the European mind against the English-
speaking peoples with their tendency to misunderstand and
misconstrue anything that borders on the mystical and the
occult. Nevertheless, an artistically designed, separate volume of
the *Sermons* was also published by Stuart & Watkins in London,
containing the translation by Baynes. Thus there are several edi-
tions in circulation by now, warranting additional light on the
text itself.†

There certainly were events in the course of Jung's career
when he might have easily regretted the youthful indiscretion of
publishing his small volume of archetypal visions. One such incident concerned the formidable and Jehovah-like Martin Buber,
who never got along well with Jung, and who, moreover,
managed to lure one of Jung's dearest disciples away from him
and into his own camp. This faithless disciple, whose name was
Martin Trüb, gave a copy of the *Sermons* to Buber, whose Old
Testament wrath rose to tremendous proportions in view of
what he considered to be Jung's Gnostic heresies. Buber
repeatedly attacked Jung and in his book *Eclipse of God* gravely
accused him of being a Gnostic. Jung was most upset about the
matter and made a somewhat ambiguous reply, denying and affirming his own Gnosticism in the same breath, as it were.‡
Another curious story concerns the Nobel Prize-winning German author Hermann Hesse and his epochal novel *Demian,* in
which Hesse incorporated many explicitly Gnostic

---

*See C. G. Jung, *Memories, Dreams, Reflections.*
†For complete publication history see Translator's Note in Appendix I.
‡Reported at the first Panarion Conference.

themes—notably some references to the Gnostic archetypal god Abraxas, which closely resemble Jung's treatment of the same figure in the *Sermons*. While Gnosticism was definitely in the air during the two decades between the two world wars, the *kind* of Gnosticism espoused by Hesse in *Demian* appears so uniquely Jungian that many suspected a connection. In fact, a Jungian analyst by the name of Lang treated Hesse around the year 1916 and may easily have passed a copy of the *Sermons* to the then-unfolding young literary genius. A sympathetic connection continued to exist between Jung and Hesse for many decades and was subsequently immortalized by the Chilean diplomat and poet Miguel Serrano in his lovely volume *C.G. Jung and Hermann Hesse.* It would seem that the little book of poetic Gnosticism, occasioned by the visit of the dead to Jung in 1916, had a greater influence and elicited more response than even Jung thought likely. All of these responses, however, concerned one subject, at once obscure and controversial, and this was of course Gnosticism.*

What in the World Are Gnostics?

The words *Gnostic* and *Gnosticism* are not exactly standard features in the vocabulary of contemporary people. In fact, more people are familiar with the antonym of *Gnostic,* which is *agnostic*, literally meaning a non-knower or ignoramus, but figuratively describing a person with no faith in religion who still resents being called an atheist. Yet Gnostics were around long before agnostics and for the most part appear to have been a far more exciting category of persons than the latter group. In contradistinction to non-knowers, they considered themselves knowers—*gnostikoi* in Greek—denoting those who have *Gnosis* or knowledge. Gnostics were people who lived, for the most part, during the first three or four centuries of the so-called Christian era. Most of them probably would not have called themselves by the name *Gnostic* but would have considered themselves Christians, or more rarely Jews, or as belonging to

---

*The reader is referred to pp. 93-95 in part III of the present work for more details of the relationship of Hermann Hesse to Jung and to the *Seven Sermons to the Dead.*

the traditions of the ancient cults of Egypt, Babylon, Greece and Rome. They were not sectarians or the members of a specific new religion, as their detractors claimed, but rather people who shared with each other a certain attitude toward life. This attitude may be said to consist of the conviction that direct, personal and absolute knowledge of the authentic truths of existence is accessible to human beings, and, moreover, that the attainment of such knowledge must always constitute the supreme achievement of human life. This knowledge, or *Gnosis,* they did not envision as a rational knowledge of a scientific kind, or even as philosophical knowledge of truth, but rather a knowing that arises in the heart in an intuitive and mysterious manner and therefore is called in at least one Gnostic writing (the *Gospel of Truth*) the *Gnosis kardias,* the knowledge of the heart. This is obviously a religious concept that is at the same time highly psychological, for the meaning and purpose of life thus appears to be neither faith, with its emphasis on blind belief and equally blind repression, nor works with their extraverted do-goodism, but rather an interior insight and transformation, in short, a depth-psychological process.

If we come to envision the Gnostics as early depth psychologists, then it immediately becomes apparent why the Gnostic teaching and practice was radically different from the teaching and practice of Jewish and Christian orthodoxy. The knowledge of the heart, for which the Gnostics strove, could not be acquired by striking a bargain with Yahweh, by concluding a treaty or covenant which guaranteed physical and spiritual well-being to man in exchange for the slave-like carrying out of a set of rules. Neither could Gnosis be won by merely fervently believing that the sacrificial act of one divine man in history could lift the burden of guilt and frustration from one's shoulders and assure perpetual beatitude beyond the confines of mortal existence. The Gnostics did not deny the usefulness of the Torah or the magnificence of the figure of the Christos, the anointed of the most high God. They regarded the Law as necessary for a certain type of personality which requires rules for what today might be called the formation and strengthening of the psychological ego. Neither did they negate the greatness of the mission of the mysterious personage whom in his disguise men

knew as the Rabbi Jehoshuah of Nazareth. The Law and the
Savior, the two most highly revered concepts of Jew and Christian, became to the Gnostic but means to an end greater than
themselves. These became inducements and devices which
might, in some fashion, be conducive to personal knowing
which, once attained, requires neither law nor faith. To them, as
to Carl Jung many centuries later, theology and ethics were but
stepping stones on the road to self-knowledge.

Some seventeen or eighteen centuries separate us from the
Gnostics. During these centuries Gnosticism became a faith not
only forgotten (as one of its interpretors, G. R. S. Mead, called
it) but also a faith and a truth repressed. It seems that almost no
group has been so relentlessly and consistently feared and hated
for nearly two millenia as were the unhappy Gnostics. Textbooks of theology still refer to them as the first and most pernicious of all heretics, and the age of ecumenism seems to have
extended none of the benefits of Christian love to them. Long
before Hitler, the Emperor Constantine and his cruel bishops
began the practice of religious genocide against the Gnostics,
their first holocausts to be followed by many more through
history. The last major persecution concluded with the burning
of over 200 latter-day Gnostics in 1244 in the castle of Mont-
ségur in France, an event which Laurence Durell described as the
Thermopylae of the Gnostic soul. Still some prominent
representatives of the victims of the latest holocaust have not
regarded the most persecuted religious minority in history as a
companion in misfortune, as the attacks of Martin Buber on
Jung and on Gnosticism indicate. Jews and Christians,
Catholics, Protestants and the Eastern Orthodox (and, in the
case of the Manichaen Gnosis, even Zoroastrians, Moslems and
Buddhists) have hated and persecuted the Gnostics with a persistent determination.

Why? Was it only because their antinomianism or disregard
for moral law scandalized the rabbis, or because their doubts
concerning the physical incarnation of Jesus and their reinter-
pretation of the resurrection angered the priests? Was it because
they rejected marriage and procreation, as some of their detractors claim? Were they abhorred because of licentiousness and
orgies, as others allege? Or might it be that perhaps the Gnostics

truly had some knowledge, and that this knowledge rendered them supremely dangerous to establishments both secular and ecclesiastical?

It is not easy to give a reply to this question, but an attempt must be made, nevertheless. We might essay such an answer by saying that the Gnostics differed from the majority of humankind, not only in details of belief and of ethical precept, but in their most essential and fundamental view of existence and its purpose. Their divergence was a *radical* one in the truest sense of the word, for it went back to the root (Latin: *Radix*) of humankind's assumptions and attitudes regarding life. Irrespective of their religious and philosophical beliefs, most people nourish certain unconscious assumptions pertaining to the human condition which do not spring from the formulative, focused agencies of consciousness but which radiate from a deep, unconscious substratum of the mind. This mind is ruled by biology rather than by psychology; it is automatic rather than subject to conscious choices and insights. The most important among these assumptions, which may be said to sum up all others, is the belief that the world is good and that our involvement in it is somehow desirable and ultimately beneficial. This assumption leads to a host of others, all of which are more or less characterized by submissiveness toward external conditions and toward the laws which seem to govern them. In spite of the countless illogical and malevolent events of our lives, the incredible sequences, by-ways, repetitious insanities of human history, both collective and individual, we will believe it to be incumbent upon us to go along with the world, for it is, after all, God's world, and thus it must have meaning and goodness concealed within its operations, no matter how difficult to discern. Thus we must go on fulfilling our role within the system as best we can, being obedient children, diligent husbands, dutiful wives, well-behaved butchers, bakers, candlestick-makers, hoping against hope that a revelation of meaning will somehow emerge from this meaningless life of conformity.

Not so, said the Gnostics. Money, power, governments, the raising of families, paying of taxes, the endless chain of entrapment in circumstances and obligations—none of these were ever rejected as totally and unequivocally in human history as they were by the Gnostics. The Gnostics never hoped that any political or economic revolution could, or even should, do away with all the iniquitous elements within the system wherein the human soul is entrapped. Their rejection was not of one government or form of ownership in favor of another; rather it concerned the entire prevailing systematization of life and experience. Thus the Gnostics were, in fact, knowers of a secret so deadly and terrible that the rulers of this world—i.e., the powers, secular and religious, who always profited from the established systems of society—could not afford to have this secret known and, even less, to have it publicly proclaimed in their domain. Indeed the Gnostics knew something, and it was this: that human life does not fulfill its promise within the structures and establishments of society, for all of these are at best but shadowy projections of another and more fundamental reality. No one comes to his true selfhood by being what society wants him to be nor by doing what it wants him to do. Family, society, church, trade and profession, political and patriotic allegiances, as well as moral and ethical rules and commandments are, in reality, not in the least conducive to the true spiritual welfare of the human soul. On the contrary, they are more often than not the very shackles which keep us from our true spiritual destiny.

This feature of Gnosticism was regarded as heretical in olden days, and even today is often called "world denying" and "anti-life," but it is, of course, merely good psychology as well as good spiritual theology because it is good sense. The politician and the social philosopher may look upon the world as a problem to be solved, but the Gnostic, with his psychological discernment, recognizes it as a predicament from which we need to extricate ourselves by insight. For Gnostics, like psychologists, do not aim at the transformation of the world but at the transformation of the mind, with its natural consequence—a changed attitude toward the world. Most religions also tend to affirm a familiar attitude of internalism in theory, but, as the result of their presence within the establishments of society, they always deny it in practice. Religions usually begin as movements of radical liberation along spiritual lines but inevitably end up as pillars of the very societies which are the jailers of our souls.

If we wish to obtain *Gnosis,* the knowledge of the heart that renders human beings free, we must disentangle ourselves from the false cosmos created by our conditioned minds. The Greek word *kosmos,* as well as the Hebrew word *olam,* while frequently mistranslated as *world,* really denote more the concept of *systems.* When the Gnostics said that the *system* around them was evil and that one had to get away from it in order to know truth and discover meaning, they acted, not only as the forerunners of innumerable alienated drop-outs from St. Francis to the beatniks and hippies, but they also stated a psychological fact since rediscovered by modern depth psychology. Jung restated an old Gnostic insight when he said that the extraverted human ego must first become thoroughly aware of its own alienation from the greater Self before it can begin to return to a state of closer union with the unconscious. Until we become thoroughly aware of the inadequacy of our extraverted state and of its insufficiency in regard to our deeper spiritual needs, we shall not achieve even a measure of individuation, through which a wider and more mature personality emerges. The alienated ego is the precursor and an inevitable precondition of the individuated ego. Like Jung, the Gnostics did not necessarily reject the actual earth itself, which they recognized as a screen upon which the Demiurge of the mind projects his deceptive system. To the extent that we find a condemnation of the world in Gnostic writings, the term used is inevitably *kosmos,* or *this aeon,* and never the word *ge* (earth), which they regarded as neutral if not as outright good.

It was on this knowledge, the knowledge one has in one's heart concerning the spiritual barrenness and utter insufficiency of the establishments and established values of the outer world, that the Gnostics relied in order to construct both an image of universal being and a system of coherent inferences to be drawn from that image. (As one might expect, they accomplished this less in terms of philosophy and theology than in myth, ritual, and cultivation of the mythopoetic and imaginative qualities of their souls.) Like so many sensitive and thoughtful persons before and after their time, they felt themselves to be strangers in a strange country, a forlorn seed of the distant worlds of boundless light. Some, like the alienated youth of the 1960's withdrew into communes and hermitages, marginal communities on the edge of civilization. Others, more numerous perhaps, remained in the midst of the great metropolitan culture of the large cities like Alexandria and Rome, outwardly fulfilling their roles in society while inwardly serving a different master—in the world but not of the world. Most of them possessed learning, culture and wealth, yet they were aware of the undeniable fact that all such attainments and treasures pale before the Gnosis of the heart, the knowledge of the things that are. Little wonder that the wizard of Küstnacht who, since his early childhood, sought and found his own Gnosis, felt close to these strange and lonely people, these pilgrims of eternity, homeward bound among the stars.

Jung and Gnosticism

From the earliest days of his psychoanalytic career until the time of his death, Jung maintained a lively interest in and had a deep sympathy for Gnostics. As early as on August 12, 1912, Jung wrote a letter to Freud about the Gnostics in which he called the Gnostic conception of Sophia a reembodiment of an ancient wisdom that might appear once again in modern psychoanalysis. He was not lacking in literature that might have stimulated his interest in the Gnostics, for nineteenth-century scholarship in Germany (though almost nowhere else) diligently devoted itself to Gnostic studies. Partly as a reaction against the rigidities of Bismarckian Germany and its intellectual as well as theological conformist effects, numerous fine scholars (Reitzenstein, Leisegang and Carl Schmidt, among others) as well as imaginative writers and poets (Hermann Usner, Albrecht Dieterich) delved into Gnostic lore, as did at least some members of the French intelligentsia (M. Jaques Matter, Anatole France). All of Jung's biographers mention his keen interest in matters Gnostic. One of the most revealing statements in this regard is quoted by his one-time associate, Barbara Hannah, who recounts his words about the Gnostics: "I felt as if I had at last found a circle of friends who understood me." The same biographer also notes that Jung developed an interest in Schopenhauer precisely because the great German philosopher reminded him of the Gnostics with their emphasis on the suffering aspect of the world, and that he approved whole-heartedly of the fact that Schopenhauer "spoke neither of the all-good and all-wise providence of a Creator, nor of the harmony of the cosmos, but stated bluntly that a fundamental flaw underlay the sorrowful course of human history and the cruelty of nature; the blindness of world-creating Will . . . ." That all of these are thoroughly Gnostic statements goes without saying. Since his interest in Schopenhauer goes back to his boyhood, we may take this to mean that Jung was in many ways a "natural" Gnostic, possessing the Gnostic attitude even before he became acquainted with some of the teachings of Gnosticism.

Although Jung quite early in his life had access to a certain amount of scholarly and poetic literature that stimulated his interest in Gnosticism, he had almost no primary source material of a Gnostic nature available. Like so many others, Jung had to rely on the fragmentary and, above all, mendaciously distorted accounts of the anti-Gnostic church fathers, especially Irenaeus and Hippolytus, for his information on the Gnostics. The ponderous wheels of academic scholarship were, with extreme slowness and even reluctance, only beginning to apply themselves to the three Coptic codices (Agnew Codex, Bruce Codex, Askew Codex) then moldering in various museums waiting to be translated and published. That Jung was able to derive so much insight and extract so much valuable information favorable to Gnosticism from the polemics of the heresy-hunting church fathers may be regarded as somewhat of a miracle in itself. Jung's contribution to Gnostic studies in general and to an enlightened, contemporary interpretation of Gnosticism in particular is little short of epochal in scope and import. That this contribution is still largely unappreciated by the increasing number of specialists in Gnosticism within the field of biblical studies is regrettable but not particularly amazing, in view of the fact that most of these scholars are the products of divinity schools and schools of religion of orthodox religious leanings. Moreover, most of them are totally lacking in any serious appreciation of psychology, especially the kind of psychology that Jung proclaimed. It has been said that war is too important to be entrusted to generals, and it might be equally just to say that Gnosticism is too valuable a tradition to be consigned to Bible scholars and quibblers over Coptic words. The lack of attention and respect accorded to Jung by some of these scholarly folk is all the more incredible, since Jung's influence is almost solely responsible for the vital project of the publication of the greatest storehouse of original Gnostic writings ever discovered in history, the Nag Hammadi Library.

The Gnostics were prolific writers of sacred lore. Their enemies noted with disapproval that the followers of the Gnostic teacher Valentinus were wont to write a new gospel every day and that none among them were esteemed much unless they wrote a new contribution to their literature. Yet, of all this profusion of texts, very few survived, due to the relentless suppression and destruction of Gnostic literature by the book-burners and heresy hunters of the Church, which with imperial support attained ascendancy over its rivals. For many centuries no original Gnostic scriptures were known to exist. It was not until the eighteenth and nineteenth centuries that travelers like the valiant and romantic Scotsman, James Bruce, began to bring back to Europe, from Egypt and adjoining localities, ancient papyrus fragments containing texts. While probably written in Greek originally, these had been translated by Gnostic scribes into Coptic, the demotic language of Hellenistic Egypt. Coptic scholars as well as persons interested in Gnosticism being rare indeed, the translation of such texts proceeded at a veritable snail's pace. Then, a near miracle occurred. In December, 1945, in the immediate wake of World War II, an Egyptian peasant, while digging for fertilizer in the vicinity of some caves in the Jabal al-Tarif mountain range near the Nile in Upper Egypt, came upon an entire collection of Gnostic codices. These treasures were apparently once part of the library of the vast monastic complex founded in that area by the father of Christian monasticism, the sainted Coptic monk, Pachomius.

Like its predecessors, the Nag Hammadi find was exceedingly slow to see the light of day. The ponderous ways of scholarship were greatly speeded up, however, by the influence of one man who was neither a Coptic scholar nor a biblical expert but merely an archaeologist of the human soul. This man was, of course, none other than Carl Jung. Jung took an early interest in the

Nag Hammadi find, and it was Jung's long-time friend and collaborator Professor Gilles Quispel who took the lead in the translation and publication of the Nag Hammadi books. On May 10, 1952, while political crises and academic wrangling had brought all the work on the manuscript to a standstill, Quispel acquired one of the codices in Brussels, and it was from this portion of the great library that most of the early translations were made, thus shaming the scholarly community into speeding up its long-delayed work. This codex, named *Jung Codex* was presented to the Jung Institute in Zurich on the occasion of the eightieth birthday of Dr. Jung, and was thus the first item from the Nag Hammadi find to be openly viewed by scholars and laymen outside the turbulent and uncooperative milieu of Egypt in the fifties. Professor Quispel himself went on record as stating that Jung was instrumental in calling attention to, and in publishing, the priceless collection of the Nag Hammadi manuscripts. There is good reason to suspect that without Jung's influence this collection might also have been consigned to oblivion by the seemingly ever-active conspiracy of scholarly neglect. (For further details of the history of the Nag Hammadi Library and Jung's connections with it see: H.C. Puech, G. Quispel, W.C. Van Unnik: *The Jung Codex*, London, M.R. Mowbray, 1955.)

What was Jung's true view of Gnosticism? Unlike most scholars until quite recently, Jung never believed Gnosticism to have been a Christian heresy of the second and third centuries. Neither did he pay attention to the endless disputes of experts about the possible Indian, Iranian, Greek and other origins of Gnosticism. Earlier than any authority in the field of Gnostic studies, Jung recognized the Gnostics for what they were: seers who brought forth original, primal creations from the mystery which he called the unconscious. When in 1940 he was asked Is Gnosticism philosophy or mythology? he gravely replied that the Gnostics dealt in real, original images and that they were not syncretistic philosophers as so many assumed. He recognized that Gnostic images arise even today in the inner experiences of persons in connection with the individuation of the psyche, and in this he saw evidence of the fact that the Gnostics were expressing true archetypal images which are known to persist and to exist irrespective of time or of historical circumstances. He recognized in Gnosticism a mighty and utterly primal and original expression of the human mind, an expression directed toward the deepest and most important task of the soul, which is attainment to wholeness. The Gnostics, so Jung perceived, were interested in one thing above all—the experience of the fullness of being. Since this was both his own personal interest and the objective of his psychology, it is axiomatic that his affinity for the Gnostics and their wisdom was very great indeed. This view of Gnosticism did not remain confined to Jung's own psychological works, but it soon entered the world of Gnostic studies by way of his aforementioned coworker, Gilles Quispel, who in his important work *Gnosis als Weltreligion* (1951) presented the thesis that Gnosticism expresses, neither a philosophy nor a heresy, but a *specific religious experience* which then manifests itself in myth and (or) ritual. It is regrettable indeed that, more than twenty-five years after the publication of this work, so few have appreciated its significant implications.

In view of these considerations, one may understandably ask the question Was Jung a Gnostic? Misguided persons, like Martin Buber, have answered yes to this question, implying thereby that Jung was both less than a respectable scientist and less than a good man within the orthodox religious meaning of the term. As the result of this derogatory use of the term *Gnostic*, many of Jung's followers, and occasionally Jung himself, have denied that he was a Gnostic. A rather typical example of this hedging was a statement made by Gilles Quispel when he stated that "Jung was not a Gnostic in the usual sense of the term." It is very doubtful, however, that there ever was even one single Gnostic *in a usual sense of the term*. Gnosticism is not a set of doctrines but a mythological expression of an inner experience. In terms of Jungian psychology, we might say that the Gnostics gave expression in poetic and mythological language to their experiences within the individuation process. In so doing they brought forth a wealth of most significant material, containing profound insights into the structure of the psyche, the content of the collective unconscious and the dynamics of the individuation process. Like Jung himself, the Gnostics described, not only the conscious and personal unconscious aspects of the human psyche, but empirically explored the collective unconscious and gave descriptions and formulations of the various archetypal images and forces. As Jung stated, the Gnostics were far more successful than the orthodox Christians in finding suitable symbolic expression of the Self, and their symbolic expressions closely parallel those which Jung formulated. While Jung did not openly identify himself with Gnosticism as a religious school, just as he did not identify himself with any religious denomination, there can be little doubt that he did more than anyone to illuminate the central thrust of Gnostic imagery and symbolic practice. He saw in Gnosticism a particularly valuable expression of man's universal struggle to regain wholeness. While it would have been both impractical and immodest for him to say so, there is no doubt that this Gnostic expression of the urge toward wholeness was duplicated only once in the history of the West, and that was in Jung's own system of analytical psychology.

What manner of Gnostic was Jung? Certainly he was not a literal follower of any one of the ancient teachers of Gnosis, which would have been an impossible undertaking in any case in view of the inadequacy of detailed information regarding these teachers and their teachings. On the other hand he, like the Gnostics of old, formulated at least the rudiments of a system of transformation, or individuation, which was based, not on faith in any outside source (whether it be Jesus or Valentinus), but on the natural, inner experience of the soul which was ever the source of all true Gnosis.

The dictionary definition of Gnostic is *knower* rather than a follower of someone else who may be a knower. Jung was certainly such a knower if there ever was one. To deny that Jung was a Gnostic in this sense would be tantamount to the denial of all the recognized data of his life and work. The most probable indication of the specifically Gnostic character of Jung's orientation, however, is none other than the treatise called *Seven Sermons to the Dead,* which, by the admission of prominent Jungians, is the fount and origin of his later work. Who but a Gnostic would or could write a work like these sermons? Who would choose to garb his personal archetypal revelations, which form the skeleton of his life's work, in the terminology and mythological framework of the Alexandrian Gnosis? Who would prefer to select Basilides rather than any other figure as the author of the *Sermons*? Who would use, with expert understanding and finesse, such terms as *Pleroma* and *Abraxas* to symbolize highly abstract psychological states? There can be but one answer to these questions: *only a Gnostic would do these things*. Since Carl Jung did all of these and indeed much more, therefore we may consider Carl Jung a Gnostic, both in the general sense of a true knower of the deeper realities of psychic being and in the more narrow sense of a modern reviver of the Gnosticism of the first centuries of the Christian era.

Jung and the Pansophic Gnosis

According to Morton Smith, the noted discoverer of the *Secret Gospel of Mark,* the term *gnostikoi* was generally used to describe persons of a Platonic and/or Pythagorean orientation, although, of course, the term *gnosis* occurs in the writings of many authors belonging to other schools, including orthodox Christian church fathers like Origen and Clement of Alexandria. The Nag Hammadi Gnostic Library contained copies of both the *Republic* of Plato and of certain Hermetic tractates which scholarly purists of contemporary vintage would never dream of including in the Gnostic corpus. All of this furnishes evidence for the contention that already in early times, when the Gnostic schools were still physically alive, Gnosticism was characterized by a considerable ecumenicity and elasticity. The members of the presumed Gnostic community in Upper Egypt would probably have defined Gnostic literature as any spiritually valuable scripture capable of producing Gnosis within the reader. Academic experts on Gnosticism may aspire to the status of purists, but the Gnostics themselves never were such, nor could they ever be. Thus in later centuries, after the destruction of the original Gnostic communities and of their scriptures, the Gnostic spirit lived on under many names and in many disguises, still serving its original and never-fading purposes. As long as there is a light within the innermost selfhood of human nature, and as long as there are men and women who feel themselves akin to that light, there will always be Gnostics in the world. We may consider the continued presence of the Gnosis as in a very large measure due to the survival of Gnostic archetypes within the collective unconscious and to the very nature of the processes of the growth and development of the psyche itself. Jung undoubtedly knew this when he referred to the process of the confrontation with the shadow (the recognition of the unacceptable, or "evil" part of ourselves) as a "gnostic process." The church fathers coined the phrase *anima naturaliter Christiana* (the soul, which is by its nature Christian), but the Gnostics with even greater validity could have said that the soul's content and path of growth are by their nature Gnostic. The undeniably archetypal character of Gnosticism is not the only cause of its survival. In addition to the Gnostic character of the unconscious, which spontaneously tends to produce Gnostic systems of reality, there also exists a historical development and continuity linking the ancient Gnostics with their heirs in later historical periods.

Underground movements seldom lend themselves as subjects for the work of the historian. Compelled to secrecy by their hostile environment, their chief preoccupation is survival, and thus they leave relatively few discernible tracks in the soil of time. Much, although not all, of Gnostic history after the third and fourth centuries is made up of speculation and intuition in lieu of facts. Still in this gossamer fabric of concealment and subterfuge, of evasions and occasional daring declarations, certain significant data stand forth with remarkable force and clarity. One of these is the life and work of the splendid Persian prophet Mani (A.D. 215-277), whose star rose just when that of the first Gnostics declined. Mani was a Gnostic both by the nature of his character and by virtue of tradition. When twelve years old he was visited by an angel who declared to him that he was chosen for great tasks. At the age of twenty-four the angel came to him again and urged him to make his public appearance and to proclaim his own doctrine. The Persian name of this angel means *twin,* and he was the spiritual twin-brother, or higher self, of Mani. The gnostic treatise known as *Pistis Sophia* recounts a similar incident in the life of Jesus, who in his youth was visited by an angel who resembled him like a twin brother and with whom Jesus merged after they embraced. These myths express the Jungian encounter between the ego and the Self, with the ensuing union of the opposites. Recent discoveries appear to indicate, however, that Mani's father, Patiq, had traveled to Syria and Palestine and there joined a Jewish or Mandaean group of Gnostic character. Thus in all likelihood Mani received a Gnostic transmission from his father or from his father's teachers.

Mani was cruelly executed by a treacherous king at the instigation of the Zoroastrian priestly establishment, but his religion continued to flourish in many lands for several centuries and became the principal carrier of the Gnostic tradition. As late as 1813 the Manichean order of the White Lotus and the Black Cloud was politically active in China, and there seem to be indications of the existence of Manichean remnants existing in Viet Nam as late as 1911. Unlike the first Gnostic teachers, Mani was a skilled organizer, and the missionaries of his church were indefatigable travelers and preachers. In Europe the Manichean Gnosis twice reared its head with bold might: once in the Balkan regions of Bulgaria and Bosnia where its votaries were known as Bogomils, and once in the south of France where the followers were known as Cathars or Albigensians. Although drowned in blood every time, their influence penetrated the cultural and religious field in many lands and helped to reinforce the underground stream of Gnostic traditions which continued to survive in secrecy.

While the spiritual heirs of Mani thus carried forth their particular Gnostic transmission openly, though against overwhelming odds, various strictly secret traditions continued to exist, especially in Europe and in the Middle East. It is with one of these covert traditions of the Gnosis that Carl Jung established a most significant link. The tradition we refer to is alchemy. In an address, delivered at the presentation of the celebrated Jung Codex of the Nag Hammadi collection to the C.G. Jung Institute, Jung singled out two main representatives of the Gnostic tradition, one being the Jewish Kabbala, while the other he called "philosophical alchemy." Jung was familiar with the Kabbala and was a frequent reader of one of its greatest works, the Latin translation of the *Zohar,* translated by Knorr von Rosenroth and known as *Kabbalah Denudata.* The principal modality of Gnosis to which Jung became greatly attached, however, was not the Kabbala but alchemy. He commented extensively in many volumes of his finest writing on its intricate symbolism and splendid transformational metaphors.

Many have wondered why Jung should have chosen the obscure and long-ridiculed occult discipline of alchemy as one of the favorite subjects of his research. The answer to the quandary, though clearly given by Jung himself, has failed to elicit the response that it warrants. For about a dozen years, from the First World War until 1926, Jung devoted himself with great zeal to the study of the literature on Gnosticism then available to him. In spite of the fragmentary and distorted character of this literary material, he became both well informed about Gnosticism and thoroughly imbued with its spirit, as proven by the content of the *Seven Sermons to the Dead.* What Jung could not find at first, however, was some sort of a bridge or link that might have connected the Gnosis of old with later periods, including the contemporary one. Some Grail-like vessel was needed wherein the precious elixir, once used by such masters as Valentinus and Basilides, was preserved and in which it was carried through the centuries to attract would-be Gnostic Parsifals in our own era. Jung's intuition declared to him that there must be such a bridge, such a connecting link in the chain of wisdom, but he could not rationally discern where it was to be sought. Then, as usual, he was aided by a dream.* In it he was carried back into the seventeenth century when alchemy still flourished in Europe. A recognition dawned on him. Here, he thought, is the missing link of the descent of the Gnosis! Thus began his great research, which eventually led him to proclaim that alchemy indeed represented the historical link with Gnosticism, and that a definite continuity therefore existed between the past and present. Jung stated that, grounded in the natural philosophy of the Middle Ages, alchemy on the one hand formed the bridge into the past, to Gnosticism, and on the other to the future, to modern depth psychology. Thus came to pass

---

*See C.G. Jung, *Memories, Dreams, Reflections.*

one of the significant hallmarks of esoteric historical exploration. Alchemy was discovered to be none other than the bridge over which the Gnosis of old traversed the ages and entered the modern world as the Jungian psychology of the unconscious. The implications regarding the connections of Jung's thought with Gnosticism, although seldom mentioned in the past, are nevertheless clear for all to see. They may be summed up as follows: Jung might be viewed as a modern-day Gnostic who absorbed the Gnosis, both by way of his inner transformation and his confirming study of Gnostic literature. He knew that in his psychology he was putting forward an essentially Gnostic discipline of transformation in contemporary guise. He needed to discover a historical connection between his own efforts and those of the Gnostic teachers of antiquity. He was also in need of a statement of the Gnostic method of transformation that was not fragmentary but contained an adequate vocabulary of psychologically valid symbols to be made useful within the context of the study of the human mind today. In alchemy he found precisely what he sought. Thus the answer to his dreams came heralded by a dream.

In alchemy Jung contacted one of the most important branches of what has sometimes been called the Pansophic Tradition, or the wisdom heritage which descended from Gnostic, Hermetic, and Neo-Platonic sources, through numerous later manifestations, to contemporary times. This Pan-Sophic, or Theo-Sophic tradition was recognized by Jung to have taken many forms throughout the ages, but also to have been particularly manifest in the late nineteenth and early twentieth centuries within the movement of modern Theosophy, enunciated by the Russian noblewoman and world-traveler, Madame H. P. Blavatsky. In such works as *The Undiscovered Self* and *Civilization in Transition* Jung clearly recognized modern Theosophy as an important contemporary manifestation of Gnosticism, and he likened it to a submarine mountain range spreading beneath the waves of the mainstream culture, with only the projecting mountain peaks becoming visible from time to time through the attention received by Mme. Blavatsky, Annie Besant, Krishnamurti and others.

As Jung repeatedly emphasized, orthodox Christianity (and, one should include orthodox Judaism as well) has demonstrably failed to satisfy the deepest and most essential needs of the soul of Western humanity. Christian theology was far too rationalistic, reductionistic and insensitive to the profound reaches of the human soul. As the church came to ally herself with one hopelessly unspiritual secular establishment after the other, from Constantine to Mussolini, so also her spirit atrophied under the baneful influence of Aristotelian logic and other structures of thought which stifled the urge of believers toward personal psychic transformation. In this climate of spiritual aridity, which persisted for some 1700 years, the desire for individuation frequently turned to the alternative spirituality of the Pansophic or Theosophic transmission which, while not exclusively Gnostic in the classical sense, contained a large component of Gnosticism.

The seventeenth century, to which Jung saw himself transported in his alchemical dream, was one of the most important points in the history of the upsurgence of this alternative tradition of spirituality. It was at this time that the movement called by Frances Yates the Rosicrucian Enlightenment brought Hellenistic alchemy into a cooperative conjunction with the Jewish Gnosticism of the Kabbala and with the Theurgic-magical methods that descended from both Gnosticism and Neoplatonism. The greatest early luminary of this spiritual counterpart of the artistic and literary Renaissance was a man with whom Jung felt an uncanny and overwhelming inner kinship, Phillippus Aureolus Theophrastus Paracelsus Bombastus of Hohenheim, who like himself was Swiss, a physician, and a man determined to unite the opposites of science and spirituality into one operative unity.

Although a flamboyant and gargantuan Renaissance man, filled with scientific curiosity as well as with spiritual aspiration—not to speak of physical and emotional appetites of equally heroic proportions—Paracelsus was in many ways a true Gnostic. Pugnacious, haughty, fiercely independent (his motto was He who can be his own, should not be another's), he nourished a sovereign contempt for the world of established power, dogma and values. A lonely and homeless wanderer, he journeyed over almost the entire known world of his time, and died mysteriously and alone in Salzburg, Austria, where even his tomb was found to be empty in later years. Very much like Jung, he looked upon illness as a spiritual phenomenon related to the universal meaning of life within a magical cosmos. His epigram "Magic is a Great Hidden Wisdom—Reason is a Great Open Folly" could be easily adapted to characterize Jung's discovery of the meaningful non-rationality of the unconscious, replete with its own symbolic magic and revealing itself in the wonders of synchronicity. At a fairly early point in his career (1929) speaking in the very house where Paracelsus was born at Einsiedeln in Switzerland, Jung repeatedly drew comparisons between the philosophy of the great occult physician and the teachings of Gnosticism. Jung recognized in the cosmogenic principle propounded by Paracelsus, and called by him Hylaster, a form of the Gnostic Demiurge, or deity subordinate to the supreme deity, sometimes considered the creator of evil. He traced the alchemical view of the archetypal potentialities concealed in matter to the Gnostic concept of the lightsparks scattered abroad in the darkened cosmos. With singular clarity, he perceived how the occult materialism of Paracelsus and of the alchemists was but a new form of the apparent extreme idealism of the Gnostics. Jung recognized that the same transformation process which the Gnostics symbolized as the journey of the soul through the aeonic regions appeared in the Paracelsian symbolism as the stage-by-stage transfiguration of the dark *prima materia* into the shining gold of the alchemical work. While apparently poles apart, the Gnostics and alchemists shared a common quest. They also opposed a common foe, orthodox Christianity, which was ever incapable of appreciating either the transformational potentialities of matter or the authentic, naturally inherent sanctity, and indeed divinity, of the human psyche. Instead of an appreciation of either or both of these alchemical and Gnostic propositions, the church chose to languish in a psychological limbo compounded of Aristotelian logic and the Semitic obsession with moral laws and commandments. Paracelsus and the alchemists were dear to Jung, for in them he saw a mighty manifestation of the Pansophic Tradition which is a descendant of ancient Gnosticism.

Paracelsus, Pico de la Mirandola, Fichino and their companions may have initiated the Pansophic fusion of the magico-philosophical disciplines of transformation. However, this Pansophic or Theosophic synthesis was brought to its greatest fruition in the seventeenth century, with the unknown authors of the *Fama Fraternitatis,* the *Confessio Fraternitatis* and of the *Chymical Wedding of Christian Rosenkreuz,* as well as the writings and activities of the English Renaissance occultists John Dee, Thomas Vaughan and Robert Fludd. The aforementioned historian, Frances Yates, proves in her most convincing scholarly works (*Giordano Bruno and the Hermetic Tradition,* as well as *The Art of Memory, The Theatre of the World* and *The Rosicrucian Enlightenment*) that Renaissance art, science, literature, and drama have an organic connection with and are, in a sense, part of the Pansophic effort. It is Hermetic and Gnostic magic, alchemy and heterodox mysticism that served as the well of the living waters from which the greatest lights of Western culture, from Galileo to Shakespeare, drew their inspiration and spiritual sustenance.

The seventeenth century thus led to the eighteenth, wherein Martinism, Freemasonry, the Illuminati and the neo-Templars carried forward the torch of the alternative spiritual tradition into the Age of Reason. The Jacobin club and other antimonarchist and anticlerical associations in France and elsewhere were politicized offshoots of the esoteric orders, bent in part on revenging the centuries of persecutions visited on the representatives of heterodox spirituality by the powers of throne and altar. When King Louis XVI was led to the scaffold, he is said to have exclaimed: "This is the revenge of Jaques de Molay!" But as thrones crumbled and altar lights were extinguished, the champions of the new dawn of the spirit came to recognize that the triumph of wisdom was still far off. New tyrants replaced the monarchs of old and churchly dogma gave way to the soul-killing materialism of an arrogant young science.

The era of darkness set in. Semimoribund religion continued to battle science, while the grimy smokestacks of the Industrial Revolution reduced peasant to proletarian and elevated merchant and usurer to capitalist. Only the artist and poet remained to fan the flickering flame of the alternate spiritual tradition. William Blake, Shelley, Goethe, Holderlin, and later W.B.

Yeats and Gustav Meyrink, as well as the painters Moreau and Mucha—following in the footsteps of the Pre-Raphaelites and of other artistic esotericists—were consciously, and at times hopelessly, championing the Pansophic tradition. Even toward the end of his life, Jung said gravely to Miguel Serrano: "No one understands, only a poet could begin to understand," thus speaking for the entire stream of esoteric transmission in its nineteenth and twentieth century plight.

The dawn always breaks at the darkest time of night. Out of the torpor of nineteenth century culture, new figures arose and, like chanticleers, they called forth magically the new-old light of the sun. Wagner, Nietzsche, Kierkegaard and numerous lesser figures, all in their own fashion, brought forth elements of the Pansophic tradition. Like a Cathar troubadour risen from the pyre of the Inquisition, Richard Wagner sang the glories of the mystical Grail and paraded the awakened gods of the pagan past. Nietzsche, the passionate neo-pagan, articulated a truly Gnostic contempt for the pusillanimous constructs of what he saw as an alienated, degenerated Christianity, while Kierkegaard, the gloomy Dane, conjured up existential anguish and alienation, duplicating the feat of the earliest Gnostics. All of these efforts, however, fell short of taking the ultimate step, taken long ago by Valentinus, Basilides, Marcion and other Gnostics, which was neither a leap of faith nor a plunge into despair, but the entry into the aionic regions of the human psyche. Here the archetypal gods await the neophyte ego to be initiated into the mystery. Depth psychology thus became the logical conclusion of an age-long process which brought the Pansophic tradition from the sunny shores of the Mediterranean to Europe and America, and from classical antiquity through the Middle Ages and subsequent centuries into the paradoxical times of the two World Wars, of Nazism, Fascism, and Marxism and the other curious elements which make up the twentieth century.

Religion, science, philosophy, art and literature were only partial approaches to the great mystery of the soul; each was like a facet in a cut gem, fragmentary in its own isolation. Only two forces emerged in the late nineteenth and early twentieth centuries which addressed themselves to the very fire in the center of the many-faceted diamond of the soul and endeavored in their own ways to understand the dynamics of the brilliancy of its light. The two forces were: modern occultism, initiated by the Theosophy of Madame Blavatsky, and modern depth psychology, initiated by Freud and carried forward into new creative dimensions by Jung. The former followed the age-old pattern of the alternative spiritual tradition, pursuing a private, or quasi-religious approach. The latter aspired to become a science, even though it came to reveal itself more as a quasi-scientific discipline, half an art and half a science. Whether this modern discipline of the soul will be able to live up to its own high expectations and fulfill its outstanding promise, only the passage of time will disclose. In the person and in the work of C.G. Jung, modern depth psychology has come very close to revealing the great secret; it has come close to perfecting the Gnostic-alchemical work. As we know, the old wizard of the mind whom the world called C.G. Jung is no longer on earth to continue the great experiment he began. His psychology is still with us, and so is his general Pansophic legacy, inherited by him from a succession of sages that includes the Gnostic elite of two millenia. The night is still long and the watchmen are few. Will the magnum opus be carried forward to a new stage toward its completion? Who will be the alchemists, the Gnostics of the future?

Jung and the New Gnosticism

If one accepts the view expressed in the foregoing, namely that Jung played the role of an authentic, contemporary link in the chain of transmission that has been called Pansophic, the core of which is Gnosticism, then certain conclusions will, of necessity, suggest themselves. One of these is that Jungian or analytical psychology cannot and must not remain restricted to the field of psychotherapeutic practice and theory, but that instead the wider cultural and spiritual implications of Jung's thought need to be explored and implemented. This necessity is made increasingly clear when one considers the mounting generalized public response to Jung's total message, which is far greater than the response of the same public to Jungian therapy alone. The academic community of experts in literature, mythology, comparative religions and kindred disciplines, as well as large segments of the educated lay public, have responded with the greatest measure of positive interest to Jung's insights, while the medical and clinical disciplines of psychology have remained relatively unimpressed and unaffected by them. (This assessment is primarily to be understood within the context of the intellectual life of America, but the European picture resembles the American to a significant degree.) Over the last two or three decades there has been a phenomenal increase in the popularity of Jung's books, but the number of practicing psychiatrists and psychologists following the Jungian discipline is still minuscule when compared to those attached to other psychological models. "Vox populi, vox Dei" (The voice of the people is the voice of God). It may well be that the gods have thus spoken through the mouths of people in many walks of life and that their judgment declares that, while only few may avail themselves of Jungian therapy, many, and perhaps all, can benefit from Jung's "Weltanschauung," his model of reality, or world-conception.

Another conclusion that should be considered is that Jung's essential message cannot be regarded as an isolated, contemporary phenomenon, but rather as an organic outgrowth, nay perhaps even the culmination, of a distinguished spiritual tradition of great antiquity as well as of timeless relevance. In short, Jung's insights need to be considered as one of the latest and greatest manifestations of the stream of alternate spirituality which descends from the Gnostics. It is to be expected that this position will find its critics and that some of these critics will be precisely persons who are quite attached to Jung's psychology and in some cases are practitioners of his therapy. To link Jung's name unequivocally with the most abominated heresy of Christian history may appear to some as a disservice rendered to Jung and to his psychology. Perhaps the timid and the faint-hearted need to be reminded that immediate advantages must often be sacrificed in order to benefit distant but larger objectives. What will it profit Jung's admirers if they should gain the whole world in terms of acceptance and academic respectability, while modern man at large still wanders in search of his lost soul?

The world, especially the Western world, is in evident need of a new Gnosis, even of a new Gnosticism. Fascinating and inspiring though it is, the old Gnosticism of 1700 years ago labors under some obvious limitations when its applicability to contemporary spiritual problems is considered. Yet, at the same time it must be evident to any unprejudiced student of Gnosticism that it still has much to offer to contemporary humanity when it is stripped of certain archaic and outdated historical features. It is because of these features that it appears imperative that Gnosticism should not be confined to the limited interests of a backward-looking antiquarianism. Some way must be found to rescue ancient Gnosticism from the ivory towers of those who delight more in the subtleties of Coptic and Greek phrases than in the living realities of the soul, to which the ancient Gnostics were in fact addressing themselves. It appears to us that such a way can be found, and that it must of necessity be composed of two main sources.

The first of these sources is the classical Gnosticism of the early centuries A.D. with the addition of significant amplifications brought forth by the various manifestations of the Gnostic impulse within the Pansophic tradition. The second element is none other than the Gnosis formulated by Jung. It may be considered likely that self-declared purists of both the Jungian and of the Gnostic variety will resist the marriage of these two elements. Resistances and objections of such a nature, however, ought to be viewed as of little importance when contrasted with the potential benefits to be derived from a creative conjunction of ancient Gnosticism and the modern Gnosis of Jung. Assuredly there may be persons who wish to confine the wisdom of Jung to the small operational arena of the consulting room, even as there will be others who will insist on locking up Gnosticism in the files of scholarly specialists and in their costly and obscure academic treatises. The fact remains that Jungian depth psychology is more than a therapeutic discipline, just as Gnosticism is more than an ancient religion. Both are the expression at their particular levels of existential reality of a Gnosis, a knowledge of the heart directed toward the inmost core of the human psyche and having as its objective the essential transformation of the psyche.

It becomes necessary for us now to give some expression to the model of reality as it appears within the texts of the ancient Gnostics, and as it may be usefully amplified by the modern statement of Gnosis offered to us by Jung. Gnosis is formless, since ultimate reality is always beyond conceptual grasp. It was precisely this perception of ultimate reality that inspired the teachers and writers of ancient Gnosticism and fired them to amazing heights of original, creative accomplishment in the spiritual field. Modern psychology and ancient Gnosticism are but pointers to truths that are actually encountered in the vital experience of personal psychic transformation. Experience itself is always individual and can never be adequately expressed or interpreted by arranging sets of concepts and doctrines, for concepts are only indications of similarities within experience. Gnostic and psychologist must both be on their guard against the danger that they might mistake formulae for wisdom, and thus fall into the same dark pit into which theology plunged headlong, and fatally.

If anyone should expect Jung to have constructed a new Gnostic "system" in the accustomed sense of the word, such an expectation would assuredly meet with disappointment. Jung, in fact, pointed the way toward a most important feature of the new Gnosticism when he said that where individual development is demanded, all methods must be abandoned. He considered individuality as unique, unpredictable and uninterpretable. In his view, all human beings are pathfinders, hewing their way through a dense forest. The established systems and forms of knowledge can do no more than put up signposts and indicate the explored roads that lead to the edge of this forest where the task of solitary exploration begins. Thus religious and quasi-religious disciplines, as well as modern psychology, can point to significant, common situations in the quest after Gnosis, but they are in reality only a shorthand of the language of the soul to be abandoned as real contact with the deeper layers of spirit is achieved. The danger of all systems is that they tend to mistake the words which serve as pointers for the realities to which they point. We may use terms of a Gnostic derivation, such as Sophia or Abraxas, or on the other hand, we may employ psychological terms, such as anima, animus and shadow, but in all instances we must be extremely careful that we do not earmark them as known because named, thus depriving ourselves of authentic Gnosis. Life is never static and the inner life least of all, so it would be improper to refer to any definable Gnosis or individuation as a final achievement. We are ever becoming, but we never become. All systems must beware of assuming that they are making true statements about reality. When they come to rationalize their symbols and begin to look upon them as truths, they will soon be fossilizing their insights and thus soon destroy their empirical value as signposts on the way. At the portal of true Gnosis all "isms," even Gnosticism, must vanish. Similarly the psychologist must be willing to sacrifice his allegiance to a psychological system when he begins to deal with true individuation.

It is interesting to note in this connection that Jung was quite critical of the representatives of the Pansophic tradition within the modern era, precisely because of their frequent tendency to mistake their own symbols for factual and philosophical truth. Most of his derogatory remarks made about Theosophy and related systems must be interpreted in this light. Modern occultists for the most part, even if thus inclined, could not give expression to their symbolic models of reality in psychological language. Jung, on the other hand, seriously questioned the usefulness of metaphysical formulations such as theirs. His endeavor was to bring everything purporting to be metaphysical into what he called "the daylight of psychological understanding," which he felt was vastly preferable to the use of nebulous power-words of academic metaphysicians and occultists. Jung, in turn, has been criticized for this approach by persons attached to the mainstream religions as well as by some esotericists (notably by the school of Renè Guènon and Frithjof Schuon in recent years), and the charge of "psychologism" was made against him for his attempt to express religious and metaphysical statements in psychological terms only. Yet it is fairly apparent that Jung acted as a Gnostic in this respect also. To name is not to know. The church has substituted faith for knowing, and some metaphysicians as well as many esotericists have come to regard speculation and elaborate systematizations of terminology as substitutes for knowing directly for oneself. To know, one must experience. This, as far as we can discern from the now increasingly available Gnostic documents, was exactly the position of the ancient Gnostics, for which reason they were held in disrepute by churchly believers and philosophical speculators alike. The occultist who uses elaborate diagrams of astral planes and etheric bodies liberally sprinkled with Sanskrit words can be as far from Gnosis as can the psychologist who employs clever two-dimensional maps of the psyche with short-hand expressions such as "the shadow," "the anima," or "the wise old man," as though these were concrete realities instead of symbolic pointers to incomprehensible mysteries in the vast recesses of the unconscious.

If we cannot expect a "system" of the conventional sort to represent the Gnosis which emerges from the conjunction of the approaches of the ancient Gnostics and of Jung, it may be at least possible for us to state certain basic axioms which could serve as the principal indicators of the message of this Gnosis. In the following we shall present a brief summary of these elements in the hope that they may state in briefest outline form the basic propositions around which all other elements of the new Gnostic reality model may constellate themselves. Some of the points here enumerated are based on a similar summary by the late Eleanor Bertine in her work *Jung's Contribution to our Time*, in which she outlines basic conclusions of Jung concerning the religious side of the psyche.

1. The first conclusion is that *a pneumatic* (spiritual, or more than personal) *element is an organic part of the human psyche*. The ancient Gnosis declared that the human being is not merely a creature of materiality (*hyle*) and of a personal mind-emotion complex (*psyche*), but that there is a third potency indwelling the soul, which is spirit (*pneuma*). It is upon the awakening of this element into effective action that Gnosis depends. Jung stated something very similar when he declared that the unconscious material of human beings inevitably reveals evidences of the highest spiritual potentiality. This spiritual component is a source of revelations, insight, and ultimately of the urge toward wholeness.

2. The second conclusion is that *this spiritual element carries on an active dialogue with the personal element of our selfhood*

through the use of symbols. The spiritual element is not a silent partner in the business of life, but demands active participation in the growth and transformation of the individual. Unlike the mind-emotion complex, the pneumatic component does not express itself in words or in ordinary feelings. Dreams, visions, altered states of consciousness and what Jung called synchronistic experiences are the most important avenues for these symbolic communications.

3. The third conclusion is that *the symbols proceeding from the pneumatic component of the soul reveal a path of spiritual or psychological development, which can be traced, not only backward toward a cause in the past, but forward to a goal in the future.* The Gnostics held that the existential condition of the human being is determined by two factors: the descent or fall of the human soul from the light-world in the past; and the soul's teleological destiny, which is its return to that light-world in glory and victory. We are not only driven by our murky past but also mightily drawn forward and upward by our splendid future. Mainstream Christianity holds the fall of man and the consequent state of original sin responsible for his present condition, even as Freudian psychology traces the present neurotic afflictions of the psyche back to infantile conditions. In contradistinction, Jung held that the psyche contains an indwelling sense of its destiny of wholeness, and that this sense to a considerable extent determines its present condition.

4. The fourth conclusion is that *prior to an arising of Gnosis* (or individuation as Jung might call it) *the human soul is dominated by many blind and foolish powers* (projections and unconscious compulsions). These powers have been mythically expressed and given names such as *demiurgoi* and *archons* by the ancient Gnostics.* While it is occasionally asserted that Jung's Gnostic statements, such as the ones contained in the *Seven Sermons to the Dead*, do not speak of a Demiurge or archons and therefore Jung could not be a Gnostic, it appears likely that such observations are based on an inability of some to appreciate the subtle code in which Jung's Gnosticism is articulated. One can-

---

*Demiurgos, or demiurge: fashioner, or architect. An inferior creator deity as distinguished from the highest God. *Archon:* ruler, a term for an inferior deity, similar to demiurge.

not help but feel that the observers making these statements simply were unable to perceive the powerful analogies and correspondences existing between Jung's concepts and the mythologems of Valentinus, Basilides and their fellows. The primary demiurge in the Jungian system is, so it would seem, none other than the alienated human ego. This conscious selfhood, having pulled itself away from the original wholeness of the unconscious, has become a blind and foolish being, unaware of its roots in the unconscious, yet desperately attempting to re-create a semblance of the over-world by effecting unconscious projections. The ego thus appears very much like an intermediary between the realm of extraverted action and the greater, unconscious matrix, within which Jung saw all external phenomena to be rooted. Like the Gnostic demiurge, the ego in its alienated, blind arrogance boldly but falsely proclaims that "there is no other God before" it—that it alone is the true determinant of existence—and that the powers and potentialities of the unconscious are unreal or non-existent. The ego-demiurge creates its own *kosmos,* but it is a flawed and distorted one, inasmuch as in it the light of the deeper selfhood is obscured and polluted by unconscious projections and compulsions. It is thus that the ego becomes a true demiurge, the foolish architect of its own foolish world.

Since in their quaintly ironic manner the ancient Gnostics frequently identified the mythologem of the Semitic creator God with their own mythologem of the demiurge, and since this Semitic creator in turn became God-the-Father to the Christians and Allah to the Moslems, it is understandable that the concept of the demiurge should create severe resentment in those who have become attached to the god image of this deity. At the same time it must be remembered that a variety of demiurgic mythologems appear in numerous religions and spiritual disciplines, thus indicating that such an idea is not merely an eccentric aberration of the abominated Gnostics. The greatest Gnosis of the East, Buddhism, gives a very clear expression of this concept when it describes the figure of Mara, the deceiver who sought to keep Gautama from attaining to Buddahood. It must be remembered also that Buddhism in the same breath affirms the psychological truth that the overcoming of the ego is the most important ingredient in the attainment of enlightenment. Other systems also give frequent mythological expression to the recognition that there is an adversary, or oppositional power, active in life, which seems bent on preventing or at least retarding the enlightenment of the soul, in order to hold it in some sort of captivity within a universe of darkness and illusion. The idea of the demiurge is not a mere weird and shocking invention of the Gnostics but an archetypal image universally present in the human psyche, and inevitably manifest in the various myths of enlightenment or liberation. The unwillingness of some religious structures to take evil seriously, and with it the image of the demiurge, has led to the psychic impoverishment of the followers of these religions. Any new Gnosis or Gnosticism emerging in our contemporary world would of necessity have to address itself to this important psychic fact and give it some useful and creative expression in present-day terms. Jung has undoubtedly paved the way in this direction by his psychological restatement of the mythic figurations once advanced by the Gnostics.

5. The fifth conclusion is that *the alienation of consciousness, along with its attendant feelings of forlornness, dread and homesickness, must be fully experienced before it can be overcome.* The detractors of classical Gnosticism forever accuse it of gloomy and "world-denying" tendencies. Jung's psychology has also had its share of accusations of gloominess and of an excessive emphasis on darkness, alienation and evil. Once again it must be recalled that there are empirical reasons related to the dynamics of spiritual liberation which make such attitudes imperative. A delightful story regarding a patient of Jung's points this up. She saw herself in a dream sinking into a dreadful mire. Overhead appeared the figure of Dr. Jung serenely floating in the aether and sternly addressing the distressed patient with the following words: "Not out, but through!" This anecdote illustrates a most important principle of Jung's and of his psychology, which is quite similar to certain principles of Gnosticism. The psyche must allow itself the experience of darkness, terror and alienation, irrespective of the pain effected by the experience. The process of individuation includes the confrontation with and experience of what Jung called *the shadow*.

This process of confrontation and experience has been characterized—once again by Jung himself—as a "Gnostic process". Another useful analogy to the modern psychological Gnostic process is the fourfold structure of the classical Greek drama: *agone* or contest; *pathos* or defeat; *threnos*, or lamentation; and *theophania*, or a divinely accomplished redemption. It is significant to note that, of the four stages of development, only the fourth and last may be described as pleasant and joyous, while the other three are characterized by struggle, defeat and mourning. Is this pessimism? Yes, but by no means a hopeless, despairing pessimism. The pessimistic view of the present existential condition of the soul or psyche is more than compensated by the hope of the potential ultimate denuément of wholeness and redemption. Similarly, in the classical ancient form of Gnosticism, the so-called cosmic pessimism (recognition of the existential evils of life in the cosmos) was set off against the glorious eschatological vision of the liberation of the soul from the bonds of darkness, oppression and ignorance and its reunion with the *Pleroma,* the transcendental fullness of being. Philosophers may argue endlessly and theologians may speculate fruitlessly about the abstract issues of the goodness or evil of the created world, but the psychologist has little reason to doubt that the psyche aspiring toward wholeness must first experience keenly and fully those unpleasant existential conditions of alienation and darkness which alone may convince it of the true necessity for growth. The sick person unaware of his or her illness is less likely to seek for means of healing than someone who experiences the symptoms of the disease. As Buddha taught suffering and the cessation of suffering, so Jungian psychological teaching recognizes that those unaware of suffering are much more likely to have their development arrested at the level of shallow, personalistic concerns than their fellows who are aware of the facts of suffering. The neurotic personality, resentful and fearful of the growing pains of the soul, tends to seek refuge in self-deception and thus frequently convinces itself that growth is really unnecessary, for things are quite satisfactory just as they are at present.

6. The sixth conclusion brings us back to the process of Gnosis and its goal, for it declares that *the goal of spiritual growth is*

expressed by images of completion in a whole, which the Gnostics often called the Pleroma (fullness) and/or the Anthropos, or Primal Man and which Jung called the Self. This Self, the representative of the fullness of being within an individual context, is unique for each individual and is formed by the integration of the little self, or ego, and the unconscious. Manifest life is indeed a process of soul-making. The *pneuma* must create for itself a vehicle for its own liberation from earthly bonds, while still engaged in the tasks and perils of earthly existence. Crucial to this conclusion is the idea that the authentic selfhood of the human being is neither created nor does it evolve in some Darwinian or quasi-Darwinian fashion, but it is alchemically integrated from the opposites of light and dark, good and evil, masculine and feminine, conscious and unconscious. It is not by simple extension or a lineal path of growth, but by the oppositional conflict and eventual reconciliation of the opposites that the fullness of being is restored within the individual soul.

7. The seventh conclusion is that *the wholeness, or Self, which is the end result of the process of spiritual growth, is characterized by all the qualities such as power, value, holiness which religious systems have always attributed to God.* This is not to say that the intrapsychic image of deity completely exhausts all the possible ways in which the numinous presence, often called God, may manifest. Still, the internal God-image is probably the most helpful and practically useful point of contact with transcendental wholeness available, and one, moreover, of which empirical evidence appears in our dreams, visions, and other creative experiences.

8. The eighth conclusion is that *the growth of the soul has as its goal a state of integrated wholeness rather than a condition of moral perfection.* This conclusion of Jungian thought links Jung and his teachings most intimately with the much condemned *antinomianism* (opposition to the law) of the Gnostics. Indeed, in ancient Gnosticism we find very clear statements of a spiritual libertarianism (not, as frequently alleged, of libertinism) which regards the individual human *pneuma* as superior to and possessing a sovereignty over the primitive law of "Thou shalt" and "Thou shalt not" promulgated by the demiurge. To imagine that one's pure, divine spirit could be even affected, and

even less lost because of transgressing against the petty laws of a cosmic tyrant appeared laughable to the Gnostics. Threats of demiurgic retribution cannot frighten the Gnostic, for the ruler of the lower world has no dominion over the *pneuma* which originates within and is destined to return to a realm superior to his own. Moreover, this freedom of the spirit of the Gnostic is much more than a mere indifferent state of permissiveness; rather it is evident that the liberating effect of this freedom from external laws and commandments is in itself a value to be cultivated, for important reasons. Through indifference to the demiurgic norms, the Gnostic thwarts the designs of the petty, tyrannical powers of the cosmos and thus makes a positive contribution to the work of salvation. Freedom makes for more and greater freedom, while subservience to the blind law of a blind demiurge creates further slavery. One cannot free oneself by bowing to the yoke but only by breaking it.

Like a true Gnostic, Carl Jung recognized that, even at best, goodness is no substitute for wholeness; he frequently said that in the long run what matters is not goodness or obedience to moral laws, but only and simply the fullness of being. Gnostic psychology has always recognized that the artificial division or splitting apart of the fullness of being into the two halves of good and evil was a plot of the tyrannical forces bent upon keeping humanity in chains. By dividing life into two separate halves and ordering the human being to cleave to one of these halves to the exclusion of the other, the demiurgic power has caused humanity to do violence against the shadow side of the soul and has caused human beings to condemn themselves to a state of incompleteness and guilt. In order to restore the *pleroma,* or experience the fullness of being, we must know evil, which is not the same as doing evil. Evil-doers in the true sense are almost inevitably persons acting under one or several compulsions of an unconscious nature. It is thus their very lack of self-knowledge, and with it their lack of knowledge of their own evil, that forces them to do antisocial and evil acts. Unconscious content not brought into the Gnosis of consciousness is forced to live itself out by way of compulsive acts performed by the ego. As a latter-day Gnostic classic has expressed it, each human being is in truth his or her own absolute lawgiver, as well as his or her own reward and punishment. Such a statement can be recognized as valid only by persons who have emancipated themselves from the one-sided pursuit of moral perfection according to external laws and commandments. No longer seeking umbrage under the written law, such persons learn how to make conscious moral choices of their own design, winning individual victories and suffering their personal defeats according to the just constellations of psychic life.

Such are, in brief outline form, some of the principal tenets of the Gnosis, both of those who in olden days were called Gnostics, and of those who, following the guidelines set forth by C.G. Jung, have become acquainted with the Gnostic nature of the human soul and its path toward wholeness. Important and useful though such summaries of ideas may be, they cannot serve as substitutes for the original Gnostic images embodied in the primary vision revealed to the inner eye of the inspired knower. C.G. Jung was, of course, just such a knower. His knowledge was amplified by his superb education and his extensive acquaintance with the literature of the Gnostics, but it did not originate therein. It is of supreme importance therefore that we should have a glimpse of some of these original insights ("initial imaginationen," as he called them) as he wrote them down in his mysterious small treatise, filled with primeval power and deepest inspiration, and called by him *Septem Sermones ad Mortuos* or the *Seven Sermons to the Dead*. The remaining and major portion of this work shall be devoted to the content of this poetic tractate, presented here in an original translation, and to the elucidation of its strange message in the light of the ideas of classical Gnosticism and of modern psychology.

II

VII Sermones ad Mortuos

(Seven Sermons to the Dead)

Seven exhortations to the dead, written by Basilides in Alexandria, the city where East and West meet.*

The First Sermon

The dead came back from Jerusalem, where they did not find what they were seeking. They asked admittance to me and demanded to be taught by me, and thus I taught them:

Hear Ye: I begin with nothing. Nothing is the same as fullness. In the endless state fullness is the same as emptiness. The Nothing is both empty and full. One may just as well state some other thing about the Nothing, namely that it is white or that it is black or that it exists or that it exists not. That which is endless and eternal has no qualities, because it has all qualities.

The Nothing, or fullness, is called by us the PLEROMA. In it thinking and being cease, because the eternal is without

---

*See Translator's Note in the Appendix.

44

qualities. In it there is no one, for if anyone were, he then would be differentiated from the Pleroma and would possess qualities which would distinguish him from the Pleroma.

In the Pleroma there is nothing and everything: it is not profitable to think about the Pleroma, for to do that would mean one's dissolution.

The CREATED WORLD *is not in the Pleroma, but in itself. The Pleroma is the beginning and end of the created world. The Pleroma penetrates the created world as the sunlight penetrates the air everywhere. Although the Pleroma penetrates it completely, the created world has no part of it, just as an utterly transparent body does not become either dark or light in color as the result of the passage of the light through it. We ourselves, however, are the Pleroma, so it is that the Pleroma is present within us. Even in the smallest point the Pleroma is present without any bounds, eternally and completely, for small and great are the qualities which are alien to the Pleroma. The Pleroma is the nothingness which is everywhere complete and without end. It is because of this that I speak of the created world as a portion of the Pleroma, but only in an allegorical sense; for the Pleroma is not divided into portions, for it is nothingness. We, also, are the total Pleroma; for figuratively the Pleroma is an exceedingly small, hypothetical, even non-existent point within us, and also it is the limitless firmament of the cosmos about us. Why, however, do we discourse about the Pleroma, if it is the all, and also nothing?*

I speak of it, in order to begin somewhere, and also to remove from you the delusion that somewhere within or without there is something absolutely firm and definite. All things which are called definite and solid are but relative, for only that which is subject to change appears definite and solid.

The created world is subject to change. It is the only thing that is solid and definite, since it has qualities. In fact, the created world is itself but a quality.

We ask the question: how did creation originate? Creatures indeed originated but not the created world itself, for the created world is a quality of the Pleroma, in the same way as the

uncreated; eternal death is also a quality of the Pleroma. Crea-
tion is always and everywhere, and death is always and
everywhere. The Pleroma possesses all: differentiation and non-
differentiation.

Differentiation is creation. The created world is indeed differen-
tiated. Differentiation is the essence of the created world and for
this reason the created also causes further differentiation. That
is why man himself is a divider, inasmuch as his essence is also
differentiation. That is why he distinguishes the qualities of the
Pleroma, yea, those qualities which do not exist. These divisions
man draws from his own being. This then, is the reason for man
discoursing about the qualities of the Pleroma, which do not
exist.

You say to me: What good is it then to talk about this, since it
has been said that it is useless to think about the Pleroma?

I say these things to you in order to free you from the illusion
that it is possible to think about the Pleroma. When you speak
of the divisions of the Pleroma, we are speaking from the posi-
tion of our own divisions, and we speak about our own differen-
tiated state; but while we do this, we have in reality said nothing
about the Pleroma. However, it is necessary for us to talk about
our own differentiation, for this enables us to discriminate suffi-
ciently. Our essense is differentiation. For this reason we must
distinguish individual qualities.

You say: What harm does it not do to discriminate, for then we
reach beyond the limits of our own being; we extend ourselves
beyond the created world, and we fall into the undifferentiated
state which is another quality of the Pleroma. We submerge into
the Pleroma itself, and we cease to be created beings. Thus we
become subject to dissolution and nothingness.

Such is the very death of the created being. We die to the extent
that we fail to discriminate. For this reason the natural impulse
of the created being is directed toward differentiation and
toward the struggle against the ancient, pernicious state of
sameness. The natural tendency is called Principium Individuationis *(Principle of Individuation). This principle is indeed the*
essence of every created being. From these things you may

readily recognize why the undifferentiated principle and lack of discrimination are all a great danger to created beings. For this reason we must be able to distinguish the qualities of the Pleroma. Its qualities are the PAIRS OF OPPOSITES, *such as*

> *the effective and the ineffective*
> *fullness and emptiness*
> *the living and the dead*
> *difference and sameness*
> *light and dark*
> *hot and cold*
> *energy and matter*
> *time and space*
> *good and evil*
> *the beautiful and the ugly*
> *the one and the many*
> *and so forth.*

The pairs of opposites are the qualities of the Pleroma: they are also in reality non-existent because they cancel each other out.

Since we ourselves are the Pleroma, we also have these qualities present within us; inasmuch as the foundation of our being is differentiation, we possess these qualities in the name and under the sign of differentiation, which means:

First—that the qualities are in us differentiated from each other, and they are separated from each other, and thus they do not cancel each other out, rather they are in action. It is thus that we are the victims of the pairs of opposites. For in us the Pleroma is rent in two.

Second—the qualities belong to the Pleroma, and we can and should partake of them only in the name and under the sign of differentiation. We must separate ourselves from these qualities. In the Pleroma they cancel each other out; in us they do not. But if we know how to know ourselves as being apart from the pairs of opposites, then we have attained to salvation.

When we strive for the good and the beautiful, we thereby forget about our essential being, which is differentiation, and we are victimized by the qualities of the Pleroma which are the pairs of opposites. We strive to attain to the good and the beautiful, but at the same time we also attain to the evil and the ugly, because in the Pleroma these are identical with the good and the beautiful. However, if we remain faithful to our nature, which is differentiation, we then differentiate ourselves from the good and the beautiful, and thus we have immediately also differentiated ourselves from the evil and the ugly. It is only thus that we do not merge into the Pleroma, that is, into nothingness and dissolution.

You will object and say to me: Thou hast said that differentiation and sameness are also qualities of the Pleroma. How is it then when we strive for differentiation? Are we not then true to our natures and must we then also eventually be in the state of sameness, while we strive for differentiation?

What you should never forget is that the Pleroma has no qualities. We are the ones who create these qualities through our thinking. When you strive after differentiation or sameness or after other qualities, you strive after thoughts which flow to you from the Pleroma, namely thoughts about the non-existent qualities of the Pleroma. While you run after these thoughts, you fall again into the Pleroma and arrive at differentiation and sameness at the same time. Not your thinking but your being is differentiation. That is why you should not strive after differentiation and discrimination as you know these, but strive after your true nature. If you would thus truly strive, you would not need to know anything about the Pleroma and its qualities, and still you would arrive at the true goal because of your nature. However, because thinking alienates us from our true nature, therefore I must teach knowledge to you, with which you can keep your thinking under control.

The Second Sermon

During the night the dead stood along the walls and shouted: "We want to know about God! Where is God? Is God dead?"

—God is not dead; he is as much alive as ever. God is the created world, inasmuch as he is something definite and therefore he is

differentiated from the Pleroma. God is a quality of the Pleroma and everything that I have stated in reference to the created world is equally true of him.

God is distinguished from the created world, however, inasmuch as he is less definite and less definable than the created world in general. He is less differentiated than the created world, because the ground of his being is effective fullness; and only to the extent that he is definite and differentiated is he identical with the created world; and thus is he the manifestation of the effective fullness of the Pleroma.

Everything that we do not differentiate falls into the Pleroma and is cancelled out along with its opposite. Therefore if we do not discern God, then the effective fullness is cancelled out for us. God also is himself the Pleroma, even as every smallest point within the created world, as well as within the uncreated realm, is itself the Pleroma.

The effective emptiness is the being of the Devil. God and Devil are the first manifestations of the nothingness, which we call the Pleroma. It does not matter whether the Pleroma is or is not, for it cancels itself out in all things. The created world, however, is different. Inasmuch as God and Devil are created beings, they do not cancel each other out, rather they stand against each other as active opposites. We need no proof of their being; it is sufficient that we must always speak about them. Even if they did not exist, the created being would forever (because of its own differentiated nature) bring them forth out of the Pleroma.

All things which are brought forth from the Pleroma by differentiation are pairs of opposites; therefore God always has with him the Devil.

This interrelationship is so close, as you have learned, it is so indissoluble in your own lives, that it is even as the Pleroma itself. The reason for this is that these two stand very close to the Pleroma, in which all opposites are cancelled out and unified.

God and Devil are distinguished by fullness and emptiness, generation and destruction. Activity is common to both. Activity unites them. It is for this reason that activity stands above both, being God above God, for it unites fullness and emptiness in its working.

There is a God about whom you know nothing, because men have forgotten him. We call him by his name: ABRAXAS. He is less definite than God or Devil. In order to distinguish God from him, we call God HELIOS, or the Sun.

Abraxas is activity; nothing can resist him but the unreal, and thus his active being freely unfolds. The unreal is not, and therefore cannot truly resist. Abraxas stands above the sun and above the devil. He is the unlikely likely one, who is powerful in the realm of unreality. If the Pleroma were capable of having a being, Abraxas would be its manifestation.

Although he is activity itself, he is not a particular result but result in general.

He is active non-reality, because he has no definite result.

He is still a created being, inasmuch as he is differentiated from the Pleroma.

The sun has a definite effect and so does the devil; therefore they appear to us more effective than the undefinable Abraxas.

For he is power, endurance, change.
—At this point the dead caused a great riot, because they were Christians.

The Third Sermon

The dead approached like mist out of the swamps and they shouted: "Speak to us further about the highest god!"

—Abraxas is the god whom it is difficult to know. His power is the very greatest, because man does not perceive it at all. Man sees the summum bonum (supreme good) of the sun, and also the infinum malum (endless evil) of the devil, but Abraxas, he does not see, for he is undefinable life itself, which is the mother of good and evil alike.

Life appears smaller and weaker than the summum bonum *(supreme good), wherefore it is hard to think that Abraxas should supersede in his power the sun, which is the radiant fountain of all life force.*

Abraxas is the sun and also the eternally gaping abyss of emptiness, of the diminisher and dissembler, the devil.

The power of Abraxas is twofold. You cannot see it, because in your eyes the opposition of this power seems to cancel it out.

That which is spoken by God-the-Sun is life;
That which is spoken by the Devil is death.
Abraxas, however, speaks the venerable and also accursed word, which is life and death at once.

Abraxas generates truth and falsehood, good and evil, light and darkness with the same word and in the same deed. Therefore Abraxas is truly the terrible one.

He is magnificent even as the lion at the very moment when he strikes his prey down. His beauty is like the beauty of a spring morn.

Indeed, he is himself the greater Pan, and also the lesser. He is Priapos.

He is the monster of the underworld, the octopus with a thousand tentacles, he is the twistings of winged serpents and of madness.

He is the hermaphrodite of the lowest beginning.

He is the lord of toads and frogs, who live in water and come out unto the land, and who sing together at high noon and at midnight.

He is fullness, uniting itself with emptiness.
He is the sacred wedding;
He is love and the murder of love;
He is the holy one and his betrayer.

He is the brightest light of day and the deepest night of madness.

To see him means blindness;
To know him is sickness;
To worship him is death;
To fear him is wisdom;
Not to resist him means liberation.

God lives behind the sun; the devil lives behind the night. What god brings into birth from the light, that the devil pulls into the night. Abraxas, however, is the cosmos; its genesis and its dissolution. To every gift of God-the-Sun, the devil adds his curse.

All things which you beg from God-the-Sun, generate an act of the devil. All things which you accomplish through God-the-Sun add to the effective might of the devil.

Such is the terrible Abraxas.

He is the mightiest manifest being, and in him creation becomes frightened of itself.
He is the revealed protest of creation against the Pleroma and its nothingness.
He is the terror of the son, which he feels against his mother.
He is the love of the mother for her son.
He is the delight of earth and the cruelty of heaven.
Man becomes paralyzed before his face.
Before him there exist neither question nor answer.
He is the life of creation.
He is the activity of differentiation.
He is the love of man.
He is the speech of man.
He is both the radiance and the dark shadow of man.
He is deceitful reality.

—Here the dead howled and raved greatly, for they were still incomplete ones.

The Fourth Sermon

Grumbling, the dead filled the room and said: "Speak to us about gods and devils, thou accursed one!"

—God-the-Sun is the highest good, the devil is the opposite; thus you have two gods. But there are many great goods and many vast evils, and among them there are two god-devils, one of which is the BURNING ONE, *and the other the* GROWING ONE.

The burning one is EROS *in his form as a flame. It shines and it devours. The growing one is the* TREE OF LIFE; *it grows green, and it accumulates living matter while it grows. Eros flames up and then dies away; the tree of life, however, grows slowly and reaches stately stature throughout countless ages.*

Good and evil are united in the flame.
Good and evil are united in the growth of the tree.
Life and love oppose each other in their own divinity.

Immeasurable, like the host of the stars, is the number of gods and devils. Every star is a god, and every space occupied by a star is a devil. And the emptiness of the whole is the Pleroma. The activity of the whole is Abraxas; only the unreal opposes him. Four is the number of the chief deities, because four is the number of the measurements of the world. One *is the beginning; God-the-Sun.* Two *is Eros, because he expands with a bright light and combines two.* Three *is the Tree of Life, because it fills space with bodies.* Four *is the devil, because he opens everything that is closed; he dissolves everything that is formed and embodied; he is the destroyer, in whom all things come to nothing.*

Blessed am I, for it is granted unto me to know the multiplicity and diversity of the gods. Woe unto you, for you have substituted the oneness of God for the diversity which cannot be resolved into the one. Through this you have created the torment of incomprehension, and the mutilation of the created world, the essence and law of which is diversity. How can you be true to your nature when you attempt to make one out of the many? What you do to the gods, that also befalls you. All of you are made thus the same and in this way your nature also becomes mutilated.

For the sake of man there may reign unity, but never for the sake of god, because there are many gods but only few men. The gods are mighty, and they bear their diversity, because like the stars

*they stand in solitude and are separated by vast distances one
from the other. Humans are weak and cannot bear their own
diversity, because they live close to each other and are desirous
of company, so that they cannot bear their own distinct
separateness. For the sake of salvation do I teach you that which
is to be cast out, for the sake of which I myself have been cast
out.*

*The multiplicity of the gods equals the multiplicity of men.
Countless gods are waiting to become men. Countless gods have
already been men. Man is a partaker of the essence of the gods;
he comes from the gods and he goes to God.*

*Even as it is useless to think about the Pleroma, so it is useless to
worship the number of the gods. Least of all is it of any use to
worship the first God, the effective fullness and the highest
good. Through our prayer we cannot add to it and we cannot
take away from it, because the effective emptiness swallows
everything. The gods of light compose the heavenly world,
which is multiple and stretches into infinity and which expands
without end. Their highest lord is God-the-Sun.*

*The dark gods constitute the underworld. They are uncom-
plicated and they are capable of diminishing and shrinking into
infinity. Their deepest lord is the devil, the spirit of the moon,
the serf of the earth, who is smaller, colder and deader than the
earth.*

*There is no difference in the power of the heavenly and the
earthly gods. The heavenly ones expand, the earthly ones
diminish. Both directions stretch into infinity.*

The Fifth Sermon

*The dead were full of mocking and cried: "Teach us, thou fool,
about church and holy community!"*

*—The world of the gods is manifest in spirituality and sexuality.
The heavenly gods appear in spirituality, the earth gods appear
in sexuality.*

Spirituality receives and comprehends. It is feminine and therefore we call it MATER COELESTIS, *the heavenly mother. Sexuality generates and creates. It is masculine and therefore we call it* PHALLOS, *the earthly father. The sexuality of man is more earthly, while the sexuality of woman is more heavenly. The spirituality of man is more heavenly; for it moves in the direction of the greater. On the other hand, the spirituality of woman is more earthly; for it moves in the direction of the smaller.*

Deceitful and devilish is the spirituality of the man who goes toward the smaller. Deceitful and devilish is the spirituality of the woman who goes toward the greater. Each is to go to its own place.

Man and woman become a devil to each other when they do not separate their spiritual paths, for the nature of created beings is always of the nature of differentiation.

The sexuality of man goes to that which is earthly; the sexuality of woman goes to that which is spiritual. Man and woman become a devil to each other if they do not discriminate between their two forms of sexuality.

Man shall know that which is smaller, woman that which is greater. Man shall separate himself from spirituality and from sexuality alike. He shall call spirituality mother, and he shall enthrone her between heaven and earth. He shall name sexuality phallos, *and shall place it between himself and the earth, for the mother and the phallos are super-human demons and manifestations of the world of the gods. They are more effective for us than the gods, because they are nearer to our own being. When you cannot distinguish between yourselves on the one hand, and sexuality and spirituality on the other, and when you cannot regard these two as beings above and beside yourselves, then you become victimized by them, i.e., by the qualities of the Pleroma. Spirituality and sexuality are not your qualities, they are not things which you can possess and comprehend; on the contrary, these are mighty demons, manifestations of the gods, and therefore they tower above you and they exist in themselves. One does not possess spirituality for oneself or sexuality for oneself; rather one is subject to the laws of spirituality and sexuality.*

Therefore no one escapes these two demons. You shall regard them as demons, as common causes and grave dangers, quite like the gods, and above all, like the terrible Abraxas.

Man is weak, therefore community is indispensible; if it is not the community in the sign of the mother, then it is in the sign of the phallos. Not to have community consists of suffering and sickness. Community brings with itself fragmentation and dissolution. Differentiation leads to solitude. Solitude is contrary to community. Because of the weakness of man's will, as opposed to the gods and demons and their inescapable law, there is need for community.

For this reason there shall be as much community as necessary, not for the sake of men but for the sake of the gods. The gods force you into a community. As much community as they force upon you is necessary, but more than that is evil.

In the community each shall be subject to another, so that the community will be maintained, inasmuch as you have need of it. In the solitary state each one shall be placed above all others, so that he may know himself and avoid servitude. In community there shall be abstinence.

In solitude let there be squandering of abundance.
For community is the depth, while solitude is the height.
The true order in community purifies and preserves.
The true order in solitude purifies and increases.
Community gives us warmth, while solitude gives us the light.

The Sixth Sermon

The demon of sexuality comes to our soul like a serpent. It is half a human soul and is called thought-desire.

The demon of spirituality descends into our soul like a white bird. It is half a human soul and is called desire-thought.

The serpent is an earthly soul, half demonic, a spirit, and related to the spirits of the dead. Like the spirits of the dead, the serpent also enters various terrestrial objects. The serpent also induces fear of itself in the hearts of men, and enkindles desire in the same. The serpent is of a generally feminine character and seeks forever the company of the dead. It is associated with the dead who are earthbound, who have not found the way by which to cross over to the state of solitude. The serpent is a whore and she consorts with the devil and with evil spirits; she is a tyrant and a tormenting spirit, always tempting people to keep the worst kind of company.

The white bird is the semi-heavenly soul of man. It lives with the mother and occasionally descends from the mother's abode. The bird is masculine and is called effective thought. The bird is chaste and solitary, a messenger of the mother. It flies high above the earth. It commands solitude. It brings messages from the distance, from those who have gone before, those who are perfected. It carries our words up to the mother. The mother intercedes and warns, but she has no power against the gods. She is a vehicle of the sun.

The serpent descends into the deep and with her cunning she either paralyzes or stimulates the phallic demon. The serpent brings up from the deep the very cunning thoughts of the earthly one, thoughts that crawl through all openings and become saturated with desire. Although the serpent does not want to be, she is nevertheless useful to us. The serpent eludes our grasp, we pursue her and she thus shows us the way, which, with our limited human wit, we could not find.

—The dead looked up with contempt and said: "Cease to speak to us about gods, demons and souls. We have known all of this in essence for a long time!"

The Seventh Sermon

At night the dead came back again and amidst complaining said: "One more thing we must know, because we had forgotten to discuss it: teach us concerning man!"

—Man is a portal through which one enters from the outer world of the gods, demons and souls, into the inner world, from

the greater world into the smaller world. Small and insignificant is man; one leaves him soon behind, and thus one enters once more into infinite space, into the microcosm, into the inner eternity.

In immeasurable distance there glimmers a solitary star on the highest point of heaven. This is the only God of this lonely one. This is his world, his Pleroma, his divinity.

In this world, man is Abraxas, who gives birth to and devours his own world.
This star is man's God and goal.
It is his guiding divinity; in it man finds repose.
To it goes the long journey of the soul after death; in it shine all things which otherwise might keep man from the greater world with the brilliance of a great light.

To this One, man ought to pray.
Such a prayer increases the light of the star.
Such a prayer builds a bridge over death.·
It increases the life of the microcosm; when the outer world grows cold, this star still shines.

There is nothing that can separate man from his own God, if man can only turn his gaze away from the fiery spectacle of Abraxas.

Man here, God there. Weakness and insignificance here, eternal creative power there. Here is but darkness and damp cold. There all is sunshine.

Upon hearing this the dead fell silent, and they rose up like smoke rises over the fire of the shepherd, who guards his flock by night.

Anagramma:

Nahtriheccunde
Gahinneverahtunin
Zehgessurklach
Zunnus.

END OF THE SEVEN SERMONS TO THE DEAD

III

Dr. Jung's Mysterious Treatise
Interpretation of the Seven Sermons

The Preamble—The Sage, the City and the Dead

Jung begins his poetic Gnostic treatise with a preamble of one poignant sentence: "Seven exhortations to the dead, written by Basilides in Alexandria, the city where East and West meet."

The first item in the proem which merits attention is undoubtedly Jung ascribing the authorship of the Sermons to the great Gnostic doctor, Basilides of Alexandria. Readers of the Sermons have often been puzzled by this statement regarding authorship, and some have even gone as far as to detect a spiritualistic or mediumistic character in the treatise on the basis that Jung himself ascribed it, not to himself, but to a long-dead personage. It needs to be remembered, however, that such a procedure is by no means unknown to mystical literature. As stated before, the Zohar is but one example of a long line of spiritually toned treatises which do not bear the name of their true author. The reason for this concealment of authorship is fairly simple: modesty. The mystical writers of by-gone centuries considered it unbecoming their station to take credit for works which they considered to have been authored by agencies superior to

59

themselves. The writers of such literature considered themselves at best as humble scribes whose task it was to put into earthly language the transcendental messages which appeared to them to emanate from a realm beyond the contemporary and the mortal. Thus it would seem that Jung was following in the footsteps of a distinguished lineage of inspired scribes who did not wish to give credit to their earthly egos for the messages emanating from their higher Selves.

The *Sermons* thus have two authors, as it were: Jung, the Swiss scribe, and Basilides, the Alexandrian prophet. Who then, one must ask, was or is this Basilides? Although one of the illustrious quaternary of great Gnostic luminaries (composed of himself, Valentinus, Marcion and Bardesanes), Basilides is an elusive figure of Gnostic history. He is said to have been at the height of his career as a teacher of Gnosis between the years A.D. 117 and 138. Of his nationality we know nothing. He may have been Greek, as his name suggests, or Syrian or even Egyptian, but he was certainly steeped in Hellenic spirituality and Hebrew scriptural religiosity alike, for he wrote twenty-four books of commentaries on the Gospels and is said to have authored a gospel himself. Like his great colleague Valentinus, he also was a poet and wrote a number of odes on spiritual themes. In him indeed, and not only in his favorite city, East and West met, for of all the Gnostic teachers his teachings have the most distinctly Eastern flavor, reminiscent at times of Buddhism.

Basilides was a disciple of Glaucias, who as a very young man sat at the feet of the controversial apostle of Jesus whom posterity has come to know as Peter the fisherman. The Christian writer Agrippa Castor stated that from A.D. 133 on Basilides was regarded as heterodox by the self-styled orthodox party within the church. His death probably occurred around A.D. 145, but his teachings survived in Egypt till the end of the fourth century, and his spirit entered European Gnosticism in the wake of the journeyings of his disciple Marcus of Memphis, who carried the Basilidian tradition as far as Spain. It is not amazing, then, that Jung had come in some ways to regard himself as a mouthpiece of this great teacher, for was his thought not mysteriously rooted in that elusive tradition of Gnosis, which survived for uncounted centuries in the fastness of the Pyrenees from whence it came, to reside in the Alps of Switzerland where Paracelsus walked before Jung? Was the Swiss doctor, after a fashion, not of "those of Basilides," as the church fathers have called the heirs of this sage of Alexandria?

Most of the information we possess regarding the content of the numerous writings of Basilides derives from the work *Philosophumena* by the church father Hippolytus. As an avid reader of the then still pitifully inadequate corpus on Gnosticism, Jung was of course well acquainted with the majestic phrases of Basilides as quoted by Hippolytus. He knew of the sublime heights to which the genius of this great man soared when describing the great, impersonal, deific fullness of the Pleroma, which in the words of G.R.S. Mead "to the narrow minds of earth seems pure nothingness, instead of being that which beggars all fullness." "The First Sermon to the Dead" indeed shows a remarkable similarity with these fragments of the works of Basilides which have survived.

Well nigh as important as Basilides himself is Alexandria, the city where East and West meet. Alexandria, the larger of the two Egyptian cities founded by and bearing the name of the invincible Alexander, was indeed the holy city of Gnosticism, which continued to inflame the imagination of poets and mystics for millenia to come, right down to the modern days of Constantine Cawafi and Lawrence Durell. In a very real sense, Alexandria was the embodied archetype of the *Polis*, the classical urban alchemical vessel of human creativity from whence arise the new aeons of transformative thought and realization. The French poet and admirer of the Gnostics, Jaques Lacarriere, has put it better than the present writer could hope to do:

> Crucible, burning-glass, mortar and blast furnace; the still wherein all heavens, all gods, all visions are mixed, distilled, infused and transfused: such was Alexandria in the second century. Look wherever you will, interrogate history from any standpoint or level whatever, and you will find all races represented there (except the Chinese, who have not yet arrived), all continents (Africa, Asia, Europe) and all ages (Ancient Egypt, whose sanctuaries are preserved there, the ages of Athens and Rome, of Judea, Palestine, and Babylon); all these elements are gathered together in this knot of the Delta, this city which is to the river what lungs are to men and branches to a tree: the place through which they breathe and the source of their inspiration.[1]

The Emperor Hadrian when journeying to Alexandria wrote to his friend Servianus that in this magnificent whirlpool of creeds and mysteries, of philosophers, mystagogues, diviners and bishops, all exclusiveness seemed to melt away and "one can see bishops, who claim to be Christians, paying homage to Serapis. There is no single priest—Samaritan, Christian or Jew—who is not a mathematician, a haruspex or alpyte. When the (Christian) Patriarch himself comes to Egypt, he worships both Christ and Serapis to keep everyone happy...." Alexandria was not a city, it was *the city*, the true *Polis* where East and West, above and below, light and darkness, met. Nay, they did more than that, they fought, debated and embraced, and out of their passionate battles and compassionate agreements arose the spiritual wonders of late antiquity: the god-taught philosophy of Ammonius; the mystic flights of Plotinus; the theurgic magic of Proclus and Iamblichus; the spiritual quantum leaps of the Neo-Pythagoreans; and last but most certainly not least, the Gnosis of Basilides, of Valentinus, of Carpocrates and of his regal wife Alexandra. Such was the glory of Alexandria, the city founded by an imperial messiah where the gods and goddesses walked with men longer than in any other city on earth. Jung traveled to Alexandria in 1935 and, among others, had the curious experience that a palmist looked at his hand and refused to say anything. (One needs to remember that Jung was attracted to Alexandria, while he shunned Rome, the eternal city of non-Gnostic Christendom, and never entered its confines.) No wonder the *Seven Sermons* came to be mystically and poetically associated with this great archetype of the city of wisdom.

One more important element needs to be illuminated here, and that is the matter of the "dead" to whom the exhortations of Basilides are addressed. Who, then, are the dead? Death and the dead have a powerful connection with the land of Egypt, in both its ancient and in its Alexandrian aspects. The transformational symbolism of Egyptian proto-psychology is inextricably interwoven with burial places, mummies, pyramids; the savior prototype of the "living One," the Lord of life and of the living, Osiris, becomes the dreaded ruler of the underworld—the judge, not of the quick, but of the dead. Death hovers with its vulture wings over the mythos of Egypt, and out of this mythos, by way of the Egyptian Gnostics, arises the curious, dramatic format of the *Seven Sermons* wherein the dead ask questions of—and at times rage against—the Gnostic master Basilides.

The Gnostic significance of the words *death* and *life*, which in his own way Jung employs throughout the *Seven Sermons*, is one which, like so many Gnostic symbols, reverses the mundane significations, and thus brings us a meaning not hitherto suspected. The celebrated *Gospel According to Thomas* of Nag Hammadi fame promises the reader that those who will understand the meaning of the words contained in this gospel "will not taste death." Victory over death, of course, remained the keynote of the message of the resurrection in exoteric Christianity as well, without, however, bringing to us any apprehension of the hidden meaning of the word "death." The Gnostic meaning of death is, if not exactly derived from them, at least closely related to the concepts of the pre-Socratics, whose psychological wisdom was greatly respected and extolled by Jung. Thus we find Heraclitus says that each of the four elements lives the death of the others. "Water lives the death of air," proclaims Heraclitus, as "air lives the death of fire." This indicates that the essence of superior life must give its vital power over to a sort of "death" when it projects itself outward and downward and incorporates its nature in organisms or forms existing on the plane below its own status. Superior principles thus become the inspiriting or life-giving principles of inferior beings. A superior entity must die away or die out to the full conscious expression of its authentic selfhood in order to give life to a kingdom of being below its own rank. The life of the body thus becomes the death of the soul, even as the life of the soul itself has been the death of the spirit. A sacrificial relationship or rather relatedness can be said to exist between the various kingdoms of being. In those teachings of Gnosticism where the incarnation, or embodiment of the Logos in the body of Jesus, is regarded as factual, this Gnosis becomes the basis of the theology of redemption. God the Son is the divine seed of the Father's life, which, like any seed, must fall into the ground and lose its life in order to regain it in the form of a new plant. When a high and blessed potential life is exchanged for the poverty of actuality, we experience the tragedy of alienation, which plays such a significant role in the myths of the Gnostics as well as in the life of the psyche, according to Jung. No wonder the Gnostic Thomas in his Gospel makes Jesus exclaim: "I wonder how this wealth has made its home in this poverty." The meaning of death then is in Gnosticism the same thing that the non-Gnostics would call the meaning of life. The bodily life of humankind is in truth a form of death, not possessing the finality of bodily death, but a death nevertheless. Thus the "dead" are revealed as none other than ourselves, the so-called and self-styled living. Lest this curious reversal of meaning should be allowed to cast yet another shadow on the reputation of the unhappy Gnostics, it is necessary to emphasize that this view of death and life was virtually universal in the ancient world, and that it was by no means just another foible of the "world-hating" Gnostics. Plotinus, who had his quarrels with at least some Gnostics, holds to this exact meaning of the word *death* when he says in his *Enneads* (I., 1viii):

> When the soul has descended into generation she partakes of evil and is carried a great way into a state the opposite of her first purity and integrity, to be entirely merged in it...and death to her is, while baptized or immersed in the present body, to descend into matter and be wholly subjected to it. This is what is meant by falling asleep in Hades of those who have come there.

Attention should be called to Plotinus' use of the expression "falling asleep in Hades" in this connection, for this expression indicates that in an esoteric sense Plotinus, like the Gnostics, regarded this incarnate existence as Hades, or hell, and that physical life was known to him as "death." Greek philosophy is replete with references to the esoteric glyph which declares that "life" is "death." Ancient philosophers stated that whatever we see when awake is death; and what we see when asleep is a dream. Plato is said to have revealed this identical view to Cebes, and commenting on the beliefs held by the practitioners of the Mysteries, the great expositor of Greek thought Thomas Taylor wrote that the Greeks "believed that human souls were confined in the body as in a prison, a condition which was denominated by genesis or generation; from which Dionysus would liberate them. This generation, which linked the soul to the body, was supposed to be a kind of death to the higher form of life. Evil is inherent to this condition, the soul dwelling in the body as in a prison or a grave...." Even the aforementioned egregious involvement of ancient Egyptian religion with the idea of death has been reinterpreted by some scholars as referring, not primarily to the souls who have departed their earthly habitation, but to the living, who philosophically, or as one might say today psychologically, might be referred to as dead. There is much indication of the possibility amounting to near fact that the three pivotal words *death, the dead,* and *to die* bore the same esoteric meaning and reference in Gnostic and other Christian scriptures as they did in the Greek philosophical discourses and in the Egyptian books of old. C.G. Jung, a man as deeply versed in classical literature as he was in Gnostic spirituality, was aware of this meaning of *death*, and *the dead* to him undoubtedly meant the unregenerate hyletic representatives of humanity, who by identifying with physicality to the exclusion of their psychic and pneumatic natures, have allowed physical life to render them spiritually dead.

The exhortations delivered by Basilides thus are indeed intended for those living dead who are without Gnosis, and who might attain to Gnosis, or true consciousness, by apprehending the meaning of the sermons which the master teacher patiently delivers to them in spite of their frequent incomprehensions and protestations.

The First Sermon—The Empty Fullness

The first significant statement that calls attention to itself in the First Sermon is the mention of Jerusalem. "The dead came back from Jerusalem, where they did not find what they were seeking." Jerusalem, the old city of peace, where both the dwelling of the Jewish God and the sites of the life and death of the Christian Son of God were located, was and continues to be much more than a mere city. Like Alexandria, it is an archetype, but its psychic charge is of a different order.* While the Egyp-

---

*For further impressions of the special qualities of Alexandria, refer to Couat: *La Poesie Alexandrine;* also the noted quadrilogy of novels by Laurence Durell: *The Alexandria Quartet.*

tian city of the Delta stands for freedom, creativity, spiritual pluralism, the Palestinian holy site denotes orthodoxy, the law, the awesome majesty of the lordly and jealous patriarch of Semitic religiosity. In Alexandria the gods and goddesses walk the streets side by side with prostitutes, bishops and fishmongers; in Jerusalem the Lord broods in his secret temple chambers, to be visited only on rare and dreadful days by the high priest. The twelfth century Calabrian abbot Joaquino da Fiore wrote that the Age of the Father had its capital in Jerusalem, while the Age of the Son came to be centered in Rome, and that both would give way to the Age of the Holy Spirit which would spread over the earth without fixed centers and capitals whatsoever. Jung would not visit Rome, but he did travel to Jerusalem. There is little doubt, however, that Alexandria, rather than the Jewish-Christian sacred city, was his spiritual home.

In this vale of alienation, the exiled children of Eve continue to make pilgrimages to Jerusalem. The ambivalence of non-Gnostic Christendom towards its Judaic roots leads to queer and contradictory phenomena. A good example of these is the case of a notorious anti-Semite preacher in America whose anti-Jewish tirades resounded over the continent for decades and who all the while was engaged in the construction of a costly replica of Jerusalem in Arkansas. Christian fundamentalism thinks nothing of reviling the Jewish people for the alleged killing of Christ while worshipping a God appropriated from the mythos of its despised spiritual ancestors. It goes almost without saying that the pilgrimages of the living dead to Jerusalem never yield many useful results. Yahweh and Christ have both departed to realms unapproachable. Jewish and Christian orthodoxies, along with their fierce prophetic offspring, Islam, are as empty of Gnosis as the demolished Temple and the barren tomb are of God. The dead journey to Jerusalem in vain and thus they are bound to return to Alexandria, to life and to Gnosis. With the loss of Gnosis in the third and fourth centuries the Alexandrian spirituality of the Gnostics—and of the almost-Gnostics of the order of Clement and Origen—gave way to the literal-minded fundamentalism of the Nicene fathers, who came to substitute the physical Jesus for the spiritual Christ.

Throughout history, some have tried to find their way back to the spiritual archetype of Alexandria, asking admission to the guardians of wisdom and asking to be taught by them. Thus the dead ever come back from Jerusalem, disspirited, disillusioned, but still filled with the crumbs of dead creeds and deadly laws which fester in them, preventing their appreciation of the messages of Gnosis.

Basilides the Gnostic thus teaches the dead, whose appreciation of his wisdom is small indeed. Still, the teacher does not deny them instruction. He judges the desires of their longing hearts rather than the remonstrations of their troubled minds. Time and again, the dead rave and howl, argue and fulminate, while the knower calmly depicts the realms of being, the gods and demons, the lights and shadows that make up the fabric of the universe and of the souls of men.

He begins with nothing. This nothing he calls the Fullness, or Pleroma. The parallels with the fragments of Basilides' words as recorded by Hippolytus are truly remarkable, and some may be recounted profitably:

> There was when naught was; nay, even that 'naught' was not aught of things that are . . . . But nakedly, conjecture and mental quibbling apart, there was absolutely not even the One . . . . And when I use the term 'was,' I do not mean to say that it was; but merely to give some suggestion of what I wish to indicate, I use the expression 'there was absolutely naught,' For that 'naught' is not simply the so-called Ineffable; it is beyond that. For that which is really ineffable is not named Ineffable, but is superior to every name that is used . . . .

> Naught was, neither matter, nor substance, nor voidness of substance, nor simplicity, nor impossibility of composition, nor inconceptibility, nor imperceptibility, neither man, nor angel, nor god; in fine, neither anything at all for which man has ever found a name, nor any operation which falls within the range either of perception or conception. Such, or rather far more removed from the power of man's comprehension, was the state of non-being, when . . . . the Deity beyond being, without thinking, or feeling, or determining, or choosing, or being compelled, or desiring, willed to create universality.[2]

Unlike the personalized creation myth of Genesis, the story of the origin of being as given to us by the First Sermon is indicative of a boundless, impersonal, indefinable and absolutely transcendental field residing at the root-base of all consciousness and unconsciousness. From this plenum eventually emerge emanations of differentiated being in series, with properties revealing the supreme field. In this fullness of undifferentiated potentialities, all opposites are still in a state of equilibrium. Only much later do they stir into gradual effective manifestation, first as two polarities, and finally many more descending from these, arranging themselves in numerous pairs, or Syzygies, descending from the potential and transcendental to the actual and imminent. In a very real sense all Gnostic systems have this basic realization in common. Not only do the emanational orders of Valentinus, Basilides and other ancient Gnostic teachers show this remarkable similarity, but the Kabbalah, with its Pleromic equivalent known as the *Ain Soph Aur,* as well as numerous Christian late Gnostic systems such as that of Jacob Boehme, all agree in this teaching. The nineteenth-century founder of one of the most potent revivals of the Gnosis of old, H.P. Blavatsky, gave utterance to an apparently ancient Tibetan or Mongolian description of the Pleroma in the first of her sublime *Stanzas of Dzyan:*

> The Eternal Parent, wrapped in her Ever-Invisible Robes, had slumbered once again for Seven Eternities.
>
> Time was not, for it lay asleep in the Infinite Bosom of Duration.
>
> Universal Mind was not, for there were no Ah-hi to contain it.
>
> The Seven Ways to Bliss were not. The Great Causes of Misery were not, for there was no one to produce and get ensnared by them.
>
> Darkness alone filled the Boundless All, for Father, Mother and Son were once more one, and the Son had not yet awakened for the new Wheel and his Pilgrimage thereon.
>
> The Seven Sublime Lords and the Seven Truths had ceased to be, and the Universe, the Son of Necessity, was immersed in Paranishpanna, to be outbreathed by that which is, and yet is not. Naught was.
>
> The causes of Existence had been done away with; the Visible

that was, and the Invisible that is, rested in Eternal Non-Being—the One Being.

Alone, the One Form of Existence stretched boundless, infinite, causeless, in Dreamless Sleep; and Life pulsated unconscious in Universal Space.... [3]

Light, Father of All, Unbegotten, Ineffable, the Unapproachable God, the Abyss, the Unknowable, the Primal Man—such are some of the names by which the aboriginal being of the Pleroma has been called by various Gnostic scriptures and teachers. Not unlike the so called Naassenes, or serpent venerating radical Gnostics, Jung quickly proceeds to a transcendentally humanistic or intrapsychic definition of the Fullness when he says very simply and directly: "We ourselves, however, are the Pleroma, because we are a portion of the eternal and the endless." Thus we are given a potent hint as to the psychological and personal applicability of what at first might appear as an abstract doctrine of a cosmogonic and theogenic significance. Even as in their personified state of the *Pantheon* (the family of all gods and goddesses), the Greeks mythologically acknowledged the existence of a state wherein the deities are united in an all-encompassing fullness, so the Gnostics in their more subtly mystical interpretation came to state that the Divine existences, along with their fashioned universes, while distinguished one from another, are the emanations of the impersonal and unknowable Fullness.

What could this Gnostic concept have meant to Jung? We can only guess, but the contents of the First Sermon may lend considerable substance to our guessing. Jung's psychology—as indicated by us repeatedly—is in some ways but a psychological restatement of Gnosticism, and as such it shows innumerable analogies and equivalencies to the ancient Gnostic systems. The place of the Divine existences is taken by the archetypes, and the sum of these archetypes is none other that the psychological analogy of the Pleroma. One of Jung's most prominent disciples and interpreters, Yolande Jacobi, states in her work *The Psychology of Jung* that to Jung the sum of the archetypes signifies the sum of all latent potentialities of the human psyche wherein resides an enormous and overwhelming store of knowledge and power which concerns, not at all personalistic psychic questions, but the most powerful relations between God, man and the cosmos. This store of our psyche is, for all intents and purposes, closed to most of us, but if we open it and wake it to new life by integrating it with consciousness, we thereby remove ourselves from our painful psychic isolation and become once again incorporated in the eternal process of the fullness of being.

The Pleroma in its psychological sense, then, is neither more nor less than the original fullness, or totality of psychic reality, from whence the differentiated ego with its multiplicity of functions and powers emanates and whither—as the result of the process of individuation—it strives to return. Yet this return must be accomplished in a special way. Jung states in the First Sermon that when the soul, failing to discriminate, extends itself beyond the cosmos, it falls into the undifferentiated state, and by becoming submerged into the Pleroma once again it becomes subject to dissolution and becomes nothing. The term individuation, or rather the principle inherent in the human being that impels us toward individuation, is explicitly mentioned by Jung in this sermon as the "natural tendency called *Principium Individuationis.*"

In the *Seven Sermons* therefore, we have one of the earliest and most poignant statements of Jung regarding individuation, the often repeated but even more often misunderstood central doctrine of his psychology. Individuation, especially as defined in the First Sermon, is, then, a very specific and distinct idea of the Western tradition, adapted by Jung to psychological use. The *Principium Individuationis* is the inherent tendency of the human psyche not to give up its light of consciousness and fall back into the internal abyss of primordial nothingness. Unlike many (although not all) the spiritual systems of the East, especially of India, the Western tradition has never envisioned a permanent dissolution of human individuality in Divinity. The West knows and desires no dewdrop-like slipping into the shining sea. Instead, Jung states here that the principle of individuation is the essence of every created being and that the undifferentiated principle and our own lack of discrimination are great dangers to us. How to remain individuals, in the classical sense of an indivisibly integrated psychic entity, an *individuum,* while at the same possessing an optimum degree of permeability toward the ineffable greatness of the Pleroma within us—this is the great task and objective envisioned by Jung which he poetically but unequivocally expresses already in the First Sermon.

There can be little doubt that under the metaphor and guise of cosmic and metaphysical statements, Jung speaks of psychology in the *Seven Sermons*. This may annoy those who relish immersion and perhaps even losing themselves in metaphysical abstractions and transcendentally toned understandings, but in our view their annoyance has little practical justification. In his *Alchemical Studies* Jung mercilessly castigated what he called the metaphysical claims of all esoteric teachings. In the same statement he vowed to deliberately bring everything that purports to be metaphysical into the daylight of psychological understanding. He unequivocally stated that to grasp anything metaphysically is impossible, that one must of necessity do so psychologically. Jung thus employed himself—often to the amazement of his public—in stripping various esoteric doctrines of their metaphysical wrappings and making them objects of psychology. By this he did not intend a process of reductionism, but rather a strict principle of psychological application of metaphysical statements. It is heartening to realize that this difficult task was successfully performed by Jung in virtually every instance, and that by addressing himself to it he broke ground for a most promising series of spiritual adventures for countless persons who wished to render the noble flights of metaphysical and occult preachments empirically useful in their own psychic lives.

The most enigmatic model for metaphysical fascinations of the mind in our age is undoubtedly the Eastern, particularly the Hindu, which consistently employs metaphysical and cosmological language to express what to Jung would appear to be psychological statements. Jung contended that the search for the wisdom of the East had almost darkened the mind of the West and that, in fact, it is a search that continues to lead countless persons astray. The alms of the East should not be accepted by us as if we were beggars, said Jung, and the thinking of the great alien cultures of the Orient should not be imitated by Westerners unthinkingly. In the words of Jung, those who, after the fashion of homeless pirates, settle with thievish intent on foreign shores are in the gravest of all dangers, that of losing their souls. (See C.G. Jung's Commentaries on *The Secret of the Golden Flower,* and also "Yoga and the West," in Jung's *Collected Works,* Vol. II, pp. 529-539.) The greatest peril we may run with such imitative exercises, however, is not merely the result of the alien cultural impact of the traditions thus imitated, but of some of their content. The approach of much Indian thinking, Hindu and Buddhist alike, appears to be the very obliteration of individual consciousness which Jung warns us about in connection with the submerging of the soul into the Pleroma. When desire is killed out by a variety of methods of meditation and contemplation, what remains is a psychic corpse from which the libidinal cosmic force of the vital surge has been artificially removed. One can perish of psychic pernicious anemia as well as from its physiological analogue, and the fulfillment of such objectives as desirelessness and egolessness may very well lead to just such a condition. The desire for self-knowledge is just as much a desire as the desire for food or sex.

As Jung expresses it in the last paragraph of the First Sermon, one should not strive after the differentiated state of personalism on the one hand or the obliteration of personality in undifferentiated sameness on the other. The rugged and anxious individualist is apt to end up in just as great a psychological trouble as the yogi seeking the egoless void. Says Jung by way of Basilides: "While you run after these thoughts, you fall again into the Pleroma and arrive at differentiation and sameness at the same time . . . . That is why you should not strive after differentiation and discrimination as you know these, but strive after your true nature. If you would thus truly strive you would not need to know anything about the Pleroma and its qualities, and still you would arrive at the true goal because of your nature." What is this nature which on its own, when not interfered with by human thinking, leads humanity to its authentic goal? It is not tranquillity, serenity or nirvanic quiet; it is not an ethereal trance born of the abnegation of desire and the mortification of the flesh; rather it is force, energy, power. This power, which was called by the early psychoanalytic movement *libido,* or pleasure, has in fact a principle of pleasure as its motivating force, even as it has the individuation principle as its driving force. Like the proverbial donkey, the psyche is drawn forward by the carrot of the *principium libidinis,* while it is urged forward by the *principium individuationis.* Thus have the gods assured that progress should be made within the human spiritual situation. They deserve gratitude for their wisdom rather than the usual guilt and shame we lavish on their gifts of life.

The variety of Gnosis propounded by Jung in his Sermons is not a technique or discipline absorbed or adapted by the human being from an external source, but rather a commitment to the experience of the forces of life, both in the outer world of nature and in the inner world of psyche. It is in a very real way what has been described as the Faustian path, outlined in Goethe's great masterpiece, which served as one of the principal sources of Jung's inspiration throughout his life. Faust finds himself in a position not unlike that of contemporary humanity. His studies and academic calling offer him modalities of approaching the life of the spirit, which consist of prescribed disciplines devised by authorities possessing prestige and outward luster. The arrival of the Mephistophelian facilitator convinces him, however, to abandon the outwardly imposed and taught disciplines of formal tradition and to plunge into the path of consciously committed action. In lieu of the safe and unspectacular path of respectability and morality, he walks the perilous but ultimately rewarding highway that leads to life's reservoir of vitality and power, the sole true source of transformation. He invokes the spirit of Earth, the amoral, energetic force of nature, which is unfettered by the inhibitions and high-sounding maxims of the intellect. He descends into chaos and tribulation, into the realms beyond the limits of convention and human laws where the seething magma of raw transformative energy resides in its unrefined and undiluted state. It is only by way of this commitment to darkness, error, suffering, along with ecstasy, passion and battle, that he attains to his ascent into the realms of light, guided by the transfigured Sophianic spirit of Margaret. It is thus that he can say that it is "wisdom's final say that freedom and life belong to that man solely who must reconquer them each day."

The Faustian spirit of Jung's Gnosis as expressed in the First Sermon is documented, not only by his existential and conscious attitude toward the temptations of submerging into the Pleroma, but also by his treatment of the subject of the dualities which form part of the Pleroma. Binaries, or Syzygies as they are more often called, are a time-honored feature of Gnosticism. Primal being was conceived as going forth from itself in a series of existences, each at a farther distance from the center. One of the chief hallmarks of these emanations is that they are represented in pairs, one male the other female, and that their names usually describe contrasting or complementary qualities of being. In Jung's Sermons the Syzygies are called pairs of opposites and some of them are enumerated in the text. Among these are: effective and ineffective; fullness and emptiness; living and dead; difference and sameness; light and dark; hot and cold; energy and matter (a rather modern pair from physics); time and space; good and evil; beauty and ugliness; one and many. The Faustian consciousness which emerges as a Gnostic type from the Sermons is definitely involved in these opposites and recognizes them as existential realities within the sphere of human life. Once again the empirical and existential orientation of Jung is quite apparent. While he states that in the Pleroma itself these pairs of opposites are not effectively real, inasmuch as they cancel each other out, in human experience they are indeed supremely and painfully real. He exclaims with true Gnostic pathos: "In us the Pleroma is rent in two." To the extent that the human psyche is involved in the world of differentiation, it is bound to experience the pairs of opposites, for they appertain to the operating and growth-producing mechanism of the differentiated realm. Still, the pairs of opposites are a hazard to the human, primarily because in its naivete the human consciousness tends to associate itself with one of the constituents of the pairs of opposites to the exclusion of the other. Thus we strive for the Good and the Beautiful, but as the result of this very striving we invoke the evil and the ugly.

Jung here enunciates a truly Gnostic and psychologically supremely important principle. One-sidedness of conscious orientation has been the bane of Western humanity in general and of modern Western humanity in particular. We forever tend to make the unjustified assumption that if we only did things right we could have one opposite without its partner. We tend to think that our inability to have only one opposite is the fault of our inadequate methods rather than of the inevitable nature of reality. As the interaction and eventual coalescence of the opposites seems to rule the macrocosm of the universe, so it also appears to govern the life of the psyche. Consciousness seeks unconsciousness, as light seeks the darkness, and as reason seeks the excitement and compensation of unreason.

Jung has repeatedly pointed out that whenever prolonged one-sidedness occurs within the conscious attitude of the individual, a countering compensatory action takes place within the unconscious. The fanatic, whose conscious commitment to a particular point of view has led to a failure to accept this compensatory potentiality, tends to move into an ever-increasing isolation from the healthy dynamics of his own deeper psyche. Fanatical commitment is by definition incapable of a healthy criticism of its own one-sidedness of attitude. The fanatic may criticize everything and everybody with the exception of himself and his own fanatical ideas. Thus a disharmony arises which, as the result of the rejection of the compensating influence, energizes the destructive power of unconscious elements, which blindly and furiously begin to take charge of the individual against his will and better judgement. Incomprehensible thoughts and moods, violent outbursts of temper, psychosomatic illnesses, hallucinatory intrusions into consciousness—all of these and many more are the result of the unwillingness of the mind to accept balance and compensation. The stone rejected by the builder becomes the cornerstone of the prisonhouse in which the builder himself comes to be confined. As with the individual, so with the culture; one-sidedness breeds insanity. The excessive conscious pursuits of rational values bring unprecedented outbursts of irrationality; rigid insistence on consciously accepted ethical maxims occasions the rise of crime and violence; and the perpetually avowed pursuit of world peace leads to the outbreak of one horrendous world war after another.

In the concluding sentences of the First Sermon Jung points the way toward the only real solution to this dilemma. Thoughts which flow to us from the Pleroma, from the undifferentiated fullness, tend to be deceptive. Philosophical, political and social theories tend to fail us because they bear the hallmark of abstractions unrelated to the actual world rather than authentic connections with our transformative creativity. In order to achieve true solutions, human beings must change, not their concepts, but themselves. Such a substantive change, however, is rooted not in theoretical information but in self-knowledge. To strive after one's true nature is thus far more useful than to strive for analytical knowledge. H.P. Blavatsky's spiritual classic *The Voice of the Silence* states: "The mind is the slayer of the real, let the disciples slay the slayer." Thinking, the function of reason, has many commendable uses and cannot be eliminated, but it also builds barriers between the personality and its unconscious matrix. In order to reach the necessary transformative self-knowledge, one needs to keep the thinking function subservient to the inspiration proceeding from the Self. Basilides, the Gnostic, thus feels it incumbent on himself to teach "knowledge" (gnosis) to the dead in order to facilitate this necessary ability to control thinking.

The Second Sermon—Helios: Image of God

It was Friedrich Nietzsche, a man to whom Jung owed much inspiration, who once said in a parable: "Precisely this is godlike that there are gods, but no God."[4] It was of course the same Nietzsche who uttered the cry "God is dead!" which in question form constitutes the principal challenge the dead hurl at Basilides, their teacher, in the opening portion of the Second Sermon. Unlike the Dionysian poet-philosopher, Jung does not affirm the death of God. To recognize Deity as a form of existential or psychological reality is important for the health of the soul, at least so Jung believed. Since God is in the soul rather than in a remote heaven it would be injurious to the health of the soul to deny Him. At the same time, this intrapsychic deity, or *imago dei* (image of god), is only one of numerous divine powers that manifest within the depths of the human spirit. Thus the godlikeness of the multiplicity of the gods is very much part of the picture of being given to us in the Sermons. In the Fourth

Sermon the teacher exclaims quite frankly: "Blessed am I, for it is granted unto me to know the multiplicity and diversity of the gods." At the same time he castigates the dead for their one-sided monotheism: "Woe unto you, for you have substituted the oneness of God for the diversity which cannot be resolved into the one."

In this multiplicity of gods or, as the Gnostic would have it, divine emanations, there are two which in the Sermons form the first pair of deities: God the Sun, or Helios, and his opponent, the Devil. Helios is described as effective fullness, while the Devil is called by him effective emptiness. This pair is the first of the mighty dualities arising within the created or emanated realm. The pair of opposites thus brought to our attention appears, at least at first sight, to be very much in the nature of a Syzygy of a radically dualistic cosmos, such as was imputed to the Gnostics by scholars of a bygone era, who thought they could discern in Gnosticism the echoes of the dualistic world-picture of Zarathustra.

Human life and experience ever plays itself out between the tension of two opposites. God and Devil, fighting heroes and villainous dragons, fratricidal Cain and murdered Abel are all representatives of the recurring motifs depicting symbolically the interaction of the opposing dualities. In his work *The Archetypes of the Collective Unconscious* Jung restates the message contained in the Second Sermon when he says: "Evil is the necessary opposite of good, without which there would be no good either. It is impossible even to think evil out of existence." Jung was insistent especially on the reality and titanic magnitude of evil, for he felt that Western humanity, beginning with Christian theology, has consistently and disastrously dwarfed the picture of evil as arising from the unconscious of humanity. In *Civilization in Transition* he wrote that evil "is of gigantic proportions, so that for the Church to talk of original sin and to trace it back to Adam's relatively innocent slip-up with Eve is almost a euphemism. The case is far graver and is grossly underestimated."[5]

Chesterton made his clerical detective, Fr. Brown, exclaim: "Of course I believe in the devil. If I did not, I should have to believe that I am the devil myself." Exoteric religion, in spite of its reductionisms and superficialities, is rooted in a now lost but once potent Gnosis, and thus the religious preachments about the opposition of God and Devil are not as lacking in psychological reality as one might at first assume. Prior to the advent of depth psychology, man had no rational alternative to the religious dogma according to which all good things come from God while all mysterious, bad things come from the Devil. With the coming of the various depth-psychological disciplines after the year 1900, it became increasingly clear to many that what were previously conceived to be extrapsychic and nonhuman sources of good and evil in reality reside in the human psyche itself. Thus God and Devil are revealed as mighty oppositional principles operating within us. Freud gave utterance to a recognition closely approximating the insights of Jung when he revised and reduced his once far more complex instinct theory to the existence of the two great instincts, named after deities of antiquity: Eros (life instinct) and Thanatos (death instinct). The Second Sermon expresses a very similar concept when it attributes fullness and generation to God and emptiness and destruction to the Devil. God the all-begetter stands opposed to the Devil the all-devourer. An ancient magical statement declared: "Demon est Deus inversus," the Devil is God turned upside down. Interestingly, the Judeo-Christian-Islamic tradition is alone in insisting on attributing the quality of moral evil to the "upside-down god." In Taoism, *yin* and *yang* are both equally void of moral qualities of good or evil, while in Hindu and Mahayana Buddhist mythology the destructive and terrifying deities are simply referred to as "wrathful" but not as "evil." The votaries of these faiths inevitably seem to recognize that it is through the cooperation of both the wrathful and the benevolent principles that humanity and the cosmos are brought to perfection and spiritual fullness.

In the Second Sermon Jung is concerned with the existence of a primal dichotomy within the psyche, a dichotomy which is united by a mysterious reconciling power of existential activity, named by Jung on the Basilidian model as *Abraxas*. The two polar deities of God and Devil are definite, because they force human beings to endure psychic conflict and to make painful decisions. Yet these conflicts and decisions do not occur in a vacuum. Life is lived in a force field of activity, of happening, and it is this stream of happening that balances and creatively reconciles the apparently irreconcilable, conflictual elements in living.

Unlike some other schools of thought, Jung never envisioned the absence of conflict as a desirable course for human consciousness. It is by the conflict of will and counterwill, of yes and no, of affirmation and negation, and in the resolution of these conflicts by decisions in the world of action that our ultimate selfhood unfolds. Moral opposites thus are as much a part of the process of growth toward wholeness as are opposites of another character. The simplistic notion represented by exoteric religion is that we have God, who is light, goodness, positiveness, affirmation, and benevolence, while on the other hand we have the principle of evil, envisioned primarily as the absence of good, an abyss of negativity, denial, malevolence. This religiosity declares that it is the duty of the human being to struggle against the negative pole and to strive toward the positive pole. Thus the good is within God, the bad outside God, and we are between the two, trying to follow the good but usually failing to do so with any degree of effectiveness. Jung was profoundly dissatisfied with this view and felt that it was psychologically unsound.

Within the context of Jung's psychological thinking, good and evil are not absolutes but man-made judgments dependent on the values impressed upon humanity by culture and religion. Moreover, even within a generally acceptable framework of more or less evident moral demands of a "natural morality," it is fairly clear that "good" and "evil" are not the two opposite poles of a linear dimensionality. Rather they might be said to resemble a circle wherein going far enough in either direction is likely to associate one with the opposite polarity. As Jung himself phrased it, in the last resort there is no good that cannot produce evil, and no evil that cannot produce good. One might justifiably ask some fairly weighty questions at this point, such as: What does this mean in practical terms? Are persons capable of valid moral choices and can they resolve the eternal moral conflicts in their lives, or should they give up in despair and discard such notions as good and evil, desirable and undesirable, altogether? To answer these questions is exceedingly difficult, for upon such an answer may depend the welfare of many individuals as well as of civilization itself. In our times Jung's psychological teachings regarding the principles underlying human action might assume an added, even a crucial importance. It is a frequently repeated truism, reduced often to the level of nauseous triteness, that the moral values of the past have either totally broken down or at least are being most seriously challenged at the present time. As humanity seeks more and more urgently for useful and valid answers within the fields of ethics and morality, these issues assume a much more than academic importance and relevance.

The key to the entire issue of the psychology of ethics is once again to be found in the fatal one-sidedness of Western culture. The Judeo-Christian ethic insists that the resolution of moral conflict must come about in the lives of persons by way of a conscious, rational choice. As long as the human being adheres to the externally revealed law and clings to the consciously recognized moral imperatives, striving to do good and abstaining from doing evil, all is well. It is all just a matter of choices made by consciousness and implemented by the rational will. If one is unwilling to follow this one-sided program, then one is accounted unworthy, sinful, subject to the directions of dark, diabolical powers. In contradistinction to this time-hallowed but disastrous attitude, Jung advances the proposition that moral conflict cannot be resolved by consciousness alone, and that traditional moral values and codes cannot be considered the ultimate authority. In addition to the conscious and its *commandment,* the unconscious and its *command* must also be taken into account. This is by no means the advocacy of moral anarchy. Jung never declared that we owe no individual responsibility to the world outside of our selfhood, and he never implied that the laws, regulations and conventions our egos encounter within their field of operation ought to be invariably disregarded. He stated, however, that in addition to the outer world responsibility is owed to the inner world. Man does not live by the bread of the conventions of society alone, but he also needs the nourishment that comes from the portion of himself that is older and far more powerful than state, church, society or

even family. We owe worship to the light, but the darkness needs
and deserves our homage also.

What constitutes an indivisible unity in the Pleroma, in differentiated consciousness appears as a dichotomy; split in two
parts, the Self, or archetype of wholeness, is subject to discernment through conflict. The much-publicized antinomianism
(lack of total subservience to the "law of God") of the Gnostics
appears here in a psychological form. Unlike the one-sided God
concept of conventional religiosity, the God-image of Jung and
his Gnosis contains will and counterwill, God and Devil. In his
truly Gnostic work entitled *A Psychological Approach to the
Dogma of the Trinity* Jung wrote:

> The ability to "will otherwise" must, unfortunately, be real if
> ethics are to make any sense at all. Anyone who submits to the
> law from the start, or to what is generally expected, acts like
> the man in the parable who buried his talent in the earth.
> Individuation is an exceedingly difficult task: it always in-
> volves a conflict of duties, whose solution requires us to
> understand that our "counter will" is also an aspect of God's
> will.[6]

The religions of the masses demand obedience to God's will,
while the Gnosis demands both obedience and disobedience. Not
all commandments come from the true God, said the ancient
Gnostics, for many come from a Demiurge, whose law may be
useful to the unenlightened (the psychics, or men of soul) but is
counterproductive to the true Gnostics (the pneumatics, or men
of spirit). The will of nature is not that of supernature; the law
of the morning which is appropriate for spiritual infants must be
broken by those who have progressed to the law of the evening,
where the light of differentiated consciousness must be dimmed
in order to admit the luminosity of the midnight sun of
individuation. The Jewish Gnosis of the Kabbalah recognized
this when it capitalized on the divine statement (in Isaiah 45:7):
"I form the light, and create darkness: I make peace and create
evil; I the Lord do all these things." In Kabbalistic writings we
encounter the teaching of the two "inclinations" (*yeser*) and the
advice that the Kabbalistic Gnostic is to love God with both of
these. The right-and left-hand pillars of the Tree of Life, and
even more the doctrine regarding the terrifying *klippoth* or evil

principles existing in conjunction with the same Tree, bring to our attention a doctrine that postulates evil as a metaphysical reality in God. Isaac Luria, the most Gnostic of all the Kabbalistic teachers, said that the root of all evil lies in the very nature of divine creation, inasmuch as God created in order to manifest everything hidden in His own mysterious nature. The Christian mystic Jacob Boehme similarly regarded God's love and wrath, His brilliant light and burning fire, as belonging inseparably together, both being the effluence of God's eternal word, for life can only be when good and evil exist together, both in God and in man. The Kabbalah as well as the more daring forms of Christian mysticism are, of course, rooted in the wisdom of the ancient Gnostics who declared in the Gospel of Philip: "The light and the darkness, life and death, the right and the left, are brothers one to another. It is not possible to separate them from one another. Because of this, neither are the good good, nor the evil evil, nor is life a life, nor death a death. Because of this each will be resolved into its origin from the beginning."[7]

We find then that the two manifest principles called in the Second Sermon God and Devil are the two Gnostic categories of our own being, which were ever experienced by those possessing Gnosis as a duality rooted in an underlying unity. The Self of Jung's psychology belongs to a transconscious realm, and therefore is not directly susceptible to conscious cognition; it is rather experienced through its good and evil emanations. The former of these might appear as the light and rectitude of the accepted values of consciousness, while the latter is the shadow that accompanies the light and acts as the demonic half of the psyche.

The reader who is relatively unacquainted with the content of Jung's formidable literary output may be disposed to recoil with some horror at the conventional bogey-man-like term *Devil* employed so early in the description of the Gnostic scheme of the *Seven Sermons*. In order to put this mythologem of the Devil into proper perspective, it may be useful to recall the importance of evil and its reality to Jung. Indeed, his recognition of the importance of evil runs like a fiery thread through his work. Evil to Jung was a psychic reality in the life of the individual and of human society and history, but he was also conscious of evil as a numinous power, existing at the deepest or highest metaphysical levels of reality. Unlike the non-Gnostic religious spirit of so much of Western religion and philosophy, he did not expect the salvation of man (individuation in Jung's terms) to arise from a rejection of evil. The "good god" of light and the "evil god" or Devil of darkness are equally ineffectual when it comes to the achievement of the human being's ultimate tasks. Above and beyond, or perhaps between these two powers, there is a third without which the two poles of existence have neither effect nor power. God and Devil are united in a terrifying and majestic divine hybrid, a veritable God-Devil whom Jung calls *Abraxas*.

The Third Sermon, Part I— *Abraxas, the Heavenly Chanticleer*

The awesome and mysterious figure of Abraxas appears first in the latter part of the Second Sermon. He is called initially "a god about whom you know nothing, because men have forgotten him." In contrast to Helios, the god of light, and the Devil, god of darkness, Abraxas appears as the supreme power of being in whom light and darkness are both united and transcended. He is also defined as the principle of irresistible activity and is the closest approximation to an active manifestation of the Pleroma one may imagine.

In order to begin to apprehend Jung's conception of Abraxas, it may be useful to look at the relatively scanty information descending to us from classical Gnostic sources that concerns this mysterious archetype. Irenaeus, the late second century bishop of Lyons and vociferous critic of the Gnostics, in one of his anti-Gnostic fulminations comments on the magical activities, images and incantations by which the Gnostics of his day addressed the angelic rulers of the various heavens: ". . .after inventing certain names as if they belonged to angels, they proclaim that some are in the first heaven, others in the second, and then try to set forth the names, principalities, angels and powers of the 365 fictitious heavens. . . ." These heavens, according to the account of the church fathers, were stated by

Basilides to be under the overlordship of Abraxas, a terrible and overwhelming deity, whose resistless might was invoked in the many representations of his person, engraved upon many talismans and amulets. These were worn to ward off the limiting influences of the rulers of the world and to assist one's rising to the transcendental state beyond all stellar and heavenly powers. These jewels, often carved from costly gems and set in precious metal, did not suffer the fate of the Gnostic codices and other monuments but were saved by the greed of men for our edification. In this manner we have received from the Gnostics, not only the name and idea, but the magical likeness of Abraxas, for Gnostic talismans bearing the figure of the god were preserved in considerable numbers. The usually oval stones all show a figure with a human body, the head of a rooster (or more seldom of a hawk), and legs fashioned like serpents. The god's hands hold a shield and a whip, the former usually inscribed with the sacred name *IAO,* reminiscent of the Jewish Tetragrammaton or four-lettered name of God, conjecturally pronounced "IAHVEH." The god is often mounted on a chariot drawn by four white horses, rushing along at great speed. The sun and moon shine overhead as if indicating that the polar opposites of night and day, silver and gold, feminine and masculine, come to an equilibrated state of dynamic union within this powerful symbolic figure.

The most frequently mentioned explanations of the symbols embodied in the Abraxas figure are as follows. The head of the rooster symbolizes vigilant wakefulness and is related to both the human heart and to universal heart, the sun, the rising of which is invoked by the matutinal clarion call of the chanticleer. The human torso is the embodiment of the principle of logos, or articulated thought, which is regarded as the unique power of the human being. The legs shaped like snakes indicate prudence whereby the dynamic rulership of universal being governs its own all-powerful energies. The shield held in the right hand is symbolic of wisdom, the great protector of all divine warriors. The whip, held in the left hand, denotes the relentless, driving power of life that spurs all existence on. The four white horses drawing the chariot, represent the tetramorphic forces whereby the universal libido or psychic energy expresses itself, variously

Illustration by Irene Malvin

ABRAXAS, rooster-headed god with serpent feet, in whom light and darkness are both united and transcended.

called the four ethers of the power of the sun, the four elements of earth, water, fire and air, and in Jungian psychological terms, the four functions of human consciousness, sensation, feeling, thinking and intuition.

Understandably, one of the most mysterious features of Abraxas is the name itself, which, incidentally, is also used in the alternative spelling of *Abrasax*. An imaginative scholar, Sampson Arnold Mackay, suggested that the name is a compound of two words, *abir* and *axis*, the former meaning bull and the second a pole, and that thus the name harkens back to a time when the cosmic new year, or vernal equinox, took place in the sign of Taurus, the heavenly bull over the North Pole or world axis. This idea, while incapable of verification, is by no means inconsistent with the known symbolism embodied in the figure of Abraxas, inasmuch as the vernal equinox has ever been regarded as the greatest point of concentration of magical power of the annual cycle, the birthday of the cosmos and of the gods, while the *abir* or *apis*, the sacred bull, was both the archaic symbol of the earth mother and the later symbol of Osiris, who as Serapis, the Osiris-bull, was one of the undoubted prototypes of the resurrected Christ in Alexandrian Christianity, and thus in Gnosticism. The equinoctial bull, therefore, would lend itself to a magical name of the power, whereby the ever self-renewing divine energy rises at the Eastertide of the cosmos, bursting forth from the subterranean night of the holy sepulchre and victoriously proclaiming the dawning of the messianic light of the triumphant Christly spirit. It is conceivable that the fertile magical imagination of the Egyptian Gnostics could make use of the name of this "bull of the North Pole" to invoke into their natures the personal psychological equivalent of this cosmic power in order to allow their own spirits to triumph over the guardian rulers who hold the human ego in their tyrannical grip.

The meaning of the Abraxas figure emerges in even greater clarity, however, when the name is decoded in accordance with the numerological principles, which in both Jewish and pagan circles enjoyed great respect in the ancient world. The numeration of Abraxas in Greek is: Alpha-1, Beta-2, Rho-100, Alpha-1, Xi-60, Alpha-1, Sigma-200; which totals 365. Similarly the Hebrew numeration yields the same total in the following manner: Aleph-1, Beth-2, Resh-200, Aleph-1, Qoph-100, Aleph-1, Samekh-60, equalling 365. It has been suggested that the number 365, being that of the days in a year, would readily offer itself as an identification of the deity that rules over the totality of time, and by whose power time is both made and unmade. The unmaking of time—like the Buddhist endeavor to escape from the grip of the monster-god Mahakala, ruler of the revolving wheel of duration—is a true Gnostic concern. In a sense it may be regarded as the hallmark of the true Gnosis, possessed only by the most highly accomplished pneumatic or spiritual individual. Abraxas, as the all-pervading energy of being, is thus the sum of and the liberator from the cycle of necessity, freeing man from the agony of time, or as Mircea Eliade called it, the terror of history. The 365 zones of the inner realm, which are outwardly manifest as the same number of days, represent the sum total of psychological obstacles which stand in the way of the freedom of the soul, causing its death-like entombment in limitation. It is thus evident that Abraxas, who is the power capable of liberating us from this cyclic bondage, would have held a great appeal for the Alexandrian Gnostic seekers after spiritual freedom. Not only does Abraxas bring freedom from the tedium of time—which brings frustration, old age, illness and ultimately death—but he also stops the wheel of the cycles. Thus, he puts an end to repetitious experience, the blind, unconscious reliving of aeons of unprofitable cosmic busy-work resulting in nothing but further involvement in concerns that are irrelevant to the soul. Between the two often-mentioned alternatives of a linear, historical ego-consciousness and a circular, ahistorical unconsciousness, Abraxas stands as the third possibility of the eternally available timeless moment, the eternal now, the recognition and utilization of which brings freedom from time both in its linear and its cyclic aspects.

In addition to its numerical value, the name Abraxas holds yet another significant secret, indicated by the fact that it is composed of seven letters. These seven letters have been taken to be related to the seven rays of creative powers of the planetary spheres, which in Gnostic systems stand for both the creativity and the restrictiveness of the cosmos. The seven rulers of the world, whose physical symbols are the seven sacred planets, are said to be acting as the guardians and at times jailers of the soul. The unenlightened or unconscious person is ruled by the planets, or rather by the psychological forces and complexes which are signified by the planets. Thus the unconscious, or non-Gnostic person, is enthralled by the force of Mars when anger invades his personality; another may be possessed by Venus when under the spell of romantic desire; the curiosity and acquisitiveness of Mercury may dominate others, and so on. Unlike the common superstitious believer in popular astrology, the Gnostic considers domination by planets and other heavenly bodies as an invasion of his spiritual privacy, an assault on the sovereign prerogatives of his royal selfhood. Abraxas, the summation and ruler of the sevenfold planetary spectrum, is thus the true archetype of man's potential of spiritual freedom and independence from unconscious psychological pressures and compulsions.

Origen, the Christian father, recounts how the Gnostic addresses the highest God (whom Basilides and Jung would no doubt call Abraxas) when in his work *Contra Celsum* he reproduces the following beautiful Gnostic prayer:

> Hail to thee, solitary King, Bond of Invisibility, First Power, guarded by the spirit of Foreknowledge and by Wisdom. From this place I am sent on, pure, already a part of the Light of Son and Father. Let grace be with me, yes, Father, let it be with me.

When the Gnostic thus spoke to Abraxas (or to any other symbolization of the transcendental Godhead superior to all intermediary powers), he was in fact addressing vibrant energy, active spiritual power, a sort of an "elan vital" of a spiritual nature. The obstructive powers have themselves in their own time and way emanated from this radiant, vibrant, supercelestial first-source, and in the course of their descent into the lower regions turned ignorant and at times malefic. Each power, or aionic emanation from the supreme God, is more benign than the one beneath it and correspondingly capable of reflecting the character of the transcendental first principle in an increasing measure. Thus, the Gnostic soul rises from sphere to sphere, from aion to aion, in its quest for communion and union with the supreme source. After all tasks are accomplished, all purifications undergone, all spells changed and all holy deeds done, at the end of the great journey, there beckons the First Mystery, the Source of all gods, worlds and men. This is the unknown, all-transcending and all-prevading one whose name—according to Basilides and his modern amanuensis C.G. Jung—is Abraxas.

This mythological framework, inspiring though it is, needs some contemporary amplification. The myth of salvation by ascension through the aions seems at first radically different from the view of salvation as held by non-Gnostic Christians. Mainstream Christianity, subsequent to the Nicene period, came to hold increasingly that salvation is the result of a single, unrepeatable event, namely the crucifixion and death of Jesus in fleshly form. Versus this view, the Gnostics adhere to a concept of salvation or liberation which appears as a repeatable event in the present, a meaningful process of spiritual growth, both on earth and in the unseen realms beyond physical reality. Carpocrates quite boldly postulated this process as continuing through a number of lives on earth, and all Gnostic schools recognized that it continues through the heavenly spheres. The Gnostic depiction of the heavenly spheres was of course angrily dismissed by the anti-Gnostic church fathers and their successors as "fantastic speculation." (Apparently the guardians of churchly dogma never considered that numerous tenets of so-called Christian orthodoxy, including the virgin birth, the incarnation and the resurrection, could seem also in the nature of "fantastic speculation.") Yet, there is much justification for this teaching in orthodox tradition. The existence of the heavenly host and of the supreme deity as the Lord of these host is an undisputable feature of the ancient Jewish religion, from which Christianity drew so much of its inspiration. The Merkabah mysticism, of the early period, and the Kabbalah, of the later dispensation of mystical Judaism, are both dilated with ideas of the heavenly mansions and of the ability of the mystic to rise through these to the throne of God. The Gnostic notion of the heavenly spheres and of the ability of the soul to ascend through these to a state of communion with an Abraxas-like First Power is quite within the basic developmental pattern of the mystical aspects of the Hebraic spiritual traditions. Neither is the concept of salvation as spiritual growth instead of as a one-time event of a divine sacrificial death an unheard-of position in mainstream Christianity. Both the gospels of Mark and Matthew contain numerous parables of Jesus which represent the kingdom of God as growth. (Mark 4: 26-29, 30-32; Matt. 13: 18-23; 24-30, 33.) Paul, the almost-Gnostic apostle, fills his letters with statements which indicate that, although he himself underwent a dramatic *metanoia* or conversion experience, he regarded this experience as the beginning rather than as the glorious end of his spiritual growth. He states that he "dies every day," that he "strains forward" to "what lies ahead" spiritually, that he "presses on toward the goal." Similarly in the Johannine literature there are numerous hints indicating that salvation is a process of the revelation of truth in the life of the individual. The two church fathers who were closest in time and geographical location to the flowering of Gnosticism and whose orthodoxy is not questioned today, Clement of Alexandria and Origen, both depicted the Christian life with the imagery of a ladder of ascent. Clement asserted that the soul progresses from faith, as one step on the way, to gnosis, which he regards as a subsequent, higher step. His vision of the true Christian, as given in his *Stromateis*, could easily have been written by Basilides, or for that matter by Carl Jung:

> Leaving behind all hindrances and scorning all the distractions of matter, he cleaves the heavens by his wisdom, and having passed through the spiritual entities and every rule and authority, he lays hold of the throne on high, speeding to that alone, which alone he knows.

Unquestionably C.G. Jung represents this "throne on high" as belonging to the highest but forgotten god whom he calls Abraxas. As we have demonstrated, this attitude toward the obscure figure of the Basilidian Gnosis is by no means unjustified. While some contemporary scholars, without true warrant, occasionally refer to Abraxas as the evil aeon, equating him thus with a demiurge rather than with the highest god, there is adequate reason to agree with Jung's position and to accept that Jung was writing very much within the fragmentary, but still adequate, parameters of the Basilidian tradition. Though very little information about Abraxas is available, and his name appears only infrequently in magical papyry and in some

Gnostic texts which show evident Egyptian influence, it appears nevertheless quite reasonable to assume that Abraxas was indeed a high and numinous archetypal figure in at least some forms of Gnosticism. By way of more or less purely technical interest, it might also be mentioned that some of the best-known Abraxas amulets contain at their base the word *Sabao*, a clear reference to the name *Sabaoth*, meaning *hosts*. It appears that some Gnostic hermeneutic efforts have utilized this word to describe another archonic being, a son of Ialdabaoth, the ignorant demiurge. In two of the Nag Hammadi treatises, *The Hypostasis of the Archons* and *On the Origin of the World*, Sabaoth is represented as a power who repented of the dark deeds of his demiurgic father, came to worship Sophia (Wisdom) and her daughter Zoe (Life) and was rewarded by receiving light and becoming the ruler of the seventh heaven and the "lord of the powers." The association of Abraxas with Sabaoth thus certainly appears significant. It may be that in some systems Sabaoth became a representative of Abraxas within certain realms, or it may be that at least in some myths Sabaoth and Abraxas became identified. In neither case can one or the other be legitimately equated with the demiurge. Thus, the objections against Jung's use of the name *Abraxas* as the highest god appear to be weakened on all fronts.

The Third Sermon, Part 2—Jung's Unknown God

The aforementioned elements of the Abraxas image make it fairly evident why Jung would have been attracted to this particular figure among the numerous denizens of the Gnostic aions. Abraxas clearly holds appeal to three Jungian principles: the union of the opposites; the striving for individuation by way of the gradual conquest on the part of consciousness of various unconscious regions; and the Jungian reformulation of Freud's concept of the libido as psychic energy or spiritual force of titanic magnitude, which is utilized by the psyche for its own mysterious purposes. No wonder Jung calls Abraxas in the last portion of the Second Sermon "the unlikely likely one, who is powerful in the realm of unreality." Truly, this weirdly wonderful figure of the rooster-headed, serpent-footed man-god must have appeared to Jung as a most welcome archetypal visitor in his lonely chamber where he was instructing the obstreperous and riot-prone dead.

It needs to be remembered, of course, that Jung was not the first or only scholar to resurrect the Basilidian divinity and make it a central figure of the Gnosis. In 1891 the German classicist Albrecht Dieterich published a remarkable work entitled *Abraxas,* based on a magical papyrus dating from the period around A.D. 350 and reposing in the Leyden Museum of Antiquities in Holland. Dieterich, rather like Jung in the *Seven Sermons,* represented Abraxas as the supreme God of the Gnostics in whom all opposites and partial realities meet. The papyrus in Dieterich's exposition puts forth a creation myth of sublime beauty and great psychological depth, which must have inspired Jung in a variety of ways.* Among other things Dieterich's *Abraxas* deals with the intriguing myth of the creation of the worlds by way of the seven laughters of God, the first of these producing light, the second the firmament, the third bringing forth the mind in the form of Hermes, the fourth generation, the fifth fate, the sixth time, and the seventh or last laughter emanating the goddess Psyche, representation of the soul, who, led by Hermes, the enlightened intellect, then fills the whole world-system with motion and energy. Dieterich's writings, including his *Abraxas,* were seminal in the truest sense of the word, for they contained under the prefigurative cloak of comparative religious terminology many concepts which came to be pivotal within Jung's psychology. The school of religious history (*Religionsgechichtliche Schule*) represented by such men as Dieterich and Usner has brought forth numerous insights from its vast storehouse of data on the motifs in various religions. These formed the *prima materia* for Jung's concept of the archetypes, as well as for such individual elements of his system as the anima, the theme of spiritual rebirth or individuation, and the union of the opposites.

---

*Jung's knowledge of and high regard for the works of Dieterich as well as for the latter's contemporary and spiritual brother-in-arms, Hermann Usner (1834-1905), the discoverer of Aphrodite in the guise of the legends of St. Marina, Pelagia, and Afra, is well attested to.

Another somewhat more controversial and obscure reappearance of the Abraxas figure is connected with the Nobelprize-winning German author and contemporary of Jung, Hermann Hesse. In his first noted work *Demian,* written under the pseudonym of Sinclair, Hesse repeatedly refers to Abraxas. Published in 1919, just after the conclusion of World War I and after Hesse's permanent move from Germany to Switzerland, *Demian* was the book that established Hesse as an author of world-wide fame. (His two previous volumes, *Peter Camenzind* and *Beneath the Wheel,* had attracted little attention.) *Demian* is a thoroughly Gnostic book, as anyone having the least knowledge of Gnosticism can easily discern. In addition to the references to Abraxas, Hesse utilizes several Gnostic themes, among them most prominently a Gnostic exegesis of the biblical story of Cain and Abel, which makes Cain appear in a light more favorable than Abel. Most remarkable, however, are the author's statements about Abraxas, which in their interpretation of the Gnostic image are extremely close to the interpretation offered by Jung in the *Seven Sermons.*

In *Demian* the young Sinclair encounters a coat of arms, in which a heraldic bird, a sparrow-hawk, figures prominently. Later, he dreams of the same design and paints it in vivid colors from memory. Ultimately he receives an interpretation of the dream and picture from his mysterious friend, Max Demian, which reads as follows:

> The bird fights its way out of the egg. The egg is the world. Who would be born must first destroy a world. The bird flies to God. That God's name is Abraxas.[8]

A teacher of classics, Dr. Follens, by way of a curious synchronicity, then expostulates on the figure of Abraxas, and concludes his lecture by saying:

> . . . it appears that Abraxas has much deeper significance. We may conceive of the name as that of a godhead whose symbolic task is the uniting of godly and devilish elements.[9]

Young Sinclair then recognizes that Abraxas in effect represents the solution to a conflict he had experienced for some time. The world being divided into good and evil, and the conventional Christian God being only the God of good, Sinclair was impressed by the necessity of worshipping the wholeness, rather than only the luminous, good side of being.

The next incident involving Abraxas occurs when Sinclair meets the musician Pistorius, a strangely Gnostic figure. This wild, brooding heretic responds to Sinclair's account of his recent interest in Abraxas, with a significant statement: "One doesn't hear about Abraxas by accident, and don't you forget it." During a subsequent encounter Pistorius preaches what amounts to a genuine, passionate Gnostic sermon to Sinclair:

> Sinclair, our god's name is Abraxas and he is God and Satan and he contains both the luminous and the dark world. Abraxas does not take exception to any of your thoughts, any of your dreams. Never forget that. But he will leave you once you've become blameless and normal. Then he will leave you and look for a different vessel in which to brew his thoughts.[10]

The possible sources of Hesse's interest in Abraxas, and more specifically of his unique approach to the subject, which closely resembles that of C.G. Jung in the *Seven Sermons,* have been the subject of bewilderment and controversy for some considerable time. (See proceedings of the First *Panarion Conference* of the C.G. Jung Institute, held in 1975 in Los Angeles, particularly the contributions of G. Quispel, James Kirsch and Gershom G. Scholem.) Admirers of Hesse are inclined to the view that Hesse brought forth the Abraxas image contained in *Demian* from his own creative imagination—and certainly no one familiar with the magical landscape of his many enchanting works would dismiss such a possibility as impossible or even improbable. On the other hand, various followers of Jung are inclined to see a direct connection between the *Seven Sermons* and *Demian.* These persons point to the fact that Hesse underwent Jungian analysis around the year 1916 and that his analyst, a certain Dr. Lang, *might* have had access to Jung's *Seven Sermons* and could have given the same to Hesse to read, so that Hesse *may* have received his Gnostic inspiration from Jung's small work. However, *Demian* was published in 1919, perhaps too early for Hesse to have included Jung's ideas on Gnosticism. Hesse is said to have denied any acquaintance with the literary corpus of ancient Gnosticism, although he was apparently never directly confronted with the question whether he knew Jung's

Seven Sermons. Miguel Serrano, the Chilean diplomat and poet who attained to considerable note as the result of his record of his two friendships with Hesse and Jung respectively, never mentions any possible connection between the *Seven Sermons* and *Demian,* although he discusses the figure of Abraxas, both in Hesse's and Jung's treatment, at considerable length.

It is curious that few if any persons seem to have considered the possibility that both Jung *and* Hesse may have experienced a typically Jungian psychological phenomenon roughly at the same point in time, namely that they met a newly emerging archetype, or to put in more poetic terms, they both had an encounter with Abraxas, as an autonomous being of great antiquity as well as of contemporary relevance. Jung amplified his Abraxas experience by way of his considerable learning in the field of Gnosticism, while Hermann Hesse relied primarily on his poetic imagination for surrounding Abraxas with the appropriate images and concepts. Yet, as it often happens, coming from two different directions the two visionaries, both presented to their readers material of such similarity and internal consistency that the reasoning mind tends to asume a direct connection. Logical explanations are not invariably correct, especially when they involve the product of non-rational, creative and imaginative processes. The emerging of a certain archetypal manifestation of Abraxas at a particularly critical time of European history (during and immediately following World War I), differing from, and yet organically linked with the original image given by Basilides and other Gnostics, would be a remarkable and meaningful phenomenon indeed. The fact that two of the most creative people of the epoch should have been chosen by the archetype simultaneously for its coming forth would be even more remarkable and pregnant with archetypal meaning, the full implications of which are still awaiting to be discovered.

In both the latter part of the Second Sermon and throughout the Third Sermon, Jung shows a powerful awareness of the potentially negative impact his image of Abraxas may have on the conventional religious mind. Thus he ends the Second Sermon with the words: "At this point the dead caused a great riot, because they were Christians." Alas, one of the first to cause a great riot because of the *Sermons,* and particularly about Abraxas, was not a Christian, but a Jew, Martin Buber! Jung calls Abraxas the truly terrible one because of his ability to generate truth and falsehood, good and evil, light and darkness with the same word and in the same deed. The concept of an all-inclusive reality, wherein the opposites exist together and from whence they come forth without the terrors of moral judgment and fearful opposition, is not palatable to the non-Gnostic mentality of the last 1700 years of Western religion. The Gnostics were repeatedly accused by their enemies of being dualists, that is, believers in two equal and opposite principles of good and evil. It may be justly advanced by Buber, or anyone else, that the figure of Abraxas in the *Sermons,* or our interpretation of the same, is lacking in the kind of moral dimension that might make it relevant to the life of the human race. Such objections are rooted principally in the fact that persons in the Western world are accustomed to the Jewish-Christian-Islamic God-concept, which is personal, and therefore moral in nature. It must be remembered that this moral aspect of the God-concept does not apply in the figurations of deity, or ultimate reality, in many other religions, particularly those of the East. Treatises of Vedanta philosophy, Buddhism, and Gnosticism regarding the ultimate deity often appear irrelevant to moral questions inasmuch as they are dealing with a reality above the dual categories of good and evil.

Jung, in his intuitive knowledge of the Gnosis, recognized that, not dualism, but the recognition of the ultimate necessity for the union of the opposites was at the heart of the Gnostic attitude. With such descriptions as "he is himself the greater Pan, and also the lesser. He is Priapos," Jung squarely identified Abraxas with the universal and undifferentiated psychic energy which he, himself, came to espouse in his work *Symbols of Transformation.* However, he also recognized that this same energy is incarnate after its fashion in the forces of the instincts, which are the lesser Pan, the blind but potent instinctual nature of humanity, symbolized by the perpetually eager and erect phallus of Priapos. The highest archetypes of the unconscious have been at times called the analogues of the instincts, and it may be equally correct to state that the instincts in turn are the correspondences of the archetypes. Thus Abraxas can be the fierce leap of the hunting lion at the moment of the kill, and simultaneously the tranquil beauty of a spring morn; he can be love and the slaying of love; he can be Christ, the holy one, as well as Judas, his betrayer. Jung said once that no healthy, well-grown tree can disavow its dark roots in the lowly earth, for by so doing it would perish. The root system of the spirit is embodied in the instincts of the psychophysiological organism of humanity. Only at our great peril can we cut ourselves off from these roots, for without them the very tree of our being will fall, and the lovely blooms of our ideals as well as the brilliantly plumed heavenly birds of the archetypal psyche will be destroyed. Yet Buber and the Christian theologians, following in the footsteps of Hippolytus and Irenaeus, accused Jung of deifying the instincts without sanctifying them. They could and would not understand that the darkness within the psyche must be accepted, understood, and ultimately reconciled with the light, in a state of wholeness that is neither light nor darkness but a condition that is both, and yet more than either.

The divine hybrid whom Jung calls Abraxas is the living and symbolic refutation of the philosophical attitude of the excluded middle, or as it may be colloquially called, the either-or philosophy. The unholy alliance of Semitic moralizing and Aristotelian logic which invaded and conquered Christendom by way of the works of Thomas Aquinas immersed Western humanity in the method of the absolute categorization of all things into an attitude to be characterized as *either this or that*. Light and dark are envisioned as being in conflict because our thinking has come to accept the idea that both cannot exist together. Life and death are imagined as polar opposites, and the human being is, of course, enjoined to choose life. Hence suicide and other forms of self-destruction, or even the destruction of a tiny foetus in the womb, appear as dreadful crimes to the Western religious mind. This sort of thinking is peculiar to the differentiated consciousness of the ego, inasmuch as the ego is dominated by only conscious motives and considerations. It is perfectly true that in the world of the conscious ego, dependent for its reality image on sense perception, things and beings are always either *this* or *that:* a chair is quite plainly not a dog, a sunny day not a rainy day, and so forth. On the other hand, the psyche, which is composed of the unconscious as well as of the conscious mind, does not deal with such sharp and clear-cut categories. Have we ever met a human being who was either wholly stupid or totally intelligent, completely decent or totally rotten? Obviously not, for in human nature, the mysteries and profundities of the psyche preclude any possible validity being attributed to such categorical judgments. In the psyche, and particularly in the unconscious component of the psyche, the opposites tend to coincide. The conscious is exclusive, for consciousness, not unlike a light beam, is defined by the surrounding darkness of unconsciousness. The unconscious, on the other hand, is inclusive; it deals in the category of "both" rather than in "either-or." Not that dualities are absent in the unconscious; far from it. We would be missing the mark indeed if we were to attribute some Advaitin non-dualism to the deeper strata of the psyche. The god Helios and his opposite number the Devil, described in the Second Sermon, are very much present in the totality of the psyche, including the unconscious. The principle of the unconscious, however, is not so much the accustomed *conflicting dualism* as the much more seldom envisioned *complementary dualism*. In the unconscious the opposites complement each other, while in consciousness they shut each other out of conscious attention or moral approval. In the unconscious—whether in the murky depths of the instinctual libido (the lower Pan, or Priapos) or in the airy heights of the numinous archetypal psyche—life is generated and regenerated by the power of Abraxas, which is impersonal, amoral, nondiscriminating, fearless, merciless, invulnerable and ever active.

In the Fourth Sermon Abraxas is mentioned as "the activity of the whole," thereby indicating that it is energy, or force, that characterizes this principle most clearly. But what is this energy used for? What are its purposes? Obviously, Abraxas exists for the perpetuating or enhancement of life, by which we must understand the life of the psyche, although physical life may not be excluded. Jesus is said to have stated that He came so that men might have this life and have it more abundantly. The dynamism of the psyche can be said to always reside at the point of equipoise between the binaries, where the balancing of the polarities liberates the energy which ordinarily would be used up in the conflict of the opposites. Not that conflict is undesirable, or evil as such. It needs to be recognized, however, that conflict is useful to and productive of the growth and enhancement of our being only when it leads to a resolution by the inclusion in lieu of the exclusion of the opposites. We may perhaps best apprehend this difficult idea when applying it within practical psychological considerations. No psychological conflict is ever truly resolved when one opposite wins out over the other. Only when the opposites are reconciled on a plane or in a dimension superior to themselves can we say that there has been a real solution. This recognition, in fact, distinguishes Jung's therapeutic method from those employed by other practitioners inspired by less profound theories. In Jungian psychology there is no easy way out of a psychic conflict by associating oneself with one polarity in the conflict. We must, as it were, not only fight on the side of the angels, but occasionally we must join the host of the fallen angels also. The two psychic antagonists must be allowed to commingle, to react upon each other, so that out of their battles and wounds, their agonies and struggles, after many transformations, there may emerge a new and changed Self. This Self will present consciousness with a solution to the problem that in all likelihood will turn out to be a true *re-solution,* a renewed, or novel and superior way of solving the conflict, which in the previous, untransformed state of the psyche would have been unthinkable and impossible.

It is perhaps not too far-fetched to suggest that this kind of subtle resolution, occasioned by a point of equipoise emerging between the two contending forces, has a profound bearing on the mystery of Abraxas, as indicated in the *Seven Sermons,* or more particularly in the Third Sermon. Between the two opposites, God and Devil, betwixt and between the night and the day, at the very crack of the dawn, stands the majestic chanticleer, the rooster-headed god of cosmic and psychic energy, drawing his strength from both the night and the day and preparing to race with his chariot drawn by the white steeds of the dawn to a world beyond earth and stars, out of time and out of mind.

Another useful example of the practical utility of the Abraxas concept may be found in the social and historical sphere. We may ask ourselves: Why are death and old age such a terrible social burden in the context of contemporary Western civilized society? Why is it that in other historical periods persons were able to live gracefully in old age and enjoy both wisdom and the respect due to wisdom, while in our times we see nothing of the sort? Why was death once a familiar acquaintance, not to say an intimate friend of humanity, while today it is an enemy no less dreaded for being politely ignored? The reason for these contemporary regrettable social phenomena might very well be found in the above-noted philosophy of the excluded middle. Our reasoning has come to declare to us with accurate but disastrous logic that life is good: therefore death must be bad. We must consequently, if we are to think rationally and logically, affirm life and deny death; we ought to cling to the former and shun the latter. If we have no reconciliation of the opposites, if we must choose in the usual "either-or" fashion, then obviously we must choose life. Thus life becomes the central affirmation of all values, while death becomes the ultimate negation of them. Since most of our value systems are centered on life, death means to us the destruction of all values of life. Death becomes not only the end of physical embodiment but of meaning, indeed of existence itself. All of this is the direct result of consciousness being dominated by ego-thinking. Since that which is conscious cannot conceive of itself not being conscious, the loss of consciousness in death must appear as the loss of existence as such. From this psychological attitude comes, not only our ignoring and rejection of death, but our rejection of the perfectly natural process of ageing, with its attendant cult of perpetual youthfulness. When we reject old age in the abstract, it is only logical that we will also reject those who appear as the carriers of the phenomenon we reject, and thus we shut away our aged into dreadful warehouses designed for their conceal-ment rather than for their care and true welfare. Let no one remind us of death, or of age, for life and youth are good, and therefore death and old age are bad—and why indeed should we be reminded of bad things?

Jung, along with the ancient Gnostics, stresses the completeness of reality. "It is the fullness of being that matters" seems to be his constant watchword, which he shouts at us again and again in a variety of ways. Jung's attitude toward death reflects this unitary approach. While he abstains from any deterministic forecasting of the fate of consciousness after the dissolution of the body, Jung continues to quietly and unobtrusively affirm the existence of some sort of a continuity beyond the grave. This attitude was rooted in his conviction regarding the mutuality and complementary nature of the opposites at the psychological level. As light is significant, not because of itself, but because of its relationship to darkness, so death becomes important because of life, and life is meaningful because of death. Death is part of life, and life is part of death. Moreover, from a classical Gnostic point of view it would be easy to argue that the author of our disastrously one-sided attitude toward death is none other than the foolish demiurge of Genesis, who in the third chapter (verse 3) of that scripture makes it appear that death is the result of man's sin. If death is the result of sin, then it follows that death must be associated with evil, and life becomes the gift of God, even as death appears as His curse. Similarly, old age is represented as a condition of labor and sorrow by Holy Writ, an affliction that is organically connected with death, the consequence of sin. It was religion and nothing else that began the great heresy of separation, of the philosophy of the excluded middle! If one is to take a Jungian psycho-historical view of this fact, one can recognize that the early, demiurgic phase of religiosity in the West was directed toward differentiation, the wrenching of consciousness from its aionial slumber in the unconscious. The Gnostic effort, on the other hand, is directed toward individuation, the reintegration of differentiated and alienated consciousness with the unconscious. Thus, conventional religion divides, while Gnosis unites. These two tendencies appear contradictory, and they most certainly are in conflict with each other, but they also represent separate developmental phases of the growth and development of the human psyche, both on the individual and the collective levels. Even as it is regarded normal for youth to be at least partially characterized by an extraverted and passionate involvement in the external world, so it is understandable that the religiosity of the adolescense of culture would be of a differentiated and extraverted character. On the other hand, maturity of the individual as well as of culture should bring with it a reflectiveness and regard for the inner realities and mysteries of the soul—in short, it should be productive of wisdom. No wonder then that the God of differentiation is a fashioner or architect (demiurge), while the principal mythic figure of the individuational spirituality of the Gnosis is Sophia, who is wisdom embodied.

The greatest resistence to the unifying or Abraxas, vision of being comes as the result of the fears of human establishments of the moral and ethical implications of such a vision. The ancient Gnostics were accused of antinomianism, or the attitude of being opposed to the moral law, especially as revealed in the Decalogue. Buber only voiced a perennial anti-Gnostic paranoia when he objected to Jung's Abraxas on the grounds that a God who is both Devil and God at the same time leads to an attitude of moral anarchy within the individual. Yet it is perfectly obvious that the sort of moral absolutism embodied in conventional religion is and must remain unacceptable to both Gnosticism and to modern depth psychology. Freud nourished a fierce hatred against religion precisely because he found that the religiously based strictures of society against the manifestations of the libido worked havoc in the lives of people, and this recognition still stands as valid. Psychology cannot and should not endorse divinely revealed moral absolutes as if they were the laws of the psyche. Gnostic religiosity would adopt a position very similar to the psychological one. Gnostics recognized the need of the individual to function within the accepted rules of the outer world, but they saw no need to build these man-made regulations into divinely instituted commandments from which there can be no deviation. Moreover, they recognized moral law and discipline as quite helpful to certain persons belonging to the category of less developed people who are in need of discipline for the strengthening of their spiritual muscle. On the other hand, they also recognized that discipline exists for the accomplishment of certain specific goals, and when these goals are met, the discipline becomes superfluous. The Gnostic is in fact not an *antinomian* (*anti*—against, *nomos*—law) but a seeker after *autonomy* (*autos*—self, *nomos*—law), inasmuch as he strives for a state of consciousness wherein his own law is declared to him day by day and moment by moment by his indwelling divine intuition. It is in the dusty, bloodied and tear-soaked arena of daily existential confrontations with life, and not in the library of Bibles, Korans and Gospels, that the Gnostic discovers the law that is applicable to his particular and individual condition. Human nature needs neither sanctification nor deification at our feeble hands; the sanctifying forces as well as the deity indwelling having been planted within it before the beginning of time and the fashioning of space.

In his description of Abraxas, Jung presents us with a veritable litany of characteristics, somewhat after the pattern of his recounting of the paradoxical attributes of the Pleroma in the First Sermon. It is readily recognized, however, that while in his description of the Pleroma he emphasized the existence of the numberless pairs of opposites which exist as equilibrated qualities of the Pleroma, in his characterization of Abraxas, he is particularly intent upon bringing forth the dynamic, over-whelming power and activity of the cosmic chanticleer. While some of the attributes of Abraxas appear as opposites (such as the delight of earth and the cruelty of heaven), their main distinguishing feature is irresistible energy. As the Pleroma represents the supreme fullness, majestically remote and quies-cent in its sovereign and numinous splendor, so Abraxas is the embodiment of this abstract fullness in cosmic and psychic activity. Yet, as mentioned before, it would be a grave misap-prehension to equate Abraxas with some sort of a conventional Gnostic demiurge. It would be much more correct to say that he is the force without which all demiurges would cease to create, and he is also the liberating force whereby wisdom and love are enabled to accomplish their work of emancipating the human soul from the thralldom of the cosmos. Above all Abraxas is *terrible*. This word, we feel, needs to be understood, less in contem-porary vernacular terms, but rather in the sense of the Ren-naissance man's *terribilita,* which was a quality to be both feared and admired and was said to appertain to all naturally great and outstanding persons. Abraxas is thus terrible in the sense that Pope Julis II or the fierce Duke Cesare Borgia were terrible; his whip is not unlike the knotted rope of Jesus whereby he dispensed the blows of his wrath to the money-changers in the Temple. This terribleness is not the hallmark of evil or of benighted arrogance, as one might find in the case of demiurge, but rather it is the natural manifestation of titanic force, which inevitably fills human consciousness with dread and trembling.

What then must human consciousness do with this terrible Abraxas? Jung's answer is clear in its awe-inspiring impact: "To see him means blindness; to know him is sickness; to worship him is death; to fear him is wisdom; not to resist him means liberation." To immerse one's consciousness in the fierce dynamism of unconscious life, either by contemplation, by thought or by religious worship, is counterproductive. The excesses of psychedelic drugs, of mind-numbing and ego-shattering substances and practices throughout the ages, bear eloquent testimony to this. Brief episodes of egolessness of an immersion of ourselves in the maelstrom of raw life-energy, we may regard as not only permissible but useful; not a few alienated persons of modern culture are indeed in need of discovering the Abraxas power within themselves, somewhat after the fashion of Hesse's *Steppenwolf*. As the fear of God has been envisioned as the beginning of wisdom, so the fear of Abraxas is said by Jung to be wisdom. This fear, as a holy commixture of awe and caution, will prevent the individual from either underestimating or foolishly provoking the titanic forces resident in the nucleus of the atom of the soul. The most important injunction to be found in Jung's sermon, however, is: "Not to resist him means liberation." To resist Abraxas, means invoking the supreme disaster. The fierce dynamism of life will not be denied; it will break into the field of consciousness by some means or other. The Romans said wisely about nature: Naturam expellas furca, tamen usque recurret (You may drive out nature with a pitchfork, but she will speedily return). Nature, whether regarded as the outer nature of elemental forces or as the inner nature of psychological forces, cannot be successfully resisted by consciousness. Wisely indeed wrote William Blake: "Sooner murder an infant in its cradle than nurse unacted desires."* Acceptance of and permeability toward the promptings and designs of the unconscious is the way to liberation, individuation, Gnosis, or whatever word may apply to describe it. Repression,

---

The Marriage of Heaven and Hell, Plate 10.

one-sidedness, the unwillingness to accept the waters of the great underground stream as they well up are sure ways to serfdom and bondage. Repression of the unconscious dynamism leads to our enslavement by the very forces we wished to repress. It is thus that whenever we do not resist Abraxas we advance our true liberation.

What should we say in summation of this Third Sermon, containing Jung's terrifyingly sublime description of Abraxas? It would be fair to say that the figure of Abraxas meant more to Jung than all the other powers and mythological figures mentioned in the *Seven Sermons*. In spite of the controversies which at times have surrounded Jung's use of the figure of Abraxas, we may be assured that this figure proves Jung's Gnosis and Gnosticism more clearly than any other item of evidence. Whether Jung's interpretation of Abraxas matches in exact detail the understanding various ancient Gnostics are said to have had of this figure is not particularly significant. The Nag Hammadi Gnostic scriptures, as well as other, earlier discoveries, clearly indicate that Gnostics were never adverse to the use of the same name or term in a somewhat different or novel context. There is no way of knowing today whether the way in which Jung treated the figure of Abraxas in the *Seven Sermons* (and, one might say, Hesse treated it in *Demian*) may not approximate some of the ancient Gnostic views more closely than some scholarly conjectures. If we accept the simple and evident proposition that Jung was a Gnostic, albeit a modern one (How could he have been any other kind?), then he acted in typical Gnostic fashion when he modified the existing Gnostic myths and mythological figures and gave them the kind of attributes and content which his own Gnosis required. This Jungian conception of Abraxas may be summed up by declaring that it represents the dynamism of the fullness of being. Certainly the image and figure of Abraxas in this Sermon is of such existential power that one can safely say that it is *alive*. The relevance of Abraxas to contemporary concerns has been most eloquently expressed by the aforementioned poet-diplomat Miguel Serrano:

The modern Christian and the Western world as a whole has now reached a point of crisis, and the choices open seem less than attractive. We neither want one of those apocalyptic catastrophes which have so disfigured our past history, nor do we want the de-humanizing path of the Orient which would result in an irremediable lowering of our standards. Perhaps then the only possibility that remains is Abraxas, that is to say, a projection of our souls both outwards and inwards, both to the light and to the deep shadows of our biological roots, in hopes of finding in the combination of the two the pure archetype. This pure archetype would be the authentic image of the god which is within ourselves and which has been sunk for so long, like Atlantis, under the waters of our consciousness. Thus Abraxas would also come to mean Total Man.[11]

As Jung declared to the same Miguel Serrano, no one truly understood him, only a poet could begin to understand. It is thus fitting that we should conclude this commentary on the Third Sermon by quoting another poet, William Blake, who in his Gnostic and prophetic visionary frenzy may well have written of Abraxas when he proclaimed:

> Where the son of fire in his eastern cloud, while the morning plumes her golden breast, spurning the clouds written with curses, stamps the stony law to dust, loosing the eternal horses from the dens of night crying: Empire is no more! And now the lion and wolf shall cease.

The Fourth Sermon— Burning Bush and Tree of Life

After having presented the awesome image of Abraxas to the dead, Jung-Basilides proceeds to teach his reluctant pupils further mysteries regarding great dual spiritual powers, which, unlike Abraxas, do not represent the union of the opposites but rather their adversary and even war-like relationship. Gnostics were forever accused of "dualism" by their opponents, and were it not for Jung's lengthy and impressive description of Abraxas in the Second and Third Sermons, a similar charge might be leveled against him on the basis of the Fourth and Fifth Sermons. Duality and unity are in fact both vitally important and coexisting principles of the functioning of psychic nature and are thus treated in the *Sermons* as well as in the later, scientific writings of the prophet of Kusnacht. The psycho-physiological organism of the human being is a unity, but within it titanic and fearsome dual forces are forever struggling for supremacy. Locked in an aeonial wrestling posture of deathly combat, body and spirit, feeling and intellect, femininity and masculinity, instinct and civilization, are forever engaged in an Armageddon, at once necessary and futile. The German soul, to which J.W. von Goethe gave such eloquent expression, seems to have expressed this Faustian duality with much greater clarity and fervor than any national psyche since the passing of the ancient Greeks. The two souls which Goethe said lived in Faust's breast were given a clear recognition by the Greeks in the cosmic-psychological figures which Jung makes reappear in the Fourth Sermon, i.e. the "burning one" and the "growing one."

The Greeks declared that two world spirits dwell in the fabric of cosmic and human life and that they stand in mortal combat one with another. This combat is of such power and magnitude that we can by no means foretell its outcome. The growing spirit is the spirit of civilization; it ever seeks to create forms wherein life may expand, may build, and make itself more secure. The burning one, on the other hand, seeks life in movement, change, adventure, battle, and at times even in conflict and violence. The growing one is peaceful, the burning one is warlike; civilization is conserving and often conservative, while the opposing dynamism is revolutionary. Both forces are part of the natural order (a consideration which may be worth mentioning in view of the periodic eruptions of Rousseauesque sentimentalizations of things we are pleased to call natural). War and peace, conservation and destruction, constructive evolution and destructive revolution are all part of nature. To identify nature with peace and serenity to the exclusion of war and fierceness is contrary to the evidence of observation. Is the peaceful sunset more natural than the erupting volcano? Is the nightingale more natural than the hawk? In the dynamism of nature, killing is as necessary as giving birth. Human moral values cannot and should not be projected unto nature for the very evident reason that they do not belong there. One may be justified in believing that peace is better than war, that compassion is preferable to cruelty, but it must be recognized that the values which underlie such judgments are derived, not from nature, but from consciousness, in the psychological meaning of the word, as opposed to the unconscious. One grand attempt at conjoining the two, the concept of "natural law" within Thomistic theology, has revealed itself as a great failure with the increasing differentiation of consciousness in history. Hygiene, sanitation, population control, or even the human concern with ecological balance in nature are all the products of consciousness and demonstrate the need to apply consciousness to the processes and developments of nature.

The burning one and the growing one are defined as god-devils in the *Sermons,* thus indicating that, although they are themselves opposites, within each we find still a contrasting and cooperative relationship of even greater oppositional forces. The flame of the burning one, whom Jung calls *Eros*, contains a union of good and evil, and so does the growth of the tree of life, which is the name he has given to the growing one. "Good and evil are united in the flame. Good and evil are united in the growth of the tree. Life and love oppose each other in their own divinity"—thus declares the Fourth Sermon. The *Sermons* bring to our attention that only in the coexistence and mutual inherence of the burning and the growing forces of being in the process of living can the secret of ultimate wholeness be discovered. Whenever the desire for security, continuity and per-manence becomes paramount in our lives, spontaneity and creativity atrophy; the growing one has managed to stifle and overpower the burning one. The perennial tragic conflicts of the establishments of society, commerce, routine toil, on the one hand, and unfettered artistic effort, on the other, are but some of the manifestations of this phenomenon. Dominance of the growing one engenders the triviality of everydayness; it places its trust and confidence in the repetitions and cyclic patterns of recurrence which ensure slow-but-sure growth. The cycle of the eternal return is the bedrock of all structures of established order. Agriculture and animal husbandry function within the cycles of biological fertility adapted to the seasons of time. Similarly the family life of human beings needs to adapt itself considerably to the cycles of birth and growth of children and the life-stages of men and women. Even such higher products of the differentiation of human consciousness as the building of cities, the pursuit of commerce and the operations of industry have their aspects of cyclicity and routine, without which their success is in jeopardy. On the other hand, the burning flame of individual creativity is ever in a state of overt or covert revolt against repetition and cyclicity. The agriculturist and industrial laborer as well as the merchant may rightly sleep the secure sleep of the righteous during the night, but the artist is more likely than not to turn to the night for his inspiration and labor and burn the midnight oil prepared for his use by the daytime labor of a prosaic society. The self-satisfied *pater familias* and doting mother peacefully rock their child on their knees, viewing him as the continuation of their own lives, the extension of their very selfhood and the fulfillment of their labors. The children of the artist, on the other hand, are not of flesh and blood but are conceived in the bridal chamber of the mind and born in the delivery room of the studio or garret. The growing one and the burning one thus live in two worlds which coexist in space but not in consciousness, which overlap in physical geography, but which are established on widely separated continents of the soul.

Another vitally present manifestation of the duality of the burning one and the growing one may be found in the two dimensions in which human relatedness tends to direct itself. One of these may be conveniently envisioned as vertical and the other as horizontal. The vertical effort directs itself toward the objective of meaning and ultimate significance and has traditionally been connected either with Divinity or with a quasi-divine or greater Self within the human being. The horizontal direction may be explained as moving towards other people who surround the individual self, to what might be called the other-people world. We must get along with the greater world of meaning, the transcendental macrocosm enshrined in the deeper recesses of our nature, and at the same time we must get along with the microcosmic world of differentiated forms of consciousness that surround us on all sides. The human being is motivated, as it were, by two forms of knowing or *gnosis*, both of which are in the nature of the biblical meaning of the word, namely involving the closest forms of intimacy and relationship. Humans appear to possess both a drive for self-knowledge and a drive for the knowledge of other persons. The drive for self-knowledge is said to motivate numerous spiritual or religious schools the world over, but its most frequently noted manifestations appear to be among several religions of India and Asia. In most of these religious systems congregational worship is nonexistent, while individual prayer, worship and meditation are advocated. Priests are guardians of temples, performers of sacrifices, but do not have the kind of social role Christian priests or ministers, as well as Rabbis and Mullahs, have assumed in the Semitic religions. Many Eastern religions appear to exist primarily for the individual's benefit; their task is to facilitate the insight, individuation, or spiritual perception of the individual. In short, they deal with relatedness to personal and ultimate meaning. In the traditions which mainly proceed from the Semitic peoples, the emphasis is primarily social. Worship is congregational in nature, and definite times of great regularity are established for activities of worship, for the most part on a weekly rather than on a merely seasonal basis. In many of these religions the ethical content has well-nigh swallowed up the metaphysics or the mysticism; the concern for "don'ts" and for "do's" is great. (It has been said in a humorous vein that the oriental religions are *be-religions,* that Judaism is a *do-religion,* and Christianity a *don't religion.*)

The two orientations to spirituality both have their light and shadow sides. In the East concern for the welfare of persons is regarded as relatively unimportant. The tendency of persons in India to shrug their shoulders in the face of human misery and suffering while taking umbrage under the concept of karma is considerable. The Buddhist attitude is much more compassionate, but in practice even in Buddhist countries one usually encounters a society with little social responsibility. On the other hand, the Western mind has been beset for centuries with the perplexities of both the theory and practice of social responsibility. Ever since Cain asked the portentous question whether he was in fact his brother's keeper, the matter of how far one must go in answering in the affirmative has been our deep concern. The Semitic religions without exception answered Cain's question affirmatively, but the practice of this affirmative precept has taken curious manifestations indeed. Some of the worst forms of economic exploitation, racial prejudice and mechanized martial slaughter originated among the peoples whose spiritual roots go back to the Semitic religions, thus indicating that practice seldom, if ever, keeps pace with theory in the life of humanity.

It takes little imagination to recognize that in the Semitic or Western forms of spiritual tradition the emphasis on the growing one is very prominent. The group, society, the people are, if not divine, at least chosen by God and thus very important in the spiritual scheme of things. The chosen people may at times appear to be a nation, as among the Jews, or a "household of the faith," as in Christianity and Islam, but the specialness of the *people* as against the *individual* is forever asserted. It is of course true that Western culture, after a certain point in history, came to champion the dignity of human personhood and to embody much individualism. It is to be doubted, however, that these developments were in any significant way the result of principles within the Judeo-Christian tradition. All of these values made significant inroads only after the Renaissance, and later after the French Revolution, when rationalism and secularism as well as humanism came to replace the rule of religious establishments.

The concern with being one's brother's keeper, of course, has done much harm along with good. Frequently we have become, not only our brother's keeper, but his jailer and oppressor as well, surrounding him with so many taboos and regulations that selfhood has withered. In our effort to create a perfect society, we have time and again subjected the individual to frightful and stifling abuses. The slaves of Rome and Greece, the serfs of the Christian Middle Ages, the tortured and executed religious and other minorities of Western society are frightful reminders of the collective horror. In all of these instances individuals were sacrificed to the alleged collective welfare of society, the burning one was extinguished so that the growing one might flourish. Curiously and significantly enough, none of these immense sacrifices offered to the Moloch of the perfect society have ever significantly improved society in either abstract or concrete terms. The distant Utopia of the *Civitas Dei,* ruled by a benign imperial father and guided by a divinely inspired loving Pope, remained as much of a mirage and a pipedream as a Thousand Year Reich and the Workers' Paradise. The worship of the growing one at the expense of the burning one has proven to be the cultus of a God that failed.

Not that the emphasis on the growing one is without merit and usefulness. The instinct for self-preservation, which along with such other instincts as the drive for self-nourishment and pro-pagation, represents one of the chief drives of the species and requires the creation of some form of society or group within which the protection of individuals against enemies may be safely accomplished. Much of civilization and culture really owes its existence to the instinct of self-preservation which forces individuals from very early and primitive times into groups. The sharing of the work-load and the company of others stimulates and brings forth cultural forces from individuals which, left to their own devices, they would never have suspected as even existing within themselves. Efficiency, utility, social organization, and eventually esthetics, beauty and fine culture are all more or less spawned by the necessity of in-dividuals to band together in groups for self-protection. Life in society therefore has a powerful and civilizing influence upon in-dividuals. Only societies have schools, artists' studios, libraries, music conservatories, churches and temples, theaters and opera; individuals in total isolation cannot produce such creations of culture. Still, with civilization comes repression, which extends, not only to the individual expression of freedoms which in groups take on an anti-social character, but to many valuable and essential expressions of the human psyche as well. No wonder Eros, the burning one, who in the words of the Sermon shines and devours, rebels against the restrictions of the growing one and bursts the bounds of order and tradition.

Culture, like the "tree of life" named by Jung in the Fourth Sermon, grows slowly and reaches stately stature only after long periods of historical development. Group life and group con-sciousness not only serve the purposes of protection and of the release of the finer forces of refinement, but they also teach humans to tolerate one another and to curb their instinctive reactions. Human society teaches individuals impulse control. The growth of the human psyche is not accomplished by fiat, and thus the external disciplines of society are indeed often helpful to persons who have achieved little or no internal discipline. External discipline is always useful to those incapable of self-discipline. The ultimate aim of human consciousness is to derive meaning from its own essential selfhood, but when this selfhood is only minimally present in the personality, significance may be derived by one's presence within a group.

At the present time most persons in modern society find themselves in a psychological position wherein they are increasingly able to derive significance from their own interior being, but are not yet ready to dispense with the significance derived from groups. Many still need some of the support which the values of the group offer, although they have already outgrown it in some respects. Even though they are not wholly themselves as yet, they no longer identify completely with others. The individuational movement away from the collective steadily asserts itself in these persons and they gradually begin to face the world alone. It is at this point that the growing one and the burning one, the collective impulse and the individual spirit, fight their greatest and most fateful battle. This is the time of life when men and women need to become heroes lest they perish. As Joseph Campbell so accurately stated in his conclusion to *The Hero With a Thousand Faces:*

> It is not society that is to guide and save the creative hero, but precisely the reverse. And so every one of us shares the supreme ordeal—carries the cross of the redeemer—not in the bright moments of his tribes' great victories, but in the silences of his personal despair.[12]

It is thus that the human being must do what at first may appear to be very close to the impossible; he must overcome nature, he must outgrow the growing one. This is not to say that either Jung or the present author tend to favor the burning one over the growing one. The process of spiritual growth, called by Jung *individuation,* requires that in its course individual values should replace collective ones. This is why the process is, in fact, called individuation: the person becomes increasingly self-directed, and therefore a real individual. Evolution, order, conditioned conscience, implanted and long-nourished values must give way to the consuming flame of the burning one. Eros must slay Logos, even slay the Word of God itself. The *command-ment* now needs to be replaced by the *command;* Mount Sinai must fade, so that the mountain peak of the interior Olympus may emerge into sight. Eros thus becomes the savior, but in his duality he is a dangerous, volatile savior, who slays as easily as he saves. Says Jung:

> (beneath the) thin veneer of culture the wild beast lurks . . . But the beast is not tamed by locking it up in a cage. *There is no morality without freedom.*[13]

The significant difference in the approaches of the growing one and the burning one consists in their treatment of freedom. Jung repeatedly stated that without freedom individuation would be a senseless mechanism, characterized by fatality rather than by fulfillment. This element of fatality is a prominent feature of the collective structures of the growing one. The Christian bows to the will of God, even as the Hindu prostrates himself before the elusive but inexorable fatefulness of karma, while the Moslem accepts the rulership of Allah in the form of Kismet. Neither are modern secularistic systems free of this fatality; Nazi Germany felt driven forward and eventually into destruction by the "law of blood," while the Marxist rulers of various countries are motivated by their conceptions of the dialectics of history. As against this fatality, individuation established a moral order of fulfillment and meaning which, while stepping outside the ramparts and motes of culturally ordained modes of behavior, freely travels along on the open road of the aeonial journey guided by the stars of inner morality and ethics shining on the firmament of the soul. As Kant poetically phrased it, "the starry heavens above, and the moral law within us" are the authentic directors of meaningful living. Our degree of morality is really never fully known to us until we retreat from externally imposed laws and regulations and allow our internal ethics to set the guidelines for its own sake and for no other reason. The spiritual liber-tarianism of the sage Lao Tzu even goes so far as to recognize the validity of this individual principle in the collective arena of the state and of society:

> The more taboos and prohibitions there are in the world,
> The poorer the people will be.

The more sharp weapons the people have,
The more troubled the state will be.
The more cunning and skill man possesses,
The more vicious things will appear.
The more law and orders are made prominent,
The more thieves and robbers there will be.[14]

In a similar vein, the Alexandrian Gnostic teacher Epiphanes, who is said to have died at the age of seventeen, the precocious son of the illustrious Capocrates and Alexandra, revered for his wisdom and loveliness of character, wrote in a treatise attributed to him, entitled *On Justice:*

Where does Justice lie? In a community of equalities. A common sky stretches above our heads and covers the entire earth with its immensity, the same night reveals its stars to all without discrimination, the same sun, father of night and begetter of day, shines in the sky for all men equally. It is common to all, rich men and beggars, kings and subjects, wise men and fools, free men and slaves. God made it to pour out its light for all the beings on this earth in order that it would be of common benefit to all: who would dare to appropriate the light of the sun to himself alone? . . .

And everything that exists, everything that lives, is subject to this law of justice and equality . . . . As for the laws of this world, it is they and they alone which have taught us to act against the law. Individual laws fragment and destroy communion with divine law. The prophet said: "I had not known sin, but by the law", and how are we to interpret his meaning, if it be not that the words "mine" and "thine" have entered into this world through the laws, and that this made an end of all community? Nevertheless, that which God created, he created for all to hold in common possession: vines, grains, and all the fruits of the earth. Has the vine ever been seen to chase away a thief, or a thievish passerby? But when man forgot that community means equality, and deformed it by his laws, on that day, the thief was born.[15]

These somewhat naive words—which are not unlike those of Antigone, Diogenes, Epicurus and Rousseau—may be too simplified for the complex, overpopulated world wherein we live, where the pestiferous horrors of crime, violence, mass insanity, the innumerable depredations of humans directed against humans distort all perspectives. Nevertheless, they are words of vision, intuition and individuation. They are the words of a

spiritual perception which rightly recognizes that lawlessness is
frequently brought about by an excess of law, and sin and evil
are brought into the world by the midwifery of taboos and commandments. Childlike and impractical as they sound to jaded
contemporary ears, the words of Lao Tzu and of Epiphanes contain a psychological insight which appears valid and substan-
tiated in twentieth-century culture. On the collective scale, as
well as on the individual plane, there is no true morality without
freedom.

What kind of freedom does man, then, possess? In a sense it
may be correctly said that freedom itself is a frightful paradox
when viewed psychologically. To be free after the fashion of the
ego alone is an unsatisfactory and deceptive freedom at best. To
say no to the responsibility of individuation, to resist *gnosis* by
way of the willfullness of the ego, is not freedom but a per-
sistence in captivity. We are not free to choose our destiny, but
our *gnosis,* or consciousness, may make us free to accept this
destiny as a task laid upon us by the law of spiritual growth. In
lieu of submitting to externally imposed laws, the individuating
person submits to this law of growth, and in so doing he takes
the responsibility for individuation in a conscious, aware
fashion. The surrender of the limited purposes of the ego to the
much larger goals of the Self—goals within which the lesser
egoic purposes are in fact meaningfully encompassed—does not
do away with the sense of freedom. On the contrary, only by
subordinating the limitations of the ego to the Self do we truly
justify our freedom and do we meaningfully validate our responsibility for our actions and decisions. At some point in life every
man and every woman must say *yes* to someone or something
greater and more meaningful than family, husband, wife, child,
society, career, country and the other ego-involved shiboleths of
mundane living. Only this *yes* will bring the truth that makes
free, only such as *yes* will bring the kind of inward greatness of
which Jung wrote:

> the man who is inwardly great will know that the long expected
> friend of his soul, the immortal one, has now really come, 'to
> lead captivity captive.'[16]

A graphic and touchingly personal testimonial of this affirmation is given to us by Dag Hammerskjold in his Diary:

I don't know Who--or What--put the question, I don't know
when it was put. I don't even remember answering. But at
some moment I did answer *Yes* to Someone--or Something--
and from that hour I was certain that existence is meaningful
and that, therefore, my life, in self-surrender, had a goal.[17]

The question of freedom, as is well known, occupies an
important position in existentialist thought, and the student of
Jung or of Gnosticism would be well advised to consider some of
these views. The existentialist Protestant theologian Paul Tillich
speaks of the "inescapability of freedom," and states that this
freedom causes a most profound unrest in the being of man, and
that all of man's being is in fact threatened by this freedom. This
inescapable freedom hangs like a threat over all of human
existence, where there are no safeguards, no certainties, no
securities of either religious or secular nature which might help
man avoid this radical exposure to the immense power of
freedom. Jean Paul Sartre, the once supremely prestigious
"pope of existentialism," referred to the human being as "condemned to freedom." In Sartre's less than cheerful phrasing,
freedom hangs over man like an undying doom, wherein, being
his own master, he is condemned to create himself. In his play
The Flies, Sartre makes his hero exclaim: "I am condemned to
have no other law but my own." Only in one's insecurity and
condemnation to utter freedom does one discover the direction
of destiny. Tillich calls the courage for this freedom a "courage
of despair," which alone can lead to an ultimate conquest of the
fear of life. Although this notion of existential fear and dread is
the consequence of a negative world-view which considers being
as blind, accidental and meaningless, still it contains
psychological truth.

Yet the commendable emphasis of these existential thinkers
on freedom is nevertheless suffering from an inadequate
recognition of the transcendental selfhood of the human being.
Tillich and Sartre do not consider that we may have anything
beyond the ego to submit to, to derive our support from. Having—in our view quite correctly—discarded the traditional
framework of dogma and religious orthodoxy with its personal
God and revealed law, they are left with only the human ego.
After stripping away the flimsy defenses of the mind, the existentialist is thrown back on his mundane, egoic selfhood; as an

ego he faces the immensity of freedom, as an ego he creates himself. In contrast with these thinkers, Jung squarely stated: "It is not I who create myself, rather I happen to myself."[18] There is a hidden operator behind our lives, even though it may not be in accord with the view of conventional religion. The words of the Delphic oracle, incised over the doorway of Jung's house in Kusnack, near Zurich, as well as on his family crypt, are of supreme importance here: Vocatus atque non vocatus Deus aderit (Called or uncalled the god will be present). Whether we affirm or deny, invoke or banish the numinous reality of the light indwelling, it will nevertheless be present, and moreover, its presence will be felt through its works. We cannot escape being destined. Our freedom is not a freedom that takes us away from the destiny of individuation, but rather it is a freedom that permits us to recognize this destiny consciously, with full gnosis. The choice is merely between two possibilities: one implies unconsciousness, and a consequent lack of freedom ensuing from the compulsive pressure exerted on us by the god, or collective unconscious; the other is an experience of meaning arising from the recognition of the individuational urge decreed by the same indwelling god. All of life is endowed by an imprint, which is nevertheless present for being concealed. The Kabbalists called it Tav, the mark of the Shekinah, or divine presence in the world; the Christian mystic Jacob Boehme called it Signatura Rerum, the seal or signature of the eternal within things. As life becomes translucent in response to the gnosis of consciousness, the hidden imprint, like a mysterious watermark in some yellowed parchment-text of concealed wisdom, appears visibly before the eyes of the astounded observer.

Freedom and restriction, the burning one and the growing one, accompany and condition the long, slow climb of the history of humanity. Man's consciousness has greatly increased in scope since its beginnings and has acquired a strong orientation toward freedom. Rational enlightenment, scientific knowledge and technological skills have made civilized man very much freer than the so-called primitive, who is almost totally held captive, but also safeguarded by the growing one, i.e. by nature and the structures of his own society. Primitive societies accord their members little freedom; conversely primitive man has little freedom from the limitations of his own unconscious. Unlike persons of a more differentiated grade of consciousness, primitive people cannot usually act on the basis of the decisions of their egos, or as we might say, at will. Rather, the primitive waits until the slumbering energies in his unconscious are aroused before acting. Hunting, sowing, war, marrying and other important events are prepared for by rituals, such as dancing and magical ceremonies, designed to stir up the unconscious forces. Before moving forward, or outward, primitive humanity thus takes a step backward, or inward into the unconscious in order to poise the psyche for the forthcoming action. Under such circumstances, primitives have almost unlimited energy for action. Fear, prudence, shyness and fatigue are banished, and the tribesmen forge ahead with their task irrespective of danger, exertion and adverse circumstances. The gods of the unconscious are riding on their backs; the divine horsemen spur them on to achievement and victory. Primitive society and its members do not suffer from the kind of psychic inertia that frequently afflicts the civilized. Either they are quiet, when the gods are silent, or they wake up the gods and then, fortified and directed by the gods, move forth into action. Civilized humanity is neither lucky nor unlucky enough to be able to follow this course. Differentiated consciousness prides itself upon its ability to exert will and to do things by force of discipline. At this level of development, consciousness is characterized by at least partial ability to make psychic energy available to the conscious ego instead of being only in a state subservient to the unconscious. Most, if not all, of the attainments of civilization depend on this availability of the psychic energy to serve the purposes of the free, conscious will of the ego; only when the impulses of the unconscious have lost their stranglehold on the psychic energy can we freely utilize this energy to build, to do and to plan in accordance with our consciously recognized ideas and ideals.

Consciousness (once again in its psychological sense), expanding in the course of the passage of time through history, is the supreme prize of evolutionary development. Not the least of the benefits bestowed by this prize is the sense of freedom it conveys. Yet the price we pay is not small, for with the increase of self-awareness and sense of freedom the original security and trustworthiness of instinct disappears. An ever-growing dependence on politics, industry, technology, on media of communication, and on ever more powerful stimuli ranging from entertainment to drugs replace the archaic dependence on the forces of nature and on the deep powers of the unconscious. Thus an increasing alienation of consciousness from the unconscious sets in, which once again brings about a decrease of freedom and an increase of aberration, suffering, and lack of psychic energy. As our liberated consciousness forgets its origin in the unconscious, the growing one-sidedness of consciousness becomes a source of more and more violations of instinct, leading to frustration, unhappiness and depression. Modern, civilized man, thus, for all his freedom, is once again in bondage. The face of the slavemaster has changed, to be sure, but the fact of bondage is nevertheless apparent. Only a people alienated from the unconscious, like that of Nazi Germany, could have been victimized by the unholy suggestive influence of a mass psychosis; or to go back farther into history, only civilized and highly rational persons like the French followers of the Enlightenment could be swept away by the bloody floodtide of Jacobinism and allow the goddess of reason to be decapitated time and again by the guillotine. The more things change the more they remain the same. Human beings possessing little differentiated consciousness are in bondage to the impulses and eruptions of the unconscious. On the other hand, the development of the conscious ego frequently brings an overvaluation of rational consciousness and of the conscious will, as well as a vitiation of instinct, which conditions in turn become the root causes of numerous neuroses and psychic illnesses. Freedom is a limited and precious prize which is jeopardized by the Scylla of unconsciousness as well as by the Charibdys of an ego-dominated consciousness.

Yet it can be safely stated that the condition of humanity regarding freedom is by no means hopeless. We need to recognize that a conscious personality or ego is vitally important to us. This alone is the safeguard against primitivism and against the mass movements of modern society, which with their propaganda first insidiously undermine and later, with draconial force, wrest the precious freedoms from individuals. At the same time it must be recognized that the ego is not alone but that within it, or through it, the shape of a mysterious "other," of a directive selfhood, can be discerned. This god, who is ever present even if not called, is the imprinter of the mark of destiny upon the ego. Ethical action, authentic morality, meaning, and above all individuation are only possible in that tenuous twilight zone, in that crack between the two worlds of the growing one and the burning one, between structure and life, endurance and change, continuity and spontaneity. The two great gods or world spirits envisioned by classical antiquity are thus rightfully brought to our attention by Jung in the mythos of the *Seven Sermons*. The Tarot Trump of the Lovers in the charming design of Arthur Edward Waite and Pamela Coleman Smith may perhaps serve as a particularly helpful symbolization of the role these two forces play in human life. Both the man and woman represented on this card have a tree behind their persons. The male figure stands before a tree that emanates fiery flames from the extremities of its branches, while the female figure is poised before a tree which is loaded with fruit. These two trees may be rightly taken as the symbolizations of the growing one and of the burning one, both of which are vitally involved in the life of humanity. Life and love oppose each other in their own divinity, only to be united in humanity. In the embrace to come, representing the union of the opposites accomplished in the arena of human life, two lovers on the Tarot Trump will be united, the force of the growing tree and of the flaming tree reconciled. In his work *The Psychology of the Transference* Jung dwelt extensively on the alchemical task of the conjunction of the opposites and stated that in their wholeness alone resides the goal of individuation. In ancient and hallowed Gnostic fashion, he referred to these opposites as the "powers of the left and right," both of which belong to wholeness. The flame of Eros and the fruit of the Tree of Life are both given to man along with the gift of life. Their reconciliation and union, however, come to him only as the gift of consciousness of the Total Self, which is the fulfillment of life, the crown of existence.

The Fourth Sermon does not stop with the enumeration of the two world spirits, Eros and the Tree of Life, but proceeds to make numerous statements regarding the powers of light and darkness in their relationship to each other. To these Basilides-Jung added certain general declarations about the unity and the multiplicity of the gods. The teacher describes the number of "gods and devils" as immeasurable, and he makes the remarkable observation that every star is a god, while every space occupied by a star is a devil. Here the existence of the fundamental principle of polarity is alluded to, whereby the bright, starry light of every bearer of consciousness is balanced and devoured by a corresponding abyss of darkness. The stars shine only while the demonic light-swallower lurking behind them develops his appetite; once his hunger has matured, the light of the star is gobbled up by the dragon of darkness. This alternating activity, denoting a tensional relationship between light and darkness, takes place within a vast, paradoxical fullness, which to earthly eyes appears as a void. This fullness is none other than the Pleroma described in the First Sermon. The ever-present dynamism of the whole, which supplies both the constructive light of the stars and the destructive force of dark space, is the fiery god of energy, Abraxas, who appears in the Third Sermon.

In the next paragraph the teacher makes what appears to be a powerful plea for polytheism, and he castigates those who "have substituted the oneness of God for the diversity, which cannot be resolved into the one." Both in this statement and in the foregoing description of the fourfold structure of the godhead, which includes the Trinity as well as evil, Jung bravely and forcefully challenges two of the most dearly cherished dogmas of Christianity and Judaism. When he asserts that "four is the number of the chief deities, because four is the number of the measurements of the world," he challenges the Christian dogma of the Trinity, as he was to do several times in his later works, notably in *Aion* and *Answer to Job*. In his affirmation of the truth of the multiplicity and diversity of the gods, he takes the entire Semitic family of religions to task, which with their emphasis on monotheism, have lost certain important psychological values. Jung has often given voice to his regard for the gods versus the one God, and his entire mythos throughout his life is far more affinitized to the god-concept of classical antiquity, particularly as modified by Christian

Gnosticism, than it is to the uncompromising monotheism of Judaism, Islam or of Calvinistic Protestantism. Were it not for the God-man Christ, the Angels and the figure of the Virgin Mary, Jung would have had far less interest in Catholicism as well; these quasi-polytheistic elements appealed to his sense of the mythic, and also validated his recognitions regarding the collective unconscious or objective psyche, with its archetypal denizens resembling nothing as much as classical gods. His comment on the changing god-concept is not without a note of sadness and nostalgia for the Olympian age:

> The gods at first lived in a superhuman power and beauty on the top of snow-clad mountains or in the darkness of caves and woods, and seas. Later on they drew together into one god, and then god became man.[19]

The God-image of a human collectivity at any given historical time or in a particular culture holds deep significance for the individuation of persons in that time and space. Personal individuation, according to Jung, is not separate from what might be called collective individuation, since the spirit of the age tends to express itself or live itself out in the individuals. Thus the God-image of an age tends to be time-bound and of a specific character; it becomes constellated in the unconscious of persons as an image of psychic totality, the Self. Jung regarded the sacred scriptures of the world, not as revelation in the orthodox sense, but, as he phrased it, "repositories of the secrets of the soul, and this matchless knowledge is set forth in grand symbolic images."[20]

Jung was disposed toward a view wherein the God-image of modern humanity appeared to be less affinitized to the image of Christ, as was the case in the earlier period of Christian history, but more closely approximating that of the Holy Spirit, who may be regarded as the final culmination and efflorescence of the Godhead in the Christian conception. Jung's psychological observations thus seem to validate the famous prophecies of the medieval Calabrian abbot Joaquino da Fiore, who predicted the coming of the Age of the Holy Spirit which was to succeed the Age of the Son, which in turn was preceded by the Age of the Father.

It is assuredly difficult if not impossible for the ordinary believer in orthodox Christianity, or for that matter in Judaism or Islam, to rethink dogmatic concepts that have been regarded as sacrosanct and unalterable for centuries without number. Jung often said that faith and psychology, while by no means incompatible, approach their object in diametrically opposite ways. What he wisely concealed most of the time, however, is the fact that *faith* is not the only avenue to spiritual truths, that in addition there also exists the way of *gnosis,* which was in fact Jung's own way, for this way of Gnosis was the avenue which he employed under the figuration of psychology, mythology, alchemy and other guises. At the same time it must be remembered that the *Seven Sermons,* representing as they do one of the very few instances where Jung's Gnosticism was able to appear without the veil of allegory or the disguise of psychological terms, brings to us statements from Jung's personal gnostic insight which are of great rarity and value.

What sort of gods and devils is Jung referring to, then, when he claims in the Fourth Sermon that there are many more gods than men, and when he describes the gods as mighty beings who, like stars, stand in solitude and are separated by vast distances from each other—unlike humans who desperately desire company, shrinking in terror from the possibility of loneliness and isolation? What gods did this self-declared knower of the multiplicity and the diversity of the gods encounter? There are two answers one might offer in response to such questions, and both would appear to be quite accurate. The first answer would declare that Jung was referring to a psychological concept unheard of until his time, namely the concept of the archetypes. According to the official account, he developed the idea of the archetypes at a fairly early period of his career while still a staff physician in the Burgholzli hospital. Here he noted the startling correspondences existing between the spontaneous imagery of some patients and the very similar imagery of ancient and distant myths and scriptures. The frequently quoted case said to be involved in this discovery was that of a deranged Swiss countryman of very limited education, whose fantasy of the winds proceeding from the tail of the sun-god exactly matched the description of a myth contained in a Mythraic liturgy, translated and published thereafter by the scholar Albrecht Dieterich on the basis of a magical papyrus reposing in a Paris museum. Since the very earliest days of his career, Jung was struck by the fact that images of universal import and great power were produced in dreams and fantasies by patients, and that these images did not belong to the realm of the personal memories and experiences of such persons, but apparently emerged from some vast, archaic, and universal storehouse of imagery, located in a deep substratum of the unconscious mind. Freud, who at that time was still an important authority figure for Jung, also came across such images, but he considered them useless "archaic residues," rather analogous at the psychic level to such residues of the biological structure as the appendix. Jung could not and would not consider such images useless. He developed the conviction that such images were in fact important and living centers of psychic life. Using the German word *Urbild* (archaic or very ancient image), he described these images as belonging to a layer of the mind which is collective rather than individual in content and which gives human beings a feeling of archaic, non-egoic identity within themselves. This layer also connects them on a profoundly impersonal level to other humans, as well as to the forces of the environment and to nature. One of the striking and memorable characteristics of the archetypes is their *numinosity,* which term has been adapted by Jung (as well as Rudolf Otto) from classical descriptions of encounters with the gods and goddesses, and which is said to be the impact of the appearance of the immortal divinities upon the minds of mortals. Thus the gods and devils referred to in the *Sermons* reveal themselves to be archetypes of the collective unconscious, or of what has since been frequently referred to as the objective psyche. In the light of this answer, many of the statements made in the Fourth Sermon make eminently good sense. The gods are indeed many, for the most important characteristic of the mysterious and vast realm of the collective unconscious is that it is teeming with a seemingly endless variety of images of beings, each with its particular character and each bringing distinct and usually significant messages from the content of the collective unconscious for recognition and assimilation. Jung's concept of the collective unconscious and of its archetypal denizens has been validated by the experiences of innumerable persons. No one who has travelled into the regions below the surface of everyday consciousness will be disposed to doubt Jung's statements regarding the existence and activities of the archetypal gods who fulfill roles not at all unlike those fulfilled by Osiris, Isis, Jupiter, Venus, Hestia and their illustrious kith and kin. The denizens of the psychic Empyrian realm are not confined to the shadowy land of dream and vision; by way of the ever-present mechanism of projection, they become living and breathing humans, merging, as it were, in a sort of incarnational process with the men and women who become their bearers. Thus the words of the teacher in the Fourth Sermon become comprehensible:

> Countless gods are awaiting to become men.
> Countless gods have already been men.
> Man is a partaker of the essence of the gods;
> he comes from the gods and goes to God.

Jung's attitude in the *Sermons* in regard to the archetypal divinities reveals a matter-of-fact orientation that parallels in some ways the attitude Buddha is said to have exhibited toward the gods. The compassionate sage of ancient India never denied the existence of the gods; rather he asserted that it is useless for humans to address them or to pray to them, for they are not free of limitation any more than humans are. Jung's view is similar:

> Even as it is useless to think about the Pleroma so it is useless to worship the number of the gods. Least of all is it of any use to worship the first God, the effective fullness and the highest good. Through our prayer we cannot take anything away from it, because the effective emptiness swallows everything.

As stated in connection with the terrible and powerful Abraxas, so in the case of the other gods it might be said that "to worship them is death; to fear them is wisdom; not to resist them means liberation." The worship of the archetypes implies their overvaluation, which frequently leads to the personality being possessed by an archetype. The ghastly apparition of spiritual pride soon rears its swollen head, and, instead of utilizing the power of the archetypes, individuals come to imagine that they have become a divine archetype themselves. Psychic inflation where persons imagine themselves godlike—rooted as they usually are in feelings of deep inferiority—makes a travesty of the individuation process and reduces the power of the gods to the level of the psychic caperings of fools and madmen.

Archetypes exist both in the light and in the shadows of the mind. In the world of light we find gods and goddesses of unquestionable numinosity and unspeakable wisdom and loveliness, while in the shadows dwell the demonic monsters nourished by the shadows of our personalities. The Fourth Sermon speaks of a heavenly world where the gods of light dwell, which stretches into an infinity of expansiveness filled with light. In the same passage the dark gods are said to constitute the underworld, which, like its heavenly counterpart, is also without end. However, its openness is of the shrinking rather than of the expanding character, for within it beings shrink into a microcosmic infinity of smallness, even as they expand into ineffable greatness in heaven.

The archetypes of the collective unconscious, however, are not the only model Jung possessed when describing gods and demons in the *Seven Sermons*. It is well known that the ancient Gnostics did not follow the example of the orthodox majority in discarding all, or even most, of the God-images of the so-called pagans. The fault Gnostics found with the majority of people in the ancient world was not that they believed in too many gods and goddesses, but that they did not believe in anything, or anything spiritual, at all. The pagan people were often called *hyletics* by the Gnostics in view of the fact that they only paid lip service to the established state religion with its numerous deities, but in reality they served only their own materialistic ends in every way. In contradistinction to these people, to whom religion was a mere useful public ritual demanded by the state, there were the followers of the mystery religions, among whom in fact the Gnostics could be numbered. The mysteries of Isis, Serapis and other deities were based on the practice of recognizing the presence of the gods and goddesses within the *mystes,* or initiates themselves. Gnostics unabashedly utilized existing mystery systems within their esoteric Christian framework and carried statues of Serapis, Mithra and Persephone in their processions at Christmas, Epiphany or on other holidays. Gnostic amulets bear the images, not only of Abraxas, but of Aphrodite, Isis, Janus and Serapis, indicating that the gods and goddesses were not regarded as evil beings whereby demonic forces ensnared the unsuspecting pagans. Gnostics could speak of gods and of God in the same breath, recognizing that the two god-images need not be contradictory but can supplement and complement each other well. The Gnostic model of the gods, therefore, is also important in the context of the *Seven Sermons* and represents a prefiguration or earlier and more numinous formulation of the psychological teaching of the archetypes. The Gnostic systems of the first three or four centuries contained a spiritual wealth of unconscious imagery unparalleled in later Christian history. The Gnostics were creators of myths, fashioners of gods and goddesses on an almost daily basis. The meaning of this should be evident to artists and psychologists alike. The Gnostic effort consists to a major extent in creating expressions and formulations for spiritual realities which spontaneously well up from the soul of the Gnostic, but which, without such images of expression, would be lost to consciousness. Since Gnosis is a realization of the Self within the unconscious, it follows that the Gnostic life is a symbolic life, and that within the context of this symbolic life, gods and demons, angels and devils are all bound to play a valuable role. Rigid monotheistic thinking seldom, if ever, lends itself to the Gnostic effort.

It is interesting to note that in the Kabbalah, which has been aptly called Jewish Gnosticism, the unitary concept is amplified and modified by the image of the Kabbalistic Tree of Life with its ten vessels, twenty-two paths and countless hierarchies of angelic, planetary, zodiacal and other attributions. Similarly, Islamic mysticism, which has appropriated many features of the Kabbalah, takes on a symbolic dimension of complex imagery, totally different from the stark, unimaginative worship of the solitary, transcendental God Allah in orthodox Muslim practice. Everywhere Gnosis appears, the many appear to supplement the one, even if not replacing it totally. "Truth did not come into the world naked, but it came in the types and images," thus declares one of the celebrated treatises of the Nag Hammadi collection, the *Gospel of Philip*. Images and images of images bring the light of the Pleroma to earth for the enlightenment and healing of human souls. To believe is vastly inferior to perceiving the symbols whereby truth is revealed. The symbols of the Gnostics were not artificially created glyphs and disguises for dogmatic or philosophical preachments; rather they resembled Jung's own concept of true symbols, which regards a symbol, not as describing something outside of itself, but as containing the mystery within its own structure. No wonder Jung stated that the Gnostics gave a better symbolic expression to the spiritual and transformative content of the unconscious than their orthodox fellows and successors. Jung regarded Gnostic symbols as natural symbols, having an organic relationship to the archetypes of the collective unconscious and being spontaneous expressions of the interior realities of the soul, from whence the religious experience originates. Thus regarding the cross and the figure of Christ as found in Gnosticism, Jung explicitly stated:

> [The Gnostic] cross had exactly the same function that the atman or Self has always had for the East . . . . [The] Gnostic Christ figure and the cross are counterparts of the typical mandalas spontaneously produced by the unconscious. They are natural symbols and they differ fundamentally from the dogmatic figure of Christ in whom all darkness is expressly lacking.[21]

It is not an exaggeration to state, then, that the Fourth Sermon, with its important imagery of the great duality of the growing one and the burning one, as well as the challenging statements regarding the existence and character of the gods of light and of darkness, reveal this Sermon as one of the most significant of the seven. This imagery holds a profound significance for the individuation, not only of persons, but of humanity. The Gnostic nature of the archetypes and their function reveal dimensions far beyond those ordinarily envisioned by psychologists or dreamt of by theologians indicating a momentous religious as well as psychological reality. When speaking of these gods one cannot help but repeat the words in which Jung himself paid tribute to the archetypes:

> I can only stand in deepest awe and admiration before the depths and heights of the soul whose world beyond space hides

an immeasurable richness of images, which millions of years of living have stored up and condensed into organic material. My conscious mind is like an eye which perceives the furthermost spaces; but the psychic non-ego is that which fills this space in a sense beyond space. These images are not pale shadows, but powerful and effective conditions of the soul which we can only misunderstand but can never rob of their power by denying them.[22]

The Fifth Sermon—
The Two Communities:
Mother City and Father Fortress

At the beginning of the Fifth Sermon, the dead ask the sage with considerable sarcasm to teach them about church and holy community. It is significant that the questioning dead are described here as "full of mocking." While in earlier sermons they are often characterized as shouting and at times even as grumbling and raving, only in the Fifth Sermon do they resort to a tone and attitude of open mockery. One cannot escape the feeling that their derisive hostility has a direct connection with the request they are making. Of all the teachings of transformative wisdom, none is as difficult to formulate and perilous to implement as a doctrine dealing with the social and communal implications of spiritual living. When Jung, by way of the dead, employs the term *church,* he does so in the ancient meaning of that term. The Greek word *ekklesia* once denoted the assembly of the electorate, or the voting constituency of citizens living in the city states of the Peloponesos and the Aegean islands. The word *church* today tends to conjure up visions of massive stone buildings with spires, and secondly of awesome and remote religious organizations claiming divine institution and guidance and having a minimal responsiveness to their constituent membership. It is easy to recognize, therefore, that the concept of the church changed greatly from the times when it consisted of a community of free spiritual citizens called to govern themselves. Well may the dead mock when questioning their teacher on such a subject!

Curiously and significantly, Jung-Basilides begins his discourse on church and community with a description of a great pair of cosmic-psychological opposites, which come to manifest themselves in the psychosexual differences that distinguish the feminine and masculine character. Not economics, nor the urge to power, nor any other much-discussed social force is regarded as the truly fundamental one by Jung in the *Sermons*. Society, or community, is made up of men and women, upon whose psychological constitution all the institutions of human living are based.

Like the Gnostics and like the Taoists, to whose archetypal concepts he was also greatly attached, Jung conceived of the structure of being as consisting of a great network of interrelated syzygies, or dual powers, extending from the most subtle and transcendental to the most concrete and material planes of existence. In the Gnostic, as well as in the Taoist systems, the manifested worlds of mind, feeling, intuition and materiality come into existence by polarization, or separation into pairs of opposites of an original wholeness. In Valentinian Gnosticism these primordial opposites are called Depth (masculine) and Silence (feminine) and in Taoism Yang (masculine) and Yin (feminine), which latter by rough translation may be named heavenly and earthly. It follows from this that all beings and things created or emanated come into existence through the attraction between these two poles. The polar opposites work in two ways: either they merge to produce something new, as in the case of ions which, being attracted to each other by their opposite electrical charges, combine into a molecule; or else, because of the field of force between them, the opposites may create something new in that field. It would appear that some sort of analogy could be drawn between the interior and exterior sides of psychological processes and the aforementioned two processes. Internally, two psychological opposites tend to combine and produce a new psychological condition, as indicated by the coming into being of the alchemical Androgyne as the result of the merging of the king and queen. Externally, when two sovereign personalities relate to each other with sufficient psychic intensity, they maintain their identities but create something new in a spiritual field of force between them.

Biological phenomena, not unlike the physical, offer another analogy. The most primitive plant or animal forms are unpolarized or sexless, their polarization or quasi-polarization being purely within the cell itself. Thus the most primitive life-forms, not unlike the Gnostic Pleroma or the Chinese Tao are unitary and unpolarized, existing in a state of primitive self-sufficiency and lack of differentiation.

The same principle of duality that is operative on the inanimate chemico-physical and on the biological-sexual levels is, of course, also apparent within the realm of the psychological. In the human being the forces of biological sexuality are conjoined with a peculiar individuality or I-ness, which in spite of appearances makes the human being quite different from other animals. The Book of Genesis, and particularly the Gnostic commentaries inspired by it, show the intuitive, psychic femininity of Eve bringing about an awakening of spiritual selfhood or I-ness in sluggish, animal-like Adam, her own masculine polar component, who is made into a "living soul" by her ministrations. It is at this point that the truly great conflicts begin for the human being. The I-ness or individuality becomes aware of differentiation and once more introduces the reality of dualities into the principles of living. The natural world becomes divided into two parts, one of which assumes the appellation of spiritual and good, the other of animal, perhaps even bestial or evil.

In no area of life is this more clearly manifest than in the matter of sex. Here the human is in a dilemma: the instinctual portion of the psyche rooted in biology causes a mechanical attraction towards any individual of the opposite sex within the same species, while a complex of aspirtions directed toward thinking and feeling and all so-called "higher" tendencies and functions, works, as it were, at right angles to the polar pull of the natural instincts. This conflict, with its numerous attendant phenomena, was noted by Freud in the early days of the psychoanalytic movement, and upon its dynamics Freud based his theory, which declares that culture or society is the product of libidinal or sexual energy diverted from its natural expression by repression. Jung was in superficial agreement with Freud on this point, but, as in so many other instances, he enlarged and transformed the rather limited ideas of his one-time mentor until they came to expand into categories of a distinctly Gnostic nature. Jung defined the libido not as a sexual force, but as a general psychic energy, which includes all human drives in addition to the sexual. Jung stated that libido is "apportioned by nature to the various functional systems, from which it cannot be wholly withdrawn," although as he said, "a small part of the total energy can be diverted from its natural flow." (See "Psychotherapy and a Philosophy of Life," in C.G. Jung's *Collected Works,* Volume 16, p. 77 ff.) While according to the Freudian model of the psyche, surplus psychic energy becomes available for purposes of culture and civilization as the result of conflict and repression, Jung's view makes a tension of the opposites responsible for surplus or excess libidinal forces. Jung squarely declares that "there is no energy unless there is a tension of the opposites." The implication is, moreover, quite clear in numerous works of Jung that the most generalized and therefore ubiquitous form of such tension is that between "matter" and "spirit." Following in the footsteps, not only of the Gnostics and Manichaeans, but of all classical ancient thinking, Jung assumes the existential reality of such a tensional opposition, and consequently of the existence of these two categories in some form. It would be expecting too much by way of abstract philosophical thinking versus psychological empiricism to have C.G. Jung offer us a definition of the categories of "matter" and "spirit." In lieu of this, he asserts that the "ultimate nature of both is transcendental, that is, irrepresentable, since the psyche and its contents are the only reality which is given to us *without a medium*." (C.G. Jung, *Answer to Job*, New York: Meridian Books, 1960, p. 15.)

It is here that the beginning of the Fifth Sermon clearly prefigures a great deal of Jung's subsequent psychological teaching. Basilides begins his discourse by saying: "The world of the gods appears in spirituality and sexuality. The heavenly gods appear in spirituality, the earth gods appear in sexuality." Thus we have represented a great duality which is at once cosmic and personal, divine and human. Matter or body (*hyle* and *soma* in Greek Gnostic terms) is represented by sexuality, while spirit (*pneuma*) is represented by the quality derived from spirit, namely spirituality. Jung was in fact quite convinced that spirit and matter were two empirically evident categories of the psyche which can be discovered by way of the examination of its structure and contents. Sense perception, as well as other functions of consciousness, attest to the existence of matter or materiality, while psychic experience largely outside the realm of the senses supports the practically universal belief in spirit or spirituality. Matter and spirit are both part of humanity's experience and they are frequently in a state of powerful opposition to each other. In his treatise *On Psychic Energy* Jung observes that:

> man living in the state of nature is in no sense merely "natural" like an animal, but sees, believes, fears, worships things whose meaning is not at all discoverable from the conditions of his natural environment. Their underlying meaning leads us in fact far away from all that is natural, obvious, and easily intelligible, and quite often contrasts most sharply with the natural instincts.[23]

The combination of polar tensions resulting from the opposition between what, for lack of more expressive terms, may be called *spirit* and *matter* produces that additional or surplus energy which human beings have at their disposal for the construction of civilization and community. Thus, when the dead mockingly ask their teacher about *ekklesia* and holy community, it is quite in keeping with Jung's psychological thinking that he initially refers them to the symbolic forces of the categories of spirit and matter, the heavenly gods and the earth gods. It is the tensional relationship and polar opposition of these two mysterious, yet potent transcendental categories that produces the energy required for culture, community, art, esthetics and religion. It is significant to note that in Jung's view the matter-spirit dichotomy is a positive force without which the creative dynamics of individual and social transformation would be unthinkable. Naive persons impressed with the need for a unitary or holistic view of life and human nature frequently reject the matter-spirit or body-psyche dichotomy as a regrettable vestige of Greek classical thinking unsuited to the present age. The one-sided and negative manner in which religion, under the impact of the primarily Semitic concept of guilt, fostered the conflict of spirit and matter is regarded by many as the bane of Western culture. When the ancient Greeks gave expression to their belief in such polar opposites as Eros and Logos, Dionysius and Apollo, Aphrodite and Minerva, they did not advocate that humans should cleave to one of these to the exclusion of the other. Instructed by the archetypal patterns embodied in their majestic myths, they accepted the reality as well as the ultimate *beneficence of conflict* in the scheme of being, and consequently in the human psyche. The Greek, Roman, and before them the Egyptian, Persian and Babylonian religious structures all recognized the transformative value of conflict and had little or no desire to escape into a state beyond the polar action of the opposites. The Greek gods fought battles and seduced maidens in fierce and joyous celebration of the value of the polarities, while Upper and Lower Egypt were transfigured as the result of the aeonial battle of Horus and Seth, while in the cosmos of Zarathustra, the host of light and darkness were battling for supremacy until the end when the world, purified by strife, is at last finally regenerated. The wisdom and magic of conflict radiates forth from every source and branch of the ancient Mediterranean wisdom.

With the coming of so-called orthodox Christianity as a dominant force of Western culture after the third century, things changed radically. No longer was the conflict of light and dark, God and Devil, spirit and flesh regarded as a troublesome but ultimately beneficent process. It was no longer acceptable and natural to follow sometimes the flesh and sometimes God, as one might expect in a world of polar dualities. Concession to the flesh became a sin against the spirit, and earthly delight became an insult to the austere majesty of heaven. The classical theurgists could readily converse with the high gods one day and with Pan and his satyrs and nymphs on another, but the medieval magician who conversed with goetic spirits from the Tartarean was regarded as a diabolist and burned at the stake. A somber pall of guilt for fleshly sin and fear of hellfire threw its shadow on the Western world and under its oppressive and terrifying cover creativity, beauty, and human warmth of feeling found it difficult to flourish. For centuries man felt comfortable only when building churches, sculpting and painting chaste madonnas of unearthly majesty, and singing psalms in austere Gregorian modes to the glory of God. Only with the partial rebirth of the spirit of antiquity by way of the Hermetic Gnosis of Giordano Bruno, Pico de la Mirandola and their fellows during the Renaissance did the arts turn from heaven to the beauties of earth and endeavor to combine these once more with the raptures of heaven. Renaissance painters could joyously paint papal mistresses and aristocratic courtesans in the role of the madonna, not because they had lost their religious devotion, but because they recovered a spiritual orientation which gloried in the convergence of the opposites, and celebrated the intersection of time and eternity in human nature. Regrettably, this relatively brief burst of Gnosis during the Renaissance gave way to long centuries of increasing materialism and the trivialization of life, which led to the confusion and despair of contemporary humanity.

Although religious preachments, as well as rationalist dogma, have lost some of their earlier influence in today's world, their principal products, namely guilt and despair, remain as prominent as ever. While the pious Christian or Jew may have felt guilty for his sins of the flesh because of the commandments of a God who was all spirit, the rationalist continued to be tormented by a very similar guilt, which resulted from yielding to desires arising from instinct, which he conceived as a sin against reason. Sigmund Freud, the rationalist, brought forth a message not unlike the one his archetypal antagonist Moses is said to have brought from Sinai. Moses and Freud are both prophets of a lonely and bitter God who recognizes no equal and therefore cannot experience the delights and dejections, the agony and the ecstasy of the opposites. Monotheistic orthodoxy and atheistic rationalism are brothers under the skin. The all-spiritual God and the all-logical deity of reason are both blind, like Saclas, the blind and foolish demiurge of the Gnostics; neither can behold the desperate need to accept his polar opposite and to relate to it in creative conflict. Both have fostered a dreary and burdensome condition of mind which is characterized by Judeo-Christian guilt augmented by Freudian neurotic hopelessness.

One way which has increasingly beckoned to Western man in recent decades has been the spirituality of the East, or more precisely of Asia, which offers several alternatives to Western one-sidedness. Some of these alternatives, such as Taoism (for which, as noted before, Jung possessed a considerable fondness) and the Hindu and Buddhist Tantric schools, have a deep appreciation of the principle of the opposites and of their creative conflictual relationship, which is symbolised both under the figure of battle and struggle on the one hand, and ritualized and sanctified sexuality on the other. In contradistinction to these movements, most of the classical Hindu schools of Vedanta philosophy and of Yoga are intent upon the overcoming of the opposites by way of various meditative yoga exercises, which are said to elevate the mind to a condition which is conceived of as non-dual and utterly beyond the categories of the opposites. These teachings, which have had a far greater popularity in the West than either Taoism or the Tantras, appear to be if anything counterproductive rather than helpful in the quest after spiritual creativity and its concomitant, the interaction of the opposites in a process of alchemical transformation. Jung characterized these and related Eastern approaches as specialists in the introversion of the psyche, which may produce relief from but not a solution to the grave psychological ailment of our culture. While being skeptical of the promised miraculous results of yoga, Jung was of the opinion that the alienation and conflicts of Western humanity itself would bring it to the threshold of a spiritual awakening. He stated that the unhappy patterns of our psychic lives will change when "claims of the spirit become as imperative as the necessities of social life. We are only at the threshold of a new spiritual epoch . . . the longing for security in an age of insecurity. *It is from need and distress that new forms of existence arise,* and not from idealistic requirements or mere wishes." (See "Yoga and the West," in C.G. Jung's Collected Works, Vol. II, p. 529ff.) Not for us the ethereal trances of the Yogis, not for us the rapturous immersion of consciousness in the abyss of the "one without a second." Ours on the other hand, must be the Great Work of the Alchemist, the Hermetic Art, named after the awesome archetype of Toth, the primeval Egyptian magician-god, rebaptized in Hellenic numinosity as Hermes the Thrice Great. This magical-alchemical spirit of the Western psyche was Jung's inspiration in all of his work, and is eminently manifest in his *Seven Sermons,* although perhaps most powerfully in the Fifth and Sixth Sermons. It is this very spirit that speaks to Goethe's Faust who had conjured it from the dynamisms of the cosmos:

> In the tides of Life, in Action's storm,
> A fluctuant wave,
> A shuttle free,
> Birth and the Grave,
> An eternal sea,
> A weaving, flowing
> Life, all-glowing,
> Thus at Time's humming loom 'tis my hand that prepares
> The garment of Life which the Deity wears![24]

These tides of life which arise in action's storm consist of the battle and embrace of the multitudes of mighty opposites: matter and spirit, instinct and instinct-inhibiting dispositions, the individual and the demands of society, feeling and thinking, masculine and feminine, spirituality and sexuality. All of these are, using Jung's word in the Fifth Sermon, "superhuman demons and manifestations of the world of the gods." The names he gives in this sermon to the great symbolic opposites are *Mater Coelestis,* the Heavenly Mother, and *Phallos,* the Earthly Father. It is remarkable that in the *Sermons,* particularly in the Fifth, Jung reverses the much more common attributions. The overwhelming majority of contemporary students, including Jungian psychologists, tend to associate the feminine, maternal principle of the psyche or of the universe with earth. "Mother Earth" like "Mother Nature" is a very common expression indeed, and the association of earth with a maternal principle appears in locales as widely separated as Northern Europe, and the America of the Indians. Conversely, the image of the "Heavenly Father" is the commonly accepted one in contemporary religion from India to the Christian churches of the West. Yet it would seem that Jung's attributions not only have merit, but hold potent and authentically Gnostic spiritual secrets as well.

In the figures of Jung's Heavenly Mother and Earthly Father we are confronted with two lofty and ancient symbols of singular illuminative power. There is no doubt that in the most ancient myths of humankind—which antedate the later arrangement of earth-mother and sky-father—the maternal, feminine principle is celestial, and the paternal and masculine is earthly. Robert Graves in his work *The Greek Myths* gives a vivid account of what is perhaps one of the oldest creation myths of the world, second in antiquity, in all likelihood, only to the Babylonian myth of Ishtar. In this, the so-called Pelasgian myth, are to be found two of the clearest prototypes of Jung's two deities in the Fifth and Sixth Sermons. The fable, which is named after Pelasgus, the first man, whose descent it recounts, tells us of the mother of heavenly chaos, Eurynome, who appeared naked from the original no-thing. She separated the sea and sky, and performed her solitary dance upon the waves. In the course of her great and presumably most seductive dance, out of the north wind, which she rubbed between her hands, there arose a great serpent by the name of Ophion. Ophion was enchanted with Eurynome's dancing and he coiled himself about her limbs and had sexual congress with her. Eurynome, having become pregnant of the serpent, changed herself into a dove, hovering over the sea. (The analogy of the image of the Holy Spirit of Christianity, hovering over the waters of Jordan at the baptism of Jesus in the form of a dove is to be remembered here.) When the time was right, Eurynome in dove form, laid the cosmic egg, which was hatched by Ophion, who coiled himself around it seven times. Out of the hatched egg came all beings and things that exist in the cosmos, including the sun, moon, and stars and all living and inanimate things. The curious divine pair dwelt on Mt. Olympus until the time when Ophion angered the goddess by arrogantly asserting that he was the creator of the universe. The divine woman in her wrath proceeded to bruise his head with her heel and managed to kick out his teeth, and she drove him from Mt. Olympus, exiling him to the regions in the interior of the earth. From the teeth of Ophion were subsequently born Pelasgus and the race of the Pelasgians. In a Gnostic context it is also important to note that Eurynome also created the seven planets, over each of which she set a syzygy of a Titan and a Titaness, so that each planet is ruled by both a male and female.

This pre-Hellenic creation myth—utilized in all probability by some of the Mother-worshipping prehistoric societies of the Near and Middle East and which might conceivably hold an appeal to feminists of leanings toward notions of female superiority—shows many similarities with Jung's scheme in the Fifth and Sixth Sermons. In the Sixth Sermon the earthly father, Phallos, is said to come to the soul like a serpent, while the heavenly mother comes as a white dove. The phallic serpent lives in the earth and consorts with the spirits of the dead, while the bird of heaven is described as "chaste and solitary." In the Fifth Sermon they are described by the German words *Geistigkeit,* which somewhat inadequately may be described as *spirituality,* and *Geschlechtlichkeit,* which is rather adequately rendered into English as *sexuality. Geistigkeit* is defined by Jung as a power that receives and comprehends, and in this sense because of its receptivity is described as feminine. *Geschlechtlichkeit* or sexuality is the giving and generating principle and is thus symbolically conceived as masculine. In Jung's later scientific writings these dual forces are primarily embodied in the concepts of Eros and Logos: the abstract-conceptual psychological tendency, and the relationship or relatedness-oriented tendency. On the individual level they appear as the so-called contrasexual images of the psyche, the anima and animus.

Upon close observation of the Fifth Sermon, one finds that the ideas presented here are far more complex and esoteric than the popularized version that found its way into the standard literature of analytical psychology. While the later Jungian literature, and to some extent even some of Jung's own statements, seem intended to veil the complexities and obscurities of this mystery of the human syzygies, the picture given us in the Fifth Sermon is replete with curious overtones of great profundity. It is always highly dangerous to attempt a rendering of Gnostic perceptions in a manner that is too simple, cohesive and inoffensive. It would appear that this was the sort of attempt made by various writers regarding the mystery of the two "great superhuman demons" depicted by Jung in the *Sermons.* For the sake of a comparison, let us present very briefly some of the elements of the popular picture presented to us by many contemporary followers of Jung.

According to the usual account, women are characterized by the principle of Eros, an ability to make connections, while men are oriented toward Logos, the function of analytical thought.

This would make it appear that the two sexes are not only generally tending toward or vaguely characterized by these psychological principles, but are in some way confined by them. Some of the most highly regarded Jungian writers in fact quite emphatically suggest such a confinement. Dr. Jolande Jacobi in her classic work *The Psychology of C.G. Jung* flatly states that, "just as the male by his very nature is uncertain in the realm of Eros, so the woman will always be unsure in the realm of Logos." One does not have to be a feminist to be uncomfortably affected by such dogmatic "certitude." To be sure, Jung himself was far more tentative and mysterious when writing about either Eros and Logos or anima and animus, as evidenced by his following statement:

> Woman is compensated by a masculine element and therefore her unconscious has, so to speak, a masculine imprint. This results in a considerable difference between men and women, and accordingly, I have called the projection-making factor in women the animus, which means mind or spirit. The animus corresponds to the paternal Logos just as the anima corresponds to the maternal Eros. *But I do not wish to give these two intuitive concepts too specific a definition.* [25] (Italics ours.)

At another place Jung, while asserting that these concepts were found to be valid and operative empirically, still cautions his readers about the tentative character of his findings:

> . . . long and varied experience was needed in order to grasp the nature of anima and animus empirically. Whatever we have to say about these archetypes, therefore, is either directly verifiable or at least rendered probable by facts. *At the same time, I am fully aware that we are discussing pioneer work which by its very nature can only be provisional.* [26] (Italics ours.)

It is suggested by the above that Jung was in a sense holding back on this vital issue; he knew more but was reluctant to reveal it. It may be argued that a considerable portion of Jung's corpus of writings bears a similar characteristic. At another place in the present volume we have described Jung's work as a "science born of mystery." Jung was both blessed and cursed with this mystery which reposed at the source of his teachings, a mystery that could not be stated once and for all in clear terms but had to be adapted time and again to the changing forms of receptivity and understanding, which alone are capable of revealing ever deeper layers of the fabric of reality.

The Fifth and Sixth Sermons reveal a model of male-female polarities in which certain fundamental qualitative differences exist between the psyches of men and women. Sexual differentiation is not merely a matter of biology but of psychology as well. There is such a thing as a feminine psyche and a masculine psyche, according to the *Seven Sermons* just as much as according to the later Jungian writers. Still, the *Sermons* depict a situation which complicates the issue and makes simple, rational conclusions difficult. There are two fundamental powers, as described earlier. One is spirituality, *Geistigkeit,* feminine in tone, which receives and comprehends, affinitized to heaven, and sexuality, *Geschlechtlichkeit,* masculine in tone, which generates and creates and is akin to earth. The deceptively easy explanation is that these are the masculine Logos and feminine Eros. Yet, the evidence is contrary to such an exposition. In this sermon the masculine principle possesses all the characteristics of Eros: it is described as sexuality, it is procreative, earthly, and microcosmic in direction. Yet it is masculine, and called by the unmistakable name *Phallos.* On the other hand, the feminine principle in the sermon is none other than Logos: it is receptive and more importantly *comprehending.* There can be little doubt, if any: the *Sermons* present us with a masculine Eros and a feminine Logos.

When bringing these categories down to a personal level, another novel picture presents itself. Both the "Heavenly Mother" and the "Phallos" are present in both men and women. There is no clear implication that either of these forces is permanently at the unconscious level; rather both seem to be operative in particular spheres of activity. Thus, the sermon states:

> The sexuality of the man is more earthly, while the sexuality of woman is more heavenly. The spirituality of man is more heavenly; for it moves in the direction of the greater. On the other hand, the spirituality of woman is more earthly; for it moves in the direction of the smaller.

Clearly we are confronted here with a constellation of spiritual forces that is substantially different from the one commonly accepted by analytical psychologists. Also, it is evident that the fourfold model here presented possesses portentous implications in the sphere of culture and community, which is the subject raised by the questioning dead in the first instance. The two great principles of *Mater Coelestis* and *Phallos* act directly upon the spiritual principles and indirectly upon the sexual principles of the masculine and the feminine psyche respectively. Logos governs the spiritual in man and the sexual in woman, while Eros in turn governs the spiritual in woman and the sexual in man. This leaves each sex with one Logos- and one Eros-oriented principle, thus affirming that there is a duality in each sex.

Let us now look at the practical psychological implications of this arrangement. The masculine mentality is directly acted upon by the feminine *Mater Coelestis,* the Goddess-Logos; the principle of *Phallos,* the God-Eros, tends to act upon the masculine psyche from the unconscious level. In the course of his ego-formation man identifies himself with mind, with law and order, with extraverted, conscious selfhood; in short, with the symbolizations and manifestations of Logos. Consequently the element of Eros, fertility, sexuality, romance, mystery, all the various facets of the subterranean Phallos, recede into the nether regions of the unconscious. Here in the underground cavern of Jung's famous childhood dream, enthroned upon a seat of power, reigns the snake-like phallic monster-god, while outside in the clear air of reason, irradiated by the effulgence of the sun of consciousness, hovers the white bird of the great goddess, the Holy Spirit, Sophia, the feminine Logos. The phallic god, being unconscious, is perceived by man only by projection. Thus men project their dark, erotic side onto women, whom they then fear and desire at the same time, precisely because they fear and desire their own unconscious Eros. Here is the true reason for the long-held distorted view of women as dangerous seductresses leading men astray, creatures filled with a dark, menacing sexuality, at once terrifying and alluring to the masculine psyche. The woman as witch, temptress, as Eve, the willing dupe of the evil serpent of the story of Genesis—these and similar figures all reveal themselves as the projections of the unconscious Eros of the masculine psyche.

Describing the condition of the feminine psyche, the Fifth

Sermon asserts "the Spirituality of woman is more earthly, for it moves in the direction of the smaller." This may be taken to mean that the conscious psyche of woman, being turned outward toward the world, or oriented toward differentiation, can relate itself freely to innumerable extraverted tasks, but may frequently do so without adducing conscious meaning to these actions. Thus the feminine psyche functions frequently on the basis of the famed "woman's intuition," namely it does the right thing but without knowing why. It might be said then that the masculine psyche tends to perceive meaning in the outer or conscious world more readily than the feminine; the latter has less need for the hard logic and conscious raciocination so often required by man, not merely because of social pressures but because of his lack of intuitive development. Lacking a natural intuitive sense, men need to address themselves to the analytical functions of reason time and again, while women achieve very frequently excellent practical results in life by way of intuitive guidance alone. It is in the area of Eros, including sexuality, that the meaning orientation of the feminine psyche manifests. This is what the sermon is saying when it calls the sexuality of woman more heavenly than that of the man, "heaven" denoting once again the *Mater Coelestis,* or Logos-Goddess. At the psychological level, it is relationship and relatedness which appears as the great carrier of feminine meaning, while at the sexual level of its expression the feminine psyche is able to discover meaning in the sexual sphere far more readily than its masculine counterpart. One might say with but a slight exaggeration that feminine sexuality has its eyes wide-open to meaning, while masculine sexuality is blind. The white bird of Logos perceives meaning and transformative truth in the sexual realm, while the phallic serpent, having grown myopic in its subterranean habitat, sees little or no meaning at all. It is in fact this blindness of masculine sexuality that makes projection of the anima so vital for man, while woman can circumvent the projection of the animus with a greater degree of frequency. A somewhat amusing account of certain aspects of this process is given to us by Jung in the following statement:

> A great feminine indefiniteness is the longed-for counterpart
> to a male definiteness and unequivocalness, which latter can

only in a measure be satisfactorily established if a man can manage to get rid of all that is doubtful, ambiguous, uncertain, and unclear in himself by projecting it on to a charming feminine innocence. Owing to the characteristic inner indifference and the feeling of inferiority which constantly masquerades as offended innocence, the man finds himself in the favorable role of being able to bear the well-known feminine inadequacies in a superior but yet indulgent way, quasi with knightly chivalry.[27]

In the above ironic statement Jung gives utterance to the distortions introduced into the image of woman as perceived by man, owing to the projection of the indefinite, ambiguous features of his unconscious, while the far more serious similar distorted projection of the Eros force, mentioned by us earlier, is documented by Jung in the following fashion:

What man has found to say about feminine eroticism, and especially about the feeling-life of women, is derived for the most part from the projection of his own anima and is accordingly distorted.[28]

The *Sermons* in fact pay homage to the feminine psyche in a manner that is clearer than found in the later literature of Jungian psychology. They declare the woman is *not* totally ruled by Eros, but rather that the principle of Logos is quite powerful in her at the unconscious level, and indeed that this situation confers certain psychic benefits on her, which tend to make her the more insightful, intuitive and spiritually aware of the two sexes. The frequently heard feminist accusation that the anima-animus cum Eros-Logos psychological model is more beneficial to men than to women thus is far less applicable to the model as found in the *Seven Sermons* than it is to the popular account of the same in contemporary literature. It is thus not true that while men can keep control of all Logos-related activities and merely add some small measure of Eros to their make-up, women will never develop Logos at all. Desirable changes in this direction undertaken in the social sphere not only meet with the approval of the spirit of this sermon, but they are clearly represented as desirable and necessary. The individuated person must learn how to rise above the blind compelling force of anima and animus and Eros and Logos. As the teacher states in our sermon:

> When you cannot distinguish between yourselves on the one
> hand, and sexuality and spirituality on the other, and when
> you can't regard these two as being above and beside
> yourselves, then you become victimized by them, i.e., by the
> qualities of the Pleroma. Spirituality and sexuality are not
> your qualities, they are not things which you can possess and
> comprehend; on the contrary, these are mighty demons,
> manifestations of the gods, and therefore they tower above
> you, and they exist in themselves.

This of course refers to the sovereign, archetypal nature of these
polarities, which should not be regarded as personalistic in
character.

The social and historical implications of this are considerable.
The suggestion arises that in the interpersonal and communal
sphere certain separate characteristics and roles for men and
women are a psychological necessity. To be sure, this does not
mean that traditional masculine and feminine stereotypes of by-
gone times need to be regarded as sacrosanct and as worthy of
preservation. The form taken by the great polarities in various
historical periods assuredly changes, for such is the nature of the
historical process. Toward the end of the Fifth Sermon the
teacher indicates that certain communities and civilizations are
under the auspices of Eros and others under those of Logos.
Following Erich Neumann's monumental psycho-historical
studies, we might postulate that the early matriarchal civilizations, with their mother-right coupled with human sacrifices and
dark, primitive sexuality, were manifestations of the principle of
Eros, while the rational and democratic organization of the later
Greek city states was overshadowed by Logos. A contemporary
application of such criteria might lead to the conclusion that the
increasing number of socialistic and communistic societies in our
contemporary world heralds an upsurgence of the community of
Eros, versus the individualistic and libertarian trend of the
democracies, which continue to be attached to Logos.

Whatever one's point of view regarding such issues, it appears
clear that in any and all of these societies an eradication of the
psychological differences between the two sexes is not going to
take place, as indeed it has never taken place in the past. A total
integration of the sexes at the external level of human society is
undeniably contrary to the Jungian model, both as represented

in the *Seven Sermons* and as found in the psychological writings of Jung and of his followers and commentators. The impetus of psychic energy operating in the masculine and feminine psyche respectively is not the same. It was Freud, not Jung, who came close to postulating a sort of psychological unisexual model when he held up the curious task of the "repudiation of femininity" as an objective within the analytical process for both men and women. There is not just one basic psychic drive, but two, which in turn manifest in a number of contrasting ways on the various levels. From these considerations it follows that current movements directed toward the revision of the status of women, or indeed of both sexes, are doomed to failure to the extent that their avowed objectives are in the nature of an integration of the sexes according to a unisexual model. Not unisex but androgyny is the true goal of the transformation of the psyche, but this androgyny, rare and precious indeed, is to be found only in the highest flowering of the soul and consequently of humanity. Unisex is a distorted and unrealistic substitute for androgyny, rather like a misshapen goat with only one horn that is paraded as a unicorn. The way to androgyny, which in an earlier period was disguised under the ciphers of alchemy, has been adequately indicated by Jung in his classic commentaries on the alchemical work *Rosarium Philosophorum,* to which he gave the prosiac name *The Psychology of the Transference.** Whether an androgynation of culture is a real possibility or not is a most difficult question to answer. Such a process could not be produced by political or social fiat but could arise only as the result of the individuation and consequent androgynation of a sufficiently large number of persons within a given society, who then could make their mark, as it were, on their community and its consciousness.

The way to the ultimate pneumatic heights of androgyny is a long and arduous path of transformation that is trod amidst much travail and suffering. Esther Harding in her monumental work *Psychic Energy* outlines four stages of this process which

---

*The entire issue of androgyny has also been most cogently explored by June Singer in her work *Androgyny* (Garden City, N.Y., Anchor Press/Doubleday, 1976).

are experienced alike by individuals and by evolving societies. The first condition is that of the identification of the ego with the demon of sexuality, with the *Geschlechtlichkeit* mentioned in the Fifth Sermon. It is an auto-erotic and narcissistic state wherein the libido is essentially self-gratifying and non-productive. This condition is attendant upon the close identification of the ego with the unconscious. The second stage brings the force of emotion and the personalization of the love-object into play. Sexuality now is always linked with emotion which attaches itself to the whole person rather than to the sexual characteristics alone. An intensification, particularly in terms of projection, brings about the next and third stage, which has often been called romantic love. In this stage of the transformation of sexuality, the love-object is a distinct and differentiated personality in the eyes of the lover, but in addition the personality of the beloved becomes now greatly colored by values projected upon it from the unconscious of the lover. The object now becomes increasingly the secret psychic one of self-knowledge, accomplished by way of the projections imposed upon the partner. The portion of the man and woman ordinarily consigned to the shadowland of the unconscious emerges in perceptible form, mingled with the personality of a living human personality. The fourth and last stage is the mystic marriage, known often under its classical name of *hieros gamos*. This thoroughly Gnostic development—which according to all indications constituted the essence of the forgotten rite of the Valentinian Gnostics, referred to in various writings as the *mystery of the bride-chamber*—still utilizes the presence of living personalities as partners. However, by way of intricate processes of modifications and transformations to which the projections are subjected, the "mystic marriage" brings about an internalization of the love-relationship. This ultimately results in the total transformation of the partners into spiritual androgynes in whom the opposites have been united by the alchemy of love, or to use the words of the Gnostic *Gospel of Thomas* "the male and the female have become a single one." Such is one of the more meaningful depictions of the long process leading to androgyny. It is quite evident that this Gnostic process has little in common with the hasty and ill-conceived politicized visions of an instant unisex society.

The individuation of humankind thus reaches on the one side into the heavens where the supernal receptive divine mother of eternal mind (the Mater Coelestis) waits to receive us, while on the other it is rooted in the subterranean power of the phallic Eros (Phallos), the earthly father, whose strength and elemental energy furnishes the force whereby we might ascend. The phallus, like a living tree, grows from the dark and moist recesses of the instinctual soil and reaches up into the limitless void of space, into the womb of the *Mater Coelestis,* the aetherial mother enthroned among the stars. The semen of the earthly phallus, the sap of the *etz chiim* (the Tree of Life of the Kabbalah) projected into the womb of the sky mother causes the fertilization of the psychological cosmic egg, out of which the new cosmos of consciousness is destined to come forth. It is thus that, as the result of the aeonial game of the dancing and battling opposites, the final union of heaven and earth begets and brings forth the androgynous *Anthropos,* the New Man, the Christ of the Gnostics, who is the paradigm of the transformed and individuated ego of every individual and of all humanity.

Out of the great tribulations of the aeons, from the fiery alchemical furnace of cosmic life, the opposites have brought into existence that which represents their union and yet is more than either of them could ever be. The dialectics of the soul has produced the living synthesis which, beyond the past categories of thesis and antithesis, points toward the future. By recognizing the celestial beloved of the Eternal Feminine, the *Sermons* join in Goethe's great ultimate vision of the *Mater Coelestis* in *Faust:*

All that is past of us
Was but reflected;
All that was lost in us
Here is corrected;
All indescribables
Here we descry;
Eternal Womanhead
Leads us on high.[29]

And in the midst of this ecstatic aspiration, the gaze of the soul is not deflected from earth, for as Jung has cogently reminded us in his *Psychology and Alchemy:* "No noble, well grown tree has ever disowned its own dark roots, for it grows not only upward but downward as well."

The Sixth Sermon—The Serpent and the Dove

In the Sixth Sermon the teacher elaborates the theme of sexuality and spirituality with special emphasis on the manifestations of these principles within the sphere of archetypal imagery in the form of the serpent and the white bird. The serpent and bird are each described as "half a human soul," and thus clearly symbolize particular embodiments of the two principles of the opposites which, when integrated in a final state of union, make up the wholeness of being toward which human consciousness moves in its effort of individuation. The serpent and bird in turn are themselves made up of a duality which is formed of the two opposites of desire and thought, the former being called thought-desire, and the latter desire-thought. This enigmatic description may be taken to indicate that the serpent of sexuality has its main principle of motivation in desire, and that its thoughts are thus ever rooted in desire; the white bird of spirituality, on the other hand, proceeds from the region of abstract thought, and its aspect of desire is still rooted in thought. The serpent is the thought of desire, while the bird is the desire of thought. Once again Jung brings to our attention the intricate and well-nigh indistinguishable intermeshing and compounding of the principles of the opposites in the psyche. Not unlike the Chinese Yin and Yang, each opposite ever contains its own opposite polarity in a state of semi-latency, from whence by way of the principle of *enantiodromia* it may emerge into the arena of growth and activity at the time appointed for this purpose by the patterns of its development. Male and female, light and dark, Eros and Logos forever combine at various levels of their interrelationship in endless series of alternating polarities, which bring all clear-cut judgments and determinations hopelessly to naught. As expressed by the Gnostic *Gospel of Philip,* neither are the good good, nor the evil evil, nor is life a life, nor death a death, for all of these opposites are brothers one to another, and each one will be resolved into its original condition at some future time. In the endless process of the combinations and recombinations of the opposites, no abiding state of freedom and spiritual stability exists. Only those who—in the words of the same Gospel—are exalted above the world are truly indissoluble and eternal. The mystery of the opposites is clearly not a matter that is subject to the discerning judgment of the human intellect. It might be said that it is not a problem to be solved but a predicament to be surmounted by Gnosis. It is thus that all Gnostic systems, whether of the third century or of the twentieth, reveal themselves to be psychological in character. The psyche, unlike philosophical reasoning, strives for the reconciliation of the opposites. This process, often paradoxical and even self-contradictory, nevertheless reveals transformative meaning, which ultimately enhances the quality of consciousness.

If the *Seven Sermons* reveal anything at all, it is that the fabric of being, both at the collective-cosmic and at the individual-human levels of its expression, is composed of an endless chain of polar opposites. The philosophical intellect desires to subject these opposites to rational analysis and thereby discern meaning in the patterns in which their relationship organizes itself. It has been the tragedy of Western culture that this persistent desire of philosophy could never be satisfied in any final and total manner. For better than two millenia, philosophical inquiry has concerned itself with the meaning of life without bringing forth what could be considered abiding guidelines to the discovery of the meaning of life. It was not without some valid reason that the late satirist Ambrose Bierce defined philosophy as a route of many roads leading from nowhere to nothing. To the extent that one is predisposed to agree with this harsh dictum, it may be profitable to consider, as Jung and before him the Gnostics were wont to do, that the question of meaning is not a philosophical or theoretical problem at all. Meaning is not a syllogism or a declaration of logic any more than it is a dogma distilled from the Torah or from the New Testament. The sciences of biology, physics or mathematics no more provide an answer to the quest for meaning than does the interpretation of the human psyche solely in terms of personal experience. Gnosis, as envisioned by such men as Valentinus, Basilides and their fellows, is the experience of totality or wholeness. This wholeness must be lived in time and must also be experienced in timelessness. The tensional relationship connecting such opposites as the personal and the impersonal, the conscious and the unconscious, the tangible and the ineffable, in accordance with the principle of the *beneficence of conflict* noted in connection with the Fifth Sermon, generate the element of meaning, which may be envisioned more as a process and less as a static condition. The general neurosis of our time, defined by Jung as a pervasive sense of futility and meaninglessness, is the result of the diminishing of the tension between the two polar opposites of being. Lacking this tension, the human being, as Jung indicated, develops the feeling that he is a helpless and haphazard creature without meaning. This meaninglessness, which may be described as existential rather than conceptual, prevents the individual from living his life with the intensity it demands if it is to be fully enjoyed. Under these conditions a certain staleness arises which is the hallmark of a life that is not the expression of the complete human being. The absence of meaning is the chief cause of psychological disturbances, which, far more frequently than childhood traumas or infantile complexes, bring the individual to the torments of neurosis. Jung frequently stated that a psychoneurosis must be understood, ultimately, as the anguish of a soul that is tormented by a lack of meaning. The aim of Gnostic thought in every age has been to oppose a certain special kind of meaning to the meaninglessness of life. This meaning is existential and experiential and is revealed in the spontaneously created and intensely lived mythic content of the soul. In practical terms this might be said to imply that the meaning of life cannot be discovered or calculated, but rather that it must be lived. The living of meaning is then a mysterious process revealed by the poetic lucidity of myth, dream and imagination rather than by the concerns of the conscious ego. In his *Memories, Dreams, Reflections* Jung referred several times to the quest for the meaning of life and of the human being, and he concluded that every answer to this grave question is but a human interpretation or conjecture, a confession or a belief. Yet it is evident from the vast corpus of his writings that in his own way he has found an answer to this same question. This answer, so he repeatedly affirmed, is to be found in a curious process, an interaction or interplay of the opposites of being as revealed in the experience of the psyche.

Here, then, we might say, is the veritable heart and center of

Jung's Gnosis. The experience of the psyche—which is the alchemical vessel within which all doves and serpents, gods and devils, burning ones and growing ones combine and recombine in an awesome and majestic dance of formations and transformations—is the maker of meaning, the creator of truth. In this recognition, Jung was chiefly inspired by the early example of the ancient Gnostics, but he was also sustained by the views of other kindred spirits throughout the ages. Well may Jung have felt gratified when toward the end of his life he was confronted with the magnificent saying of Jesus contained in the then recently discovered *Gospel of Thomas:* "There is light within a man of light, and it lights up the whole world. If he does not shine, there is darkness." Like Valentinus of old, Jung held the view that humanity itself manifests the divine life and the divine revelation, and that the true church, or *ekklesia,* is that portion of humanity that recognizes its own divine origin. Jung assented to the quaint saying of the early church: "Outside the church there is no salvation" (extra ecclesiam nulla salus), but under *church* he understood the community of conscious persons, or as Valentinus might have called them, those "considered more skillful." The statements of the teacher in the latter portion of the Fifth Sermon regarding the usefulness of community must be interpreted in this light. The gods, the Sermon instructs us, force us into a community, for the weakness of the human will easily deflects the individual from his own chosen design of individuation. While thus recognizing the value of a certain kind of community, Jung remains very much the true Gnostic when he insists on the equal value of the status of the "solitary" or "single one," a person highly extolled by *The Gospel of Thomas* and other Gnostic works. Community of like-minded seekers after Gnosis and the spiritual individualism or "solitude" of the Gnostic are not only compatible but are necessary complements to each other, as stated in the closing lines of the Fifth Sermon:

> In community there shall be abstinence. In solitude let there be squandering of abundance. For community is the depth, while solitude is the height. The true order in community purifies and preserves. The true order in solitude purifies and increases. Community gives us warmth, while solitude gives us the light.

The accusation once made by the orthodox against the
Gnostics, that the Gnostic effort is opposed to community—
today not infrequently voiced by social activitists of various hue
against the so-called narcissism of psychological transformation—reveals itself thus as an unjust and fallacious contention.
Not community but an *unconscious community* is objectionable
in the eyes of the Gnostic. The orthodox Christian opponents of
the Gnostics were wont to insist that humanity is sinful, cor-
rupted, and therefore needs a means beyond its own power to
return to God. These means they held to be revealed in their
purged and distorted canonical scriptures and enshrined within
the community of believers, the "ark of salvation." Today the
social activists similarly proclaim that only in the social concerns
of community and society is there true fulfillment. The political
party, the social movement, thus becomes the new ark of salvation, and the individual is once again reduced to a figure of
negligible worth, destined to become useful only by way of his or
her attachments to causes and purposes which transcend the
legitimate value of the individual mind. Jung, like Valentinus,
was quite willing to endorse participation in community as long
as the community unit could justly be regarded as an aid to and
instrument of self-knowledge and a necessary balancing agent
offsetting the excesses of individualism.

Religious orthodoxy—which has so profoundly influenced all
thinking in our culture that even atheists cannot escape its
aura—has ever held that the experience of the human psyche
could not possibly effect anything resembling salvation because
it is essentially sinful. The word for *sin* used in ancient Christian
sources is the Greek word *hamartia,* which interestingly enough
is derived from the art of archery and denotes "missing the
mark." The view of traditional Jewish and Christian teaching is
that human beings are by nature extremely poor spiritual
archers; they forever tend to miss the mark. Humanity suffers
distress, illness, sorrow and deprivation, because it was
prevented by the will of the Creator from ever truly hitting the
bull's eye on the cosmic target. Thus, all it can do is trust in a
deliverance that comes from an external source, namely the saving mission of Jesus. God became man in order to save man, but
man may never become god to save himself. It is not only
dissimilarity that separates the Divine from the human, but the

terrible burden of human sin.

Jung was the last person on earth to disagree with the contention that *in a certain sense* human beings may truly be regarded as sinful. Neuroses and other psychological troubles are to some extent in the nature of moral failings. To live up to the soul's higher potential is an inbuilt moral goal of human life, and when we fail to achieve this fundamental moral goal we *do* suffer. The gods visit retributions on those who stop growing in spirit. Achieving consciousness from the unconscious is to some extent a moral goal, and our failure to achieve it is a moral failing. Yet, these moral categories of failure and psychological disturbance are in turn rooted in something deeper that may be defined as *a-gnosis* or ignorance. The sublime Valentinian *Gospel of Truth* of Nag Hammadi fame depicts this psychological fact in poetic terms when it says that ignorance brought about anguish and terror, and that anguish in turn solidified into a fog-like substance which prevented everyone from seeing. The same Gospel defined this kind of life, caused by ignorance, as a nightmare in which the soul experiences terror and confusion and instability, along with doubt and division. Unlike the orthodox, the Jungian and Gnostic model of reality envisions a time and an occasion for the human being when it may cast aside this benumbing and bewildering fog of ignorance, and in the words of the *Gospel of Truth,* it may leave the works of this ignorance behind like a dream in the night. The kinship of these mythological statements regarding ignorance with depth-psychological views is perfectly obvious and has been duly noted by some interpreters of the Gnostic scriptures, notably by Elaine Pagels (*The Gnostic Gospels*). When humans are lacking in psychological insight, they are tyrannized by the impulses of the unconscious, and their ignorance brings upon them failures of diverse kinds—emotional, physical and moral. When a healthy degree of self-knowledge is achieved, the quality of contact with the unconscious in turn and proportionately enhances the quality of consciousness, and with it the life of the entire person. To quote once again, the *Gospel of Thomas:*

> If you bring forth what is within you, what you bring forth will save you. If you do not bring forth what is within you, what you do not bring forth will destroy you.[30]

Jung has shown that the greatest help for humanity in its state of spiritual distress, its condition of forlornness, is to be found in interior spiritual experience. By way of this kind of experience, the individual not only acquires various grades of *gnosis*—insight, consciousness, awareness of the true realities of being—but also receives *pistis*, trust, experiential faith, which alone ensures the survival and continuity of the effort of individuation. Jung described the acquisition of this quality of *pistis* in the following manner:

> [This kind of experience] cannot be disputed. You can only say that you have never had such an experience, whereupon your opponent will reply: "Sorry, I have." And there your discussion will come to an end. No matter what the world thinks about [this kind of experience], the one who has it possesses a great treasure, a thing that has become for him a source of life, meaning, and beauty, and has given a new splendour to the world and to mankind. He has *pistis* and peace. Where is the criterion by which you could say that such a life is not legitimate, that such an experience is not valid, and that such *pistis* is mere illusion? Is there, as a matter of fact, any better truth about the ultimate things than the one that helps you to live? That is the reason why I take careful account . . . of the symbols produced by the unconscious.[31]

It is here that our considerations must return to the two chief symbols of the Fifth and Sixth Sermons, the complementary and yet opposed principles of sexuality and spirituality, depicted respectively as the serpent and the white bird. The *pistis* Jung speaks of in the above passage assuredly does not guarantee what popular religion calls "peace of mind," not in the longer perspective in any case. So long as individuation takes place, peace in the mind or soul is at best but a breathing-space between the past conflict and the conflict to come, a temporary lull between two battles in the aeonial creative war. No matter how greatly one's life has been enriched by one or several encounters with the unconscious, the psychic fact still remains that *only conflict* leads to meaning, and only *more conflict* brings yet greater meaning. The experience of meaning—which is what gnosis is all about—is not equivalent to lack of suffering; yet the *pistis* of the self-aware consciousness can fortify us against the perils of the opposites, against the fang of the serpent and the claw and beak of the bird. The dangers of the irrational and the rational, of instinctuality and spirituality, are thus offset against the resilience of the gnostic soul, which, overcoming all these dangers, continues to experience newly discovered summits of insight and transformation and undergoes the reconciliation of new sets of opposites once more.

The serpent symbolism of the Sixth Sermon presents initially somewhat of a puzzle to the student of Gnosticism, particularly if the student is imbued with Gnostic serpent lore as found in some of the Nag Hammadi scriptures. In several of these tractates the serpent of Genesis is regarded as a wise and holy counselor, indeed a messenger or manifestation of the supernal Wisdom, Mother Sophia, who is intent upon rescuing the first human pair from the bondage in which the creator is holding them. In the works *On the Origin of the World* and *The Hypostasis of the Archons* the story is told of Eve's cooperation with the wise and benign serpent, who, far from being a Satanic deceiver, is an enlightener and liberator, persuading Eve to eat the fruit which opens her and Adam's eyes and bestows consciousness on them. If we contrast the serpent of the demon sexuality described in the Sixth Sermon with the serpent of paradise in the Gnostic myths, a significant difference appears. The Gnostic serpent of paradise is wise and well intentioned. The serpent of the Sixth Sermon, on the other hand, is called a whore who consorts with the devil and with evil spirits, a tyrant and a tormenting spirit who leads people astray to keep bad company. One might almost be tempted to accuse Jung-Basilides of having accepted the orthodox rather than the Gnostic image of the serpent! Still, the issue is more complicated than that.

In the aforementioned Gnostic tractates the serpent has a curious dual title, which is *wild beast* and also *instructor*. The treatise *On the Origin of the World* declares in fact that the interpretation of *wild beast* is *the instructor*. Linguistic scholars feel that this curious statement has to do with the fact that the two words are derived from the same word in the Aramaic language. Similarly, we are told, the name *Eve* as well as the words for *serpent* and *instruct* all have a similar ring in Aramaic, and it is therefore more than likely the Gnostic writers intended to convey a similarity in character or underlying meaning by employing a wordplay—a procedure not uncommon in the ancient world. Thus a dual role of the wise serpent begins to reveal itself. (See John Dart, *The Laughing Savior*, New York: Harper and Row, 1976, p. 72.) This duality befits the archetypal amphibian symbolism rather well, for the serpent, with its ability to move with equal ease on water and on the surface of the earth, has always stood as a primal symbol of duality and of the co-inherence of the opposites in one and the same being or principle. In *Psychology and Alchemy* Jung commented extensively on the symbolism of the serpent, and at times gave recognition to the possibility that at least part of the symbolism of serpent-lore involves the obscure myth of the Gnostic *Anthropos* or divine man embodied in nature. This teaching, gathered mainly from accounts of the church fathers, particularly from those by Hippolytus, concerns the prototype of true humanity that appears in the heavens before the creation of the world, and in some variations of the myth eventually comes to enter the earth and the realm of nature itself. The Anthropos is originally androgynous and eventually divides into two parts, the feminine which comes to reside in the sky, and the masculine, which enters the earth. Yet in the usual Gnostic fashion both principles retain a certain androgynousness, and thus the phallic serpent of the earth is still feminine in an interior sense, while the celestial bird-woman conceals a masculine core. It is this perennial inseparability of the contrasexual polarities that makes Gnostic and Jungian thought into the despair of all who wish for clear-cut divisions and differentiated images to construct logical systems and devise rational theories. The masculine earth-god Phallos thus manifests at a lower level as the serpent, which in spite of its phallic symbolism is also feminine in character. It appears that the so-called *ophite* Gnostic mythology of which Hippolytus speaks described a being very similar to the phallic serpent of the Sixth Sermon. This being—often likened to the winged phallus of Hermes, or the phallus of the mutilated god-pharaoh Osiris emerging from the water, where it was cast by the dismembering hand of Set—is the primal divine man concealed in the earth and waiting to rise from this terrestrial concealment. The other portion of the anthropos, allied to the heavenly mother, even as the first one is associated with the earthly father, has ascended into the heavens. This is none other than the white bird of the Sixth Sermon. The two *anthropoi,* one of the earth, the other of heaven, were very important to Jung's personal myth. Jung seems to have discovered an echo of this mystery in the statement of St. Paul's first letter to the Corinthians, the Latin version of which he appropriated for his tombstone: "Primus homo de terra terrenus: secundus homo de caelo coelestis" (The first man is of the earth, earthly; the second man is heavenly and from heaven). I.Cor. 15:47.

Thus we come to the recognition that according to Jung's Gnosis, and certainly not without a precedent in the ancient Gnosis, one needs to recognize that there are two aspects of the primordial anthropos which meet in the human soul. One of these is a serpent, outwardly phallic but inwardly feminine, permeating all nature and embodying, as it were, the hidden or underground divinity concealed in the recesses of physical nature and in the instinctual forces of the human psyche itself. This is the phallic god whom Jung met as a small boy in a visionary dream, the monstrous chthonic worm enthroned on his subterranean royal seat; the god whose image marked his spiritual outlook for the rest of his life. In his *Memories, Dreams, Reflections* he described this Gnostic Anthropos permeating nature as a symbol of a peculiar conjunction of the opposites which takes place in the natural world and which with singular insight he characterized as the "union of spiritually alive and physically dead matter." Once again Jung's intuitive insight revealed an aspect of Gnosis that for the most part remained concealed from the scholars. The "official" picture given us of the Gnostic view of nature has ever been one of contempt and disgust, whereby, according to the biased interpreters, Gnostics approached the world of external nature. However in the early part of the twentieth century in the so-called Oxyrynchus Papyrus a fragment of the *Gospel of Thomas* came to the attention of the interested readers which declared in the words of Jesus: "Raise the stone and thou shalt find me, cleave the wood and I am there." Still few were wont to recognize that the Gnostics did not condemn nature, but rather they condemned only the *kosmos* or system imposed on both human and external nature by the demiurge. Jung, on the other hand, following the directive received in the vision of his childhood, perceived the phallic serpentine Anthropos enthroned on the wisdom seat of nature. In his above-quoted autobiographical reflections, Jung reveals himself time and again as a sincere lover and admirer of nature. Speaking with the nostalgic wisdom of old age he exclaims: "Yet is so much that fills me: plants, animals, clouds, day and night, and the eternal in man. The more uncertain I have felt about myself, the more there has grown up in me a kinship with all things." Jung had also stated (in a comment to Barbara Hannah) that a regard for nature was one of the qualities so regrettably repressed in our culture by the Christian religion, some of the other great repressions being sexuality and the creative imagination.

Jung the Gnostic, like other persons of Gnostic orientation before him, loved nature, but not for the conventional reasons which have usually appeared in humanity. Pantheistic paganism loved and still loves nature for its own unconscious reasons; it dimly senses that nature conceals some awesome and holy mystery, though it has no conscious notion regarding the essence or the workings of that mystery. Judeo-Christian orthodoxy also professes a certain regard for the "world" (although more seldom for nature) and calls it *God's world,* holding that an extra-cosmic and supernatural creator made the world and it is His and therefore good. (One wonders whether by this reasoning hell might by considered "good" also, since the same good Creator is responsible for its existence?) Of all attitudes toward nature, the Gnostic one is perhaps the most intriguing, for it is not rooted in the mere vague intuition of primitive unconsciousness, and even less in the regard for the Creator-demiurge of Genesis. This attitude—which impelled the alchemists to speak of the "light of nature" and impelled Goethe to use the term *God-nature*—loves nature not because of its external appearance or its creator, but because of an over-whelming, mysterious, unknowable and yet ever-present Divinity that resides concealed in nature itself. While to the orthodox Christian this is God's world in the sense that it has been fashioned and is now owned by the God of the Bible, to the Gnostic, the alchemist and the magician, and of course to Jung, this is God's world, because *God lives in it.* This indwelling God is none other than the Anthropos, the primordial god-man, now inhabiting the earth and at some future time rising from its depths in a gloriously cosmic resurrection. There is a hidden spirit in the world, in nature, in rocks, caves and waters. It slithers in the dark passages of the subterranean realm, and it swims in the streams and lakes which nourish the earth. It rises serpent-like in the cells of the plants and it animates (i.e. en-souls) the moving creatures, who by virtue of its animating influence are known as animals.

It is not generally known, although quite undeniable, that the recognition of this mysterious, hidden presence in the natural world was kept alive by the pan-sophic or alternative reality tradition, and that it was at least in part through this tradition—the fount and origin of which is in Gnosticism—that Jung received his great interest in alchemy and kindred disciplines, which are all founded on the belief in the light of nature, the *lumen naturae*. It is curious to note how even medieval Christianity, with its loss of Gnosis, did not abandon the notion of the light of nature, but tended to retain it as an auxiliary source of spiritual illumination, existing side by side with divine revelation. Nourished by the convictions of magicians and alchemists like Albertus Magnus, Agrippa von Nettesheim and Paracelsus, the churchly scholastics and monastics continued to recognize that the world of beasts and birds, of fields and streams held potent spiritual secrets, even "gleams of prophecy," as Agrippa called them. The verdict of medieval and Rennaissance thinking was well summed up by Paracelsus when he wrote: "Moreover, the light of nature is a light that is lit from the Holy Spirit and goeth not out, for it is well lit."

In the human being, this earthly Anthropos or indwelling light of nature is embodied in the portion of the unconscious that is associated with the instincts. It goes without saying that in Western culture, but in almost all other cultures as well, this instinctual unconscious is to a great extent dominated by sexuality. It is for this reason that Jung connects the serpent of earth with the phallus, or the demon of sexuality. It is significant in this respect that Jung made his clearest and most convincing statement regarding the Anthropos in his book *The Psychology of the Transference*, a work dealing specifically with the alchemy of love. We could do no better than to quote his own words from this source:

> This "lower" spirit is the Primordial Man, hermaphroditic by nature and of Iranian origin, who was imprisoned in Physis. He is the spherical, i.e. perfect, man who appears at the beginning and end of time and is man's own beginning and end. He is man's totality, which is beyond the division of the sexes and can only be reached when male and female come together in one. The revelation of this higher meaning solves the problem created by the "sinister" contact and produces from the chaotic darkness the lumen quod superat omnia lumina. (The light which rises above all lights.)...
>
> The revelation of the Anthropos is associated with no ordinary religious emotion; it signifies much the same thing as the vision of Christ for the believing Christian. Nevertheless it does not appear *ex opere divino* (as the result of a divine act) but *ex opere naturae*: not from above but from the transformation of a shade from Hades, akin to evil itself and bearing the name of the pagan god of revelation.[32]

Understandably, Jung also recognized the lower Anthropos as embodied in the enigmatic but transformative figure of Mephistopheles in Goethe's *Faust*, who with the power of the instincts, particularly of sexuality, draws the hero from his alienated intellectual pursuits and into the arena of transformation in the real world of the opposites. It is perhaps easier for us at this point to recognize why Jung states in this sermon that the serpent consorts with the devil and tempts people to keep what might be called bad company. Fear, desire, the projection of inner powers onto material objects, the tyranny and torment of transformation, all of these are brought to us by the Anthropos in his terrestrial aspect. As indicated before, individuation has little in common with serene quietude or the absence of suffering. The serpent provides us with conflict, and conflict makes for the relatedness and the reconciliation of the opposites. Jung also states in our sermon that the serpent descends into the deep and there either paralyzes or stimulates the phallic demon. Here we find the two necessary extremes of *askesis*, or transformative skill, as they appear in Gnostic practice—at least as this practice reveals itself to us in the available sources. The instinctual forces of the psyche need to be brought into a condition of extraordinary stimulation in order to be utilized for purposes of intense transformation. *Askesis* (spiritual skill) is distinct from its caricature, asceticism, for it strives for the extraordinary as against the ordinary activity of psychic energy. When the force of the serpent expresses itself according to the ordinary, trivial patterns of everyday living, the results are not transformative. Only when either by rigid control or extraordinary activity the libidinal forces become activated to the point of ecstasy will the *opus contra naturam*, the work against ordinary natural patterns, be accomplished. Similarly, Jung tells us in the Sermon that the serpent, by eluding our grasp and by stimulating us to pursuit, shows us hidden ways which with our limited wit we would never discover. Mephistopheles, the wise devil of psychic energy, thus ever tempts and guides Faust to avenues and modalities of individuational activity which would never have been available to the unimaginative scholar of Goethe's dramatic vision. The usefulness of the enigmatic serpent of earth thus becomes apparent; troublesome and painful as its venom may prove to our health of limb and peace of mind, it is our mighty aid in the process of Gnosis.

The serpentine Anthropos of the Gnostics received yet another intriguing analogue in the Indian myth of the snake-goddess Kundalini, whose psycho-physiological evocations in yoga practices have received an increasing literary and practical notice in recent decades. Very much like the Anthropos, Kundalini is envisioned as a divine being that has entered the dark, moist recesses of the earth, from whence it is destined to rise to the summit of existence, there to meet its divine twin from whom the goddess has been separated for aeons unnumbered. During her journeys in the earth, the pilgrim-goddess has assumed the form of a snake, and in this adaptable, swift reptilian body she managed to survive the countless perils which attend earthly life. In the microcosmic analogy of the human body, the habitat of the divine serpent is said to be at the base of the spinal column, where under ordinary circumstances the goddess sleeps and dreams of her celestial origins. When the time of awakening has come, she coils herself around the spine as around the trunk of a tree and begins her aeonial journey of ascent to the supernal regions, where above the crown of the head, seated on an aetherial lotus throne, her spouse, the great god Shiva, awaits her. Miguel Serrano, the distinguished Chilean writer who was once in diplomatic residence in India, gave us a moving and profoundly Gnostic image of the Kundalini-Anthropos in his splendid poetic account of the spiritual world of India, entitled *The Serpent of Paradise*, from which we shall quote some brief passages here:

> Before the serpent curled itself round the Tree of Paradise it lived in the liquid depths beneath the roots of the tree. Then, like the spine of a man which rises up from the dark and sensitive regions of his waist towards the freely moving upper torso, the Serpent stretched itself up to the upper branches, where its pale, cold skin could be warmed by the sun. In the secret depths from which it emerged it enjoyed a type of elemental power and pleasure, but when it encountered the force of the sun it seemed to recoil and expand at the same time. The result was a conflict of light and darkness, for the force of the Serpent is both liquid and frozen; it poisons and it deifies. Some call the poison of the Serpent, God; others call it Immortality.[33]

Jung, too, concerned himself with the myth of Kundalini and perceived in it a symbol of human individuation. He interpreted the system of Kundalini Yoga as a symbolic journey from division to wholeness, using the human body as a medium for the projection of the transforming unconscious content. Serrano, with his keen awareness of Jungian archetypal imagery, gave utterance to some of these individuational elements of the Indian symbolism of the serpent when he wrote:

> As the Serpent of Paradise rises from the liquid depths in which the Tree itself is rooted, so man too produces his physical sons from these dark and murky regions. These sons of the flesh are destined to die, but the sons of the spirit which are born during man's maturity are capable of reaching eternity by becoming the sons of death.... By the time man has lived half of his life he must prepare to give birth to a son in the spirit; that is to say, to a son of death. This son can be born only by marrying the Serpent or by playing Shiva's phallus and Krishna's flute. And he alone can carry us over the sea of death. He will give us passage on his phosphorescent barge or will allow us to rest on the wings of the Plumed Serpent.
>
> A man who has married this Serpent has a strange, otherworldly appearance. His face has the repose of one who has

taken pleasure in being poisoned, and he reflects the calmness of death. He appears to be immersed in dreamy waters, where he swims with the fish of God. His eyes, though closed, emanate an indescribable joy, and there is the shadow of a smile on his lips; for it has been his privilege to descend to the dark roots of pleasure and to be able to return to a spiritual union. In the palace that rests on the top of the Tree of Paradise he has met someone for whom he has been waiting for a long time, and the joy of this encounter has made tears stream down his cheeks. The fruits formed from those tears are at one liquid and ice-like, and when they fall they make a noise like that of tinkling bells.[34]

Such is the process of individuation and the character of the successfully individuating person as poetically described by Serrano. The images thus evoked for our contemplation can be said to have a profound relationship to Gnosticism in both its ancient and its modern, i.e. Jungian, manifestations. Opponents of the Gnostics have made much of the hatred the Gnostics are said to have felt for the process of birth and the procreation of children. The recent discoveries have for the most part helped to dispel some of the confusion regarding this subject by demonstrating that the Gnostics were not opposed to marriage or the bearing of children *as such*, but that they had certain psychological views regarding these matters which closely parallel those voiced above by Serrano. The unconscious, according to Jung, has a fatal tendency to live itself out in physical acts bearing a symbolic relationship to the content which the unconscious needs to bring into consciousness. Within the context of the individuation process, it becomes imperative for persons to give birth to themselves as new and regenerated beings. It is obvious that the process of physical birth is the grand symbol of this interior birth. Therefore the Gnostics warned people, particularly women, that they should not mistake this biological event for the greater psychological reality which lies concealed in its symbolism. Already the canonical Gospel of Luke contains two passages (11: 27-28 and 23:29) which indicate that Jesus appears opposed to the unconscious attitude of women towards themselves as mere givers of birth to physical children. In the *Gnostic Gospel of Thomas* this theme appears with even greater clarity and within a somewhat more unified context:

A woman from the multitude said to Him: Blessed is the womb
which bore Thee, and the breasts which nourished Thee. He
said: Blessed are those who have heard the word of the Father
(and) have kept it in truth. For there will be days when you will
say: Blessed is the womb which has not conceived, and the
breasts which have not suckled.[35]

While the archetype of birth obviously would have a special role
in the life of women, the psychological problem of individuation
versus the unconscious living out of spiritual patterns of growth
affects the lives of both sexes. We have, in effect, another example here of individuation as the alchemical *opus contra naturam*
(work against nature). Nature, the Anthropos as the serpent of
earth, injects into us the venom that may either paralyze or
awaken. If we follow the promptings of the serpent blindly and
unconsciously, we will be led to further unconsciousness and will
be lulled into aeonial sleep by the pleasant feelings afforded us
by physically living out the interior realities. The "sweet lure of
the flesh" referred to by some Gnostic writers is, in fact, the lure
of the archetypes expressed unconsciously within a fleshly context. The sons of the flesh are destined to die, as Serrano wisely
states in the passage quoted above, which means that physical
acts which consist of the unconscious expression of archetypal
realities are like abortions which have no spiritual promise of
growing to real maturity. On the other hand, when one gives
birth to a son in the spirit, such a son ensures the immortality of
the spiritual parent. The son in the spirit, which is the new self,
born usually in the second half of life, becomes the carrier of the
life of the spirit. He who discovers the meaning of the words of
the Logos will not taste death, says the *Gospel of Thomas*. If we
discover the meaning of life, then and then only are we worthy
of life and will be able to escape the death of unconsciousness.
From these psychologically valid considerations, the reduc-
tionist minds of some persons have drawn the erroneous conclusion that the physical expression of interior, transformative
forces in itself is evil, and that the flesh must be mortified in
order to release the spirit from its deadly embrace. The Gnostic
scriptures, like Jung's Sermons, teach that the physical expression of spiritual realities *alone*, without the presence of consciousness, is counter-productive, or at best useless. They never

intended to declare that life should be lived *only* in mind and that the body and its experiences should be declared as evil. Still, all who taught the development of consciousness felt it necessary to warn against the tendency of the nether Anthropos to lure consciousness into the dark depths of terrestrial sleep, where the dead dwell, and where the malign spirits of unredeemed psychic energy roam. The Sixth Sermon refers to the dead who are earthbound, who have not found the way by which to cross over to the state of solitude, and says that the serpent is associated with these. One can readily see that what is meant here is the forces of unconsciousness and disunion, which are nourished by the kind of attitude that ensues when one leads a life of blind instinctuality. True *askesis* (skill) consists in the ability to combine the experiences of natural human living with a constant discovery of meaning. When this becomes possible, then the physical acts prompted by instinctuality no longer stand opposed to the realities which seek their expression through them. It is at this time that life becomes increasingly a ritualized expression of the consciously performed drama of individuation. Asceticism in the sense of a hostile denial of the value of the forces of the instinctual nature is thus a perversion and a crude reductionism. The figure of the earthly serpent in the Sixth Sermon demonstrates this.

Somewhat more remote from our everyday experience is the other principle of the dual Anthropos as represented in the Sixth Sermon. This is the white bird from heaven, which almost inevitably conjures up the image of the Holy Spirit in the form of a dove. As the serpent embodies the lower, or feminine of the elements, i.e. earth and water, so the dove or white bird is the expression of the element of air through which it flies, and of the solar fire which is the luminary of the heavens from whence it descends. As the serpent symbolizes instinct, sexuality, procreation, and the light hidden in nature, so the bird stands for thought, spirit, transcendence. The one dwells in the earth and slithers about within its holes; the other flies high above the earth, looking down upon it, as one might be inclined to imagine, with a mixture of bewilderment and bemused contempt. The cold-blooded serpent, with its fierce power to strike without the least sign of warning, and the warm-blooded, frail and gentle bird of the air together make up the strange dual aspect of the redeeming power of the Anthropos. The *principium individuationis*, the creative urge toward psychic redemption, is embodied in these two curiously different, yet complementary figures. As Hippolytus noted when writing of the Gnostic Anthropos, this saving principle is most closely related to the divinity, whom the Greeks and Romans knew as Hermes and Mercurius respectively. From the point of view of the symbolism of the *Sermons* it is interesting to note that this god, while flying in the air with wings attached to his helmet and sandals, also bears the staff of two serpents, which in turn is surmounted by a winged globe. In his previously noted psychological commentary on the alchemical work *Rosarium Philosophorum* (to which he attached the prosaic title *The Psychology of the Transference*), Jung gives us a splendid description of the ambivalent and yet subtly exciting figure of the swift-winged and light-footed divinity, whom the alchemists recognized as the great facilitator of the conjunction of the opposites:

> The alchemists aptly personified it as the wily god of revelation, Hermes or Mercurius; and though they lament over the way he hoodwinks them, they still give him the highest names, which bring him very near to deity.... Yet it would be an altogether unjustifiable suppression of the truth were I to confine myself to the negative description of Mercurius, impish drolleries, his inexhaustible invention, his insinuations, his intriguing ideas and schemes, his ambivalence and—often—his unmistakable malice. He is also capable of the exact opposite, and I can well understand why the alchemists endowed their Mercurius with the highest spiritual qualities, although these stand in flagrant contrast to his exceedingly shady character. The contents of the unconscious are indeed of the greatest importance for the unconscious can be most dangerously deceptive on account of its numinous nature. Involuntarily one thinks of the devils mentioned by St. Athanasius in his life of St. Anthony, who talk very piously, sing psalms, read the holy books, and—worst of all—speak the truth. The difficulties of our psychotherapeutic work teach us to take truth, goodness, and beauty where we find them. They are not always found where we look for them: often they are hidden in the dirt or are in the keeping of the dragon.[36]

The white bird of heaven represents the spiritual and respectable portion of Mercury, even as the serpent of earth, the phallic caduceus, symbolizes his dangerous and mischievous side. Both together, however, stand for the creative and redemptive wisdom, which reconciles heaven and earth and brings about the transformation of the substances within the vessel of the alchemist.

As indicated earlier, the serpent in the sermon is described as feminine, though messenger of the subterranean god Phallos, while the bird is masculine but proceeds from the celestial mother, *Mater Coelestis*. It is interesting to note that in Gnostic sources references can be found to the Holy Spirit as a feminine being. Jung was fascinated by the figure of Wisdom as it appears in such Hebrew writings as Proverbs, Ecclesiasticus, and particularly in the Book of the Wisdom of Solomon. In his *Answer to Job* he referred to the content of all of these books in considerable detail, and saw in them an earlier manifestation of the new Jerusalem, the heavenly city which in the Apocalypse of St. John appears as the bride of the Lamb. Jung unhesitatingly identified this figure with the feminine aspect of the Gnostic Anthropos: "She is the feminine Anthropos, the counterpart of the masculine principle," so he wrote in *Answer to Job*, and indicated that it is this principle which needs to be brought into the view of the soul in order to effect the reconciliation of matter with spirit.

At another place in the same work he called her the "feminine numen of the metropolis...the mother-beloved, a reflection of Ishtar." The word *numen* means deity, and the Heavenly Mother thus is revealed as the goddess of the great city in the heavens, which is in itself a most interesting archetype to contemplate. We may recall that in the Fifth Sermon it is stated that human communities are necessary because of man's weakness, and that if they are not in the sign of the mother, then they appear in the sign of the Phallos. When communal life is governed by primitive needs and instinctuality, which appears largely true of traditional and archaic rural village life, it serves as a natural arena for the living out of the patterns of the unconscious. Villagers are happy to the extent that they are supported by the great, underlying patterns of collectivity as manifest in outer nature and in their community life. Like the cosmic and nature-worshipping forms of religion, so the rural community life can be happy and comforting, but is lacking in creative and transformative forces of growth. The rural individual is by nature conservative and shuns the novelty of unaccustomed ideas and experiences. The Latin word *paganus*, freely translated, means a backward country bumpkin, and its English equivalent, *heathen*, similarly means a dweller in the outlying backwashes of civilization. Such persons, the ancients already believed, have little attraction to heroic consciousness, which involves adjusting to new experiences. It was thus that, in contradistinction to rural unconscious patterns, they developed and spiritually exalted the archetype of the *Polis* or *Metropolis*, the image of consciousness-making known as the city.

Historians inform us that the development of cities represented a tremendous step in the development of cultures, to be likened perhaps to quantum leaps or jumps in the realm of physics. Babylon, Egypt, Greece and Rome changed from areas inhabited by primitive dolts to great nations of philosophers, prophets, artists and statesmen with the growth of cities. The change in ancient Egyptian civilization particularly appeared so sudden and dramatic, that the more imaginative and less rational authors speculated on its colonization by escaped inhabitants of Atlantis or, in the mode of the space-age mythos, by colonists from advanced civilizations in outer space. Whatever the circumstances, all are agreed that the city was one of the most creative achievements of humanity.

Not only were cities the abode of commerce, industry, architecture, learning and other great products of the human mind, but the city became a spiritual archetype of consciousness. Not even the pastoral and rural people of the Hebrews remained immune from the influence of this archetype. It was the holy city of Jerusalem, where the *Beth-El*, the residence or dwelling place of God, came to be established. First, the Jews, but later the Christians and Muslims associated it with the religious archetype of the holy or divine city. It was not to the land or the rivers and hills of Judea that the lamentations of the prophets were addressed, but to the city:

> How shall we sing the Lord's song in a foreign land?
> If I forget thee, O Jerusalem,
> let my right hand wither!

Let my tongue cleave to the roof of my mouth
if I do not remember thee,
if I do not set Jerusalem
above my highest joy! (Psalms 137)

By the time of the gnostically influenced Apocalypse of John, the holy city had clearly revealed itself as a celestial archetype, part woman, who acts as the Bride to the Lamb, and part mandala, made of precious stones, "like a jasper, clear as crystal." (Rev. 21:10-111). This is the city from whence, as from the mother, the white bird flies to humanity. The winged messenger of the Goddess, of Sophia, Barbelo, Ishtar, of Mary the Virgin, brings messages from the holy ones who have gone before, who have attained to citizenship in the heavenly Metropolis. Conversely, the bird carries the words of humanity up to the mother. The messenger carries not only her blessing but our supplications as well.

It is interesting to note in this respect that Jung's preoccupation with the feminine city-mandala was a profound and lifelong one. Like his Gnostic forebears, he looked upon the city as the archetype of consciousness, of the divine thought in manifestation. Like Alexandria of old, the crucible of ancient Gnostic, Hermetic and Neo-Platonic thought (see chapter dealing with the preamble of the Sermons), so the archetype of the city remained to Jung the abode of wisdom, spirituality and creative consciousness. He considered the city an aspect of the wisdom-woman Sophia, of whom he said: "who was with God before time began, and at the end of time will be reunited with God through the sacred marriage."

Toward the end of his life Jung perceived a sign of the times of great significance in the declaration of the assumption of the Virgin Mary made by Pope Pius XII. At the same time when Protestant theologians, and even some Catholic ecumenicists, threw up their hands in horror because of this new evidence of old papal mariolatry, Jung hailed the Pope's apostolic constitution, *Munificentissimus Deus*, as an evidence of the long-delayed recognition on the part of Christendom of the celestiality, if not outright divinity, of the feminine. In *Answer to Job* he went on record, writing that this recognition was welling, or pushing upwards from the depths of humanity's unconscious and that it could have a deeply beneficial effect on human affairs in terms of world peace. The elevation of the Virgin, he said, was an evidence of a very real "yearning for peace which stirs deep down in the soul," and it would act as a needed compensation to the "threatening tension between the opposites."

The Sixth Sermon says that the mother intercedes and warns but has no power against the gods. Still, her presence and, more importantly, the *conscious recognition* of her presence and of her role as mediator and agent of compensation could avert further dreadful wars and revolutions which are the result of the threatening tension of the opposites in the world. The celestial maternal mandala expresses itself in many forms. The ancient Gnostics see it as Sophia, Barbelo, or as Mary Magdalene; Jung as the heavenly city foursquare and as God's forsaken daughter and wife; and some present-day men and women, imbued with the mythos of the space age, fix their gaze upon the skies where they perceive mysterious flying objects which the press—with its customary sense of the ludicrously prosaic—came to name *flying saucers*. In *Flying Saucers, a Modern Myth* Jung recognized that these objects are usually of round shape and that tasks of world-wide beneficial significance are ascribed to them. Like the figure of the Virgin, whom the Pope declared to have been bodily assumed into the heavens, so these mechanical mediators between heaven and earth are said to be intent upon preventing the nuclear Armageddon and bringing the galactic olive branch of world peace to the cantankerous children of earth. As the teacher said in the Sixth Sermon: "(The bird) brings messages from the distance, from those who have gone before, those who are perfected." (A curious variant of the myth, proclaimed largely after Jung's time, has the saucers swarming forth from secret openings in the earth and appropriately threatening humankind with destruction, thus compensating our minds for the imbalance of beneficent saucer lore.)

It is not impossible that in our own days the two great constituent parts of the ultimate mandala of wholeness are once again approaching union. The serpent of earth, released from chthonic concealment, raises his crowned basilisk-head toward the sky. Centuries of desperate sexual repression are beginning to give way to tendencies which are inclined to let the phallic serpent roam with a greater degree of freedom on the surface of consciousness. The long-suppressed feminine nature of the serpent is demanding its due also; the fact of feminine sexuality, along with all of its manifestations, is receiving attention and acceptance from men and women alike. As above, so below: the white bird of heaven moves closer to the range of our vision, while the ruddy serpent of earth raises mightily from the depths.

The serpent in the psyche is matched also by the serpent of matter itself. There is much evidence indicating that whenever the mind confronts an unknown or severely repressed force within itself, a corresponding constellation arises in the outer, physical world. Thus the phallic serpent of the psychic ground calls to the fiery snake of the nucleus of the atom, and the unleashing of the libido in the collective soul is compensated by the rising of the mushroom-cloud over Hiroshima. The terrible basilisk has risen in all its awesome fury and beauty, and no human force will compel it to retire into its former underground recesses. Well may the earth tremble, for the conquering serpent has come.

There is one more grand design, one final alchemical vessel in which the two opposites, the dove and serpent, must meet: it is the human being, the new and the eternal Anthropos. In the starry height, in the seventh region of heaven, the archetype and prototype of the Anthropos rides in his solar chariot. The head of the bird joined to serpent feet by a human torso and arms reveals the figure of Abraxas as the union of sky and earth, of the bird and the snake. "In this world," say the *Sermons*, "man is Abraxas." From the Gnosis of humanity a new Abraxas is born.

It is perhaps no mere coincidence but an evidence of synchronicity that the Cherub of the Aion of Aquarius has the form of a man. In his work *Aion*, Jung gave a psychological endorsement of the theory of the Zodiacal Age, or Aion of Aquarius. The sign of Aquarius has as its zodiacal symbol the man pouring from a vessel of water. This figure is equated by medieval and Kabbalistic lore with the cherubic emblem of the element of air, which is the exalted man. Jung, in his studies of the mandala geometric designs which arise from the depths of the unconscious, came to the conclusion that in these mandalas, like the above-mentioned cherub, one can find the expression of the Anthropos or "complete man." In *Psychology and Alchemy* he reiterated the same thought and stated that the quaternary symbols of the mandala indicated the "god within" the psyche. He also noted, not without dismay, that the mandalas drawn by contemporary persons almost never contain a god-image in the center of the design, as might have been the case in earlier periods. He wrote: "There is no deity in the mandala, nor is there any submission or reconciliation to a deity. The place of the deity seems to be taken by the wholeness of man." And later he continued in a poetic vein:

> The gods first lived in superhuman power and beauty, on the top of snowclad mountains or in the darkness of caves, woods and seas. Later on they drew together into one god, and then that god became man. But in our days even the God-man seems to have descended from his throne and to be dissolving himself in the common man.[37]

In the Aion of Aquarius the Anthropos has become personal and human. No longer does god wear the mask of the lion, the eagle and the bull, or even of the dual fish of non-Gnostic Christianity. Man has become Abraxas, and in the words of the Seventh Sermon, he may give birth to and devour his own world. The birth of a new world of spiritual humanism may be anticipated and welcomed by men and women of good will without misgivings. Not so with the devouring. The Aquarian peril is the inflation of the ego of humanity with the god-like power, which now may readily invade it in the absence of a god in the mandala. Not only do individuals fall victim to the presumptuous sacrilege of ego-inflation, but the State, too, becomes inflated, resulting in totalitarianism which assumes the dimensions of a monstrous hypertropy, crushing the freedom of the individual soul. The greatest peril of the human race—as Jung recognized in such works as *The Undiscovered Self, Modern Man in Search of a Soul*—will not be the pollution of the planet by the waste of unwisdom or the much-dreaded nuclear holocaust. It will be the already present inflation of totalitarian states which, with their enforced mass-mindedness and claims of control over the lives of men and women, duplicate the evils of the archons of creation, of which the

Gnostics spoke. Collective inflation at the level of the state and individual inflation in the form of materialism and deadly rationalism are but two sides of a coin, that of Judas' ransom for the betrayal of man's divinity. Wrote Jung:

> In the same way that the State has caught the individual, the individual imagines that he has caught the psyche and holds her in the hollow of his hand.[38]

Jung recognizes here that materialism and rationalism have come to advance the one-sidedness of consciousness, which, by way of its negation of the transcendent element in the psyche, leads to alienation from its own deeper roots in the collective unconscious. This alienation, in turn, renders it vulnerable to inflations of a positive or negative nature. The modern secularist state, devoid of all dependence on spiritual realities beyond the mundane sphere, represents a close analogue of this individual predicament.

Still, in spite of, and paradoxically perhaps because of these dangers of individual and collective inflation, the growth of the new Gnostic Anthropos proceeds apace and according to the preordained pattern of the transpersonal order. The peril of tyranny increases the vigilance of the lovers of freedom; the oppressions exercised by unwisdom strengthen the dedication of the wise. The tortured mystic poet Hölderlin said truly that peril brings salvation into manifestation. As always in history, there is no way back. If the gods have indeed departed from the center of the contemporary mandala, in their stead we may have to accept humanity. This humanity, this Anthropos at the center of the mandala, should not, must not be a puny product of nineteenth century rationalism; it must not be a statistically designed consumer-robot drafted by corporation executives; or an outdated Marxist image of the proletarian revolutionary who naively believes that the basic evils of human nature can be solved by political force and economic change. Rather, the new man and woman must be like Abraxas: with head overshadowed by the Logos of wisdom and insight, with swift feet that possess the instinctual force and libidinal resilience of the serpent. These opposites in turn must be joined and welded together by qualities of true and undisguised humanity, a humanity for which no moral, economic or political apologies are required.

The hope exists that the Anthropos may come into his own in this Aion of the Water-Bearer. The promises of earth and the prophecies of heaven converge and nourish the expectations and longings of humanity. Osiris, the old Anthropos, lies slain and dismembered on the field of aeonial battle, while Isis is once more great with the seed of his resurrected shadow. And while in the divine womb foetal Osiris stirs, opening his hawk's beak, Thoth, Lord of magic and transformation, patiently awaits the birth of the conquering hero of light. It is always thus, in the death-enshrouded mists of ancient Khem, in the chaste twilight of cathedrals and in the neonlights of the metropolis of the world of today. The Anthropos is ever reborn; he is the ever coming one; the aeonial offspring of the magical womb of time. We, the spiritual cells in the body of this Great Man, are ever becoming but never become; we are perpetually being perfected but never reach perfection. It is not up to us to know the designs of the fulfillment of time. Ours is to watch and to wait, to labor and to hope, strengthened by wisdom and led by gentleness. For have we not been told, *in illo tempore*, in those times, which were and are and are still to come, to be wise as serpents and gentle as doves?

The Seventh Sermon—
Homeward Bound Among the Stars

The Seventh Sermon is the briefest, but by no means the least of the exhortations addressed by Basilides to the recalcitrant dead. While the earlier teachings utilize archetypal themes, the Seventh Sermon addresses itself directly and undisguisedly to the phenomenon of the human being. It is of course true that all of the sermons deal with man, that *Pleroma*, God and Demon, *Abraxas*, and all the other great symbolic motifs are in reality within the individual. Nevertheless, the *mythos* of the *Sermons* is so constituted that these themes appear to be exterior to the psyche. It is always thus: the mind projects its own deepest and most potent content unto the seemingly external screen of worlds visible and invisible. The heavens teem with the gods and goddesses who had their first and most significant residence on the Mt. Olympus of the human mind. The silvery moon reflects the mysterious luminosity of the unconscious, while the red planet Mars bears the imagery of the fierce power embodied in the warrior soul of man. Venus in her dual aspects of Lucifer and Hesperus reminds of the alpha and omega of the soul's diurnal cycle, which has its beginning and ending in love. The creation myths of all peoples describe, not the formation of the universes and earthly globes with waters, plants, and animals, but the birth of consciousness from the vast womb of that internal space we today call the unconscious. Similarly, the inspiring tales woven around the lives of the wise and holy souls in human history declare, not humanity's historical salvation by Krishna, Buddha or Christ, but rather the redemption of the suffering mind by the paradigm of the individuated ego.

As above so below: as with good so with evil. The ancients rightly declared *Homo homini lupus*, man is a wolf unto man; the human being has no greater enemy than himself. Evil persons obviously do exist in the world outside of us, but our relationship with them is curiously and mysteriously interdependent with the sad failures and the woeful inadequacies concealed within ourselves. The villain without is the inseparable identical twin of all that is undesirable and villainous within ourselves. As we valiantly go about ridding the world of villains, failing to first rid ourselves of the villain inside our crusades remain doomed to failure. It is thus that wars waged to make the world safe for freedom leave humanity in an increased state of slavery, and revolution brings fiercer tyrants to the helm than those it brought to their fall. *"Selten kommt etwas besseres nach"* (seldom does anything better follow) is an old and tested popular saying in the German tongue, and it is not so much a product of cynicism as it is of wisdom derived from experience.

In the course of history and of their individual lives, men have tended to confuse change with transformation. This confusion brings disaster in its wake, for to change without being transformed is an exercise in futility. The alchemists, whom Jung regarded so highly, held that the natural world of the four elements does not transform itself, it merely changes. Following the hints given by the pre-Socratics, particularly Heraclitus, they said that the elements forever war with each other but remain essentially the same in the midst of their battles. Only when the *opus contra naturam*, the great work against nature, is undertaken by the alchemist do the elements change in such a way that ultimate transformation becomes possible. When earth, water, fire and air of the natural world no longer exist in their hitherto known forms, then, and only then can transformation take place. Thus the world of change needs to be replaced by the world of transformation, and the work of nature must be turned into the work against nature.

With the ceasing of meaningless change and the coming of meaningful transformation in the individual, the deceptive drama of projections diminishes. The human mind no longer need contemplate itself in the paradoxes of the Pleroma, or in the awesome dualities of Gods, Devils, Burning Ones and Growing Ones, or even in the serpentine sexuality of earth and the winged spirituality of heaven. With the transformation of the magical cosmos within the retort of the alchemist, the fiery spectacle of Abraxas loses its power over consciousness. As man becomes a living philosophers' stone, he becomes prepared to face the light of his own inner nature without the reflected lights of its projected images. The human Self returns unto itself and can at last recognize itself as the only existential reality of being, the quintessence of all that was and is and ever shall be. The light of the Pleroma has descended through the seven spheres and has come to rest in the human psyche itself. The *Seven Sermons* lead us—according to this preordained and profoundly archetypal pattern of the septenaries—from the abstract to the existential, from the image and the image of the image to the image-maker, ourselves.

The figure of man as given in the seventh and last Sermon is a curious and paradoxical one. In perfect accord with the statements of the Hermetic and Gnostic sources, Jung first describes man as a unique link between the macrocosm and the microcosm. These two worlds, one called the great and the other the little, have occupied an extremely significant position in the symbol system of the alternative-reality tradition throughout its long history. Beginning with that highly revered document known as the Emerald Tablet, which speaks of heaven above and heaven below and stars above and stars below, to the grimoires of the ceremonial magicians revived in Victorian and Edwardian times by various secret fraternities, the greater and the lesser cosmos has played an important role. The pentagram or five-pointed star, so popular in heraldry both ancient and modern, served since times immemorial as the symbol of the lesser, or *microcosm*. Its five points were related to innumerable symbolic analogies, from the five extremities of the human body to the five wounds on the body of Christ. It is interesting to note that the two great antagonists of our world, the United States and the Soviet Union, both employ the five-pointed, microcosmic star as their heraldic emblem: the former in typical pluralistic fashion by representing each one of its states by such a star on the flag of its union; the latter by placing a single star next to the hammer and sickle on its blood-red banner.

In contrast to the *microcosm* or lesser world, there was always recognition given to the greater world or *macrocosm*, to which the six-pointed star or hexagram was assigned. It was often said that the hexagram symbolizes a balanced structure of Pleromic perfection, while the pentagram, as an unbalanced design, stands for the growing and transforming aspect of the lesser world. The Seventh Sermon defines the human being as a portal through which the outer and inner or greater and lesser worlds are connected. It is interesting to note that the *microcosm* and *macrocosm* are defined here as two eternities, one inner and the other outer. "Small and insignificant is man; one leaves him soon behind, and thus one enters once more into infinite space, into the microcosm, into the inner eternity." The implications of this statement are many, and only some can be alluded to in the following brief expositions. It is helpful to keep in mind that the terms *macrocosm* and *microcosm*, both in Jung's writings and in Hermetic literature in general, sometimes denote the world outside of man and the world inside man: at other times they refer to the world of transcendental being and of the lower sphere of personal experience.

The mystery of the two eternities of *microcosm* and *macrocosm* which meet in the human psyche is closely related to what Jung in his later works came to call *synchronicity*, a concept with more extensive implications than is commonly assumed. There was a time when the principle of causality was regarded as absolutely valid in scientific thought and the possibility of an acausal principle connecting events in time would have appeared a total impossibility. As long as the operational sphere of scientific endeavors was largely restricted to the earth, or at most to the solar system, the causality principle was not seriously challenged. As soon as empirical, scientific enquiry began to extend into the cosmic realm of space and into the subatomic realm of matter, the absolute validity of causality began to break down. It was not philosophy or religion or even psychology, but rather the physical sciences themselves that shattered the absolutism of the causal principle. Once these sciences had accepted the statistical validity of natural laws, the exceptions to these laws which were brought to light by the statistical method demanded notice. Exceptions with regard to cosmic space on the one hand and the subatomic realm on the other, multiplied to such a degree that the absolute validity of causality, as hitherto held, collapsed before them. It is most significant to note for our purposes, however, that the post-Newtonian restructuring of reality had come about primarily because of the thrust of observation in the realms of the infinitely great and the infinitely small. Here, then, are at least two manifestations of what the Seventh Sermon calls "the inner eternity" and the "outer eternity."

What Einstein and his fellows accomplished in the physical sciences, notably in theoretical physics, Jung brought into focus in the realm of psychology. The functioning of human life contains a large number of phenomena—so Jung came to recognize—which are conditioned not only by consciousness but also by the unconscious. These phenomena, like the observations of Einstein, need a principle other than ordinary causality for their explanation. There are some events which are not caused, or, as Jung himself wrote: "The connection of events may in certain circumstances be other than causal, and requires another principle of explanation." ("Synchronicity, An Acausal Connecting Principle," in C.G. Jung's *Collected Works*, Vol. 8, par. 819.) In the above work (par. 843), Jung tells of an experience in synchronicity. At the very moment a patient was telling him a dream about a golden scarab, a scarab-like insect, called a rose-chafer, tapped gently against the window. Thus two distinct events, i.e., a dream of a scarab and the appearance of the rose-chafer, were connected together by a similarity of meaning, though, of course, causally without any connection at all. The inner event (the dream) was fortified and brought into meaningful focus by the outer event (the insect on the window).

Jung called this other principle that supplements and in some cases replaces causality by the name of *synchronicity*, and he defined it as a "coincidence in time of two or more causally unrelated events which have the same or similar meaning." The latter statement is of crucial significance, for it points to the all-important human factor of meaning, which we have encountered time and again in our considerations of the *Sermons*, and which is ever present in the corpus of Jung's scientific writings as well. In Jung's model of reality, *man is the maker of meaning*. Human consciousness is of enormous importance in history and in psychology because it is the giver of meaning, the bestower of meaningful light upon the darkness of the material and psychic worlds. Meaning is—as stated earlier on in our commentaries on the *Sermons*—not some sort of objective, measurable commodity but partakes of profoundly subjective valuations at all times. The very concept of synchronicity as enunciated by Jung is subject to frequent misunderstandings just because of this subjective factor, which is often neglected by those who scrutinize synchronistic phenomena. When Jung spoke of "coincidence in time," he did not mean thereby a mere simultaneity dependent on mechanical clock time. The kind of simultaneity he referred to is relative or subjective simultaneity, which is far more subtle and meaningful. Time and space are relativized in certain experiences of the psyche, which implies that their subjective reality is altered in accordance with meaning. The meaningful part of a synchronistic experience is never the mere connection of events in objective astronomical time, but rather in the power of meaning residing in the subjective image in the psyche, which relates itself dynamically to an outer event. Aniela Jaffe, one of Jung's closest collaborators in the later portion of his life, explains this vital fact in the following manner:

> It is...a *relative simultaneity*, to be understood as the subjective experience of an inner image coinciding with an outer

event. Only in this experience is the time difference abolished, since the event, whether in the past or future, is immediately present. It may happen that an inner image and outer event are connected together by an objective, clock-time simultaneity, for which reason Jung chose the term synchronistic rather than synchronous, and spoke of synchronicity and not synchronism.[39]

There is little doubt that Jung regarded the principle of synchronicity as of great importance. Yet by the same token he exercised great caution and restraint in making it public. There is much evidence indicating that Jung had formulated the theory of synchronicity as early as 1930, for he mentioned both the concept and the term in his memorial address for the great Chinese scholar Richard Wilhelm, when he spoke of the psychological rationale of the workings of the oracle classic, the *I Ching*. It took Jung no less than twenty-two years to return to the subject of synchronicity. He finally published his epochal essay on the subject, together with a lengthy essay on a related topic, written by the Nobel prize-winning physicist Wolfgang Pauli. It is this work and Jung's association with Pauli which brought to the fore certain considerations significantly related to the cryptic foreshadowings of these later theories, which we find also in the *Sermons*, particularly in the Seventh Sermon.

The Seventh Sermon declares that "man is a portal through which one enters from the outer world of the gods, demons and souls, into the inner world—from the greater world into the smaller world." The outer world of gods, demons and souls might be taken to mean the realm of projections and synchronistic experiences which attach themselves to the realm of sense perception, while the smaller world might in this case describe the interior, psychic and psychoid regions of the unconscious of the individual. It is in this relationship of the seemingly exterior and the seemingly interior, of the greater world and the smaller world, that the momentous implications of the synchronicity theory become gradually evident. How does a synchronistic phenomenon occur? By way of the coming into the foreground of an archetype, says Jung. The essential requirement for the occurrence of synchronistic phenomena is not a natural psychic gift, or some yogic exercise, or a great emotional exaltaton, (although any or all of these may be present as secondary agencies). It is rather the constellation of an archetype within an active situation of the psyche, wherein powerful, usually emotional, energies are able to move the unconscious, and with it the archetype, into the foreground of consciousness. The gods, demons and souls mentioned in our Sermon are such archetypes, reflected on the screen of the macrocosm of sense-perception. Within the human being as a portal or doorway, these archetypal forces and images meet their corresponding aspects from within the microcosm of the interior of the psyche. Inner eternity and outer eternity meet in man. The allusions to this remarkable phenomenon in Jung's formulation of the principle and theory of synchronicity are cryptic. In this formulation Jung makes the archetype appear far more physical, or at least potentially physical, than we would be wont to assume from reading some of his other writings. Why does a synchronistic phenomenon partake of both a physical and a psychic aspect? Because it is arranged by an archetype, and archetypes themselves are not purely psychic (of the nature of the psyche, the stuff of dreams) but rather psychophysical, or psychoid (only partly psychic)—so says Jung once again. The unexpected, and therefore dramatically impressive parallelism of psychic and physical events is due to a characteristic of the archetype, which Jung calls *transgressivity*. Thus an archetype is capable of manifesting in a dual fashion, appearing internally as a psychic image and externally as a physical event, at times even as a physical object. In spite of this split, there is nevertheless always an underlying unity between the dualities or antinomies of the archetype; indeed, on this unity depends the all-essential experience of meaning, which is the distinguishing mark, if not actually the purpose, of the synchronistic event. Says Aniela Jaffe:

> As we know, a thing becomes conscious only when it becomes distinct from another thing. Consequently synchronistic phenomena, in which parallel psychic and physical events are distinct from each other yet are connected by their equivalence and thus form a meaningful whole, must be regarded as the coming-to-consciousness of an archetype. In general, coming-to-consciousness is an intrapsychic process: the characteristic distinction of one thing from another takes place in the thoughts, dreams, and intuitions of an individual. It is different with synchronistic phenomena. Here the antinomies and

parallelisms, the various facets of the archetype that is coming
to consciousness, are torn asunder. They manifest themselves,
psychically and nonpsychically, at different times and in different places.....This nascent coming-to-consciousness is so
thoroughly peculiar and puzzling that our reason struggles
against recognizing the conformity of events which belong
together. Yet in the border territories of the psyche, that is to
say, wherever the unconscious intervenes, we can no longer
count upon the clear and logical connections which are man-
datory in the world of consciousness.[40]

The archetype then, when manifesting in a synchronistic
phenomenon, is truly awesome if not outright miraculous—an
uncanny dweller on the threshold. At once psychical and
physical, it might be likened to the two-faced Roman god Janus.
The two faces of the archetype are joined in the common head of
meaning, which is the chief characteristic of human individuation.

Far-reaching as this recognition might appear in itself, it is not
yet the greatest and most portentous of the insights that emerge
from the field of synchronicity. Jung's vision derived from these
considerations is hinted at in the following statement: "I am
inclined in fact to the view that synchronicity in the narrower
sense is only a special instance of general acausal
orderedness—that, namely, of the equivalence of psychic and
physical processes." ("Synchronicity," C.G. Jung's *Collected
Writings*, Vol. 8, par. 965.) It is undoubtedly too early to
perceive the great and joyous news (the real "Evangel") that
might come forth on the basis of these hints. Nevertheless, the
idea of a general principle of an acausal order underlying all
psychic as well as physical phenomena is perhaps one of the
most promising and exciting discoveries of our time. The small
indications given to us by Jung and by his collaborator,
Wolfgang Pauli, allow us a glimpse of a cosmic-psychological
orderedness without divisions. The abiding predicament of the
oppositional dichotomy of body and mind, of matter and spirit,
even of nature and supernature might conceivably find their
resolution in such a proposition. The dual forces—which were
for so long, and no doubt understandably, represented by the
greatest thinkers and most exalted mystics as essential and irreconcilable—might thus reveal themselves as but equivalencies
rooted in the same acausal orderedness and manifesting an iden-

tical content of meaning. The *psyche* that animates and the *physis* that is animated may both be but two glorious pawns on a numinous chessboard of transcendental, self-subsistent meaning, moved to and fro by powers unnamed and unknowable that reside in a Pleromic state of the fullness of being. If indeed there is an a priori orderedness embracing both poles of universal being and manifesting an acausal connection of meaning between these poles, then we might perhaps even have to revise the sad truism of the *Sermons*, which declares that in us the Pleroma is rent in twain. The seamless garment of deity, so long the plaything of the gambling minions of the demiurge, might be restored, the wholeness of the Pleroma reestablished. Like Isis and Thoth who patiently gathered the disjointed members of their Lord Osiris and magically brought them together in the body of a reunited godhead, so Jung and other pioneers in the mysteries of synchronicity might win the aeonial battle against the forces of dispersion and fragmentation that afflict life in this lower aeon. Man, the portal, the doorway in whose meaning the archetypes of microcosm and macrocosm meet and celebrate their long-sought reunion, could truly become the alchemist, the magician, the priest of a gnosis that would bring realization never before experienced and seldom even envisioned in the fondest dreams of the seers. While the contributions of Jung to the spiritual progress of the human race are more than numerous, this particular contribution could prove to be the most portentous of all. Lest we be accused of rhapsodizing about phantasies motivated by mere wishes, we might contemplate the following statement by the aforementioned Nobel laureate in physics, Wolfgang Pauli:

> Although in physics there is no talk of "self-reproducing archetypes" but of "statistical natural laws with primary probabilities," both formulations meet in the tendency to expand the old, narrower idea of "causality" (determinism) into a more general form of "connections" in nature. The psychophysical problem (i.e., of synchronistic phenomena) also points in this direction. This approach permits me to expect that the concepts of the unconscious will not go on developing within the narrow frame of their therapeutic applications, but that their merging with the general current of science in investigating the phenomena of life is of paramount importance for them.[41]

As yet the truly epochal significance of the principle of synchronicity is evident only to the very few. Western thought, imbued with the conviction of the absolute validity of causation for many centuries, finds it well-nigh impossible to give up the principle of causality for acausal connections. Still, parallelisms of psychic and physical events continue to occur, according to their mysterious ever-recurring patterns. The physical sciences as well as psychology are increasingly pushing forward into regions that are beyond the ordinary range of direct observation and of conventional logic. From the vastness of macrocosmic space and from the minute infinity of microcosmic atoms and subatomic structures, there arises the vision of an autonomous order behind the physical phenomena. In the psychological macrocosm of projections as well as in the corresponding microcosm of psychoid archetypal forces, we find revealed a reality behind the phenomena of the psyche analogous to that revealed in the realm of physics. As Jung stated in *Aion*:

> Sooner or later nuclear physics and the psychology of the unconscious will draw closer together as both of them, independently of one another and from opposite directions, push forward into transcendental territory, the one with the concept of the atom, the other with that of the archetype.[42]

It is not given to us to perceive the future development of the theory and the principle of synchronicity. It is fairly apparent, however, that the existence of synchronistic phenomena gives us powerful indications of a possible psychophysical unity underlying the traditionally separate categories of being, which were named matter and spirit, or body and mind. Jung gave us a clear and prophetic indication of a new and unitary model of reality, in which causal and acausal connections are reconciled along with spirit and matter:

> Since psyche and matter are contained in one and the same world, and moreover are in continuous contact with one another and ultimately rest on irrepresentable, transcendental factors, it is not only possible but fairly probable, even, that psyche and matter are two different aspects of one and the same thing.[43]

The long-lost unity of the world is thus gradually brought within the reach of humanity. The disunion and the dichotomies of contemporary living, the fragmentation of the once valid but no longer viable reality-models may be on the verge of a unitary synthesis. The significance of the synchronicity principle thus can be seen to extend far beyond psychology and physics; it may in fact herald the dawn of a creative and unitive answer to one of the greatest philosophical and religious questions ever posed by the human mind.

Even as Jung intimates in the Seventh Sermon that the two eternities might be reconciled and later presents us with the implications of his principle of synchronicity, so he also draws our attention in the same Sermon to the greatest and most ancient predicament of the spiritual life: man's relationship to God, the great question which still remains. The Sermon gives expression to this in the lyrically exquisite sentence: "In immeasurable distance there glimmers a solitary star on the highest point of heaven. This is the only God of this lonely one. This is his world, his Pleroma, his divinity." And later, after an allusion to the Abraxas-like creative and destructive role of the human being, the teacher continues with the description of the relationship of God and man: "This star is man's God and goal. It is his guiding divinity: in it man finds repose. To it goes the long journey of the soul after death; in it shine all things which otherwise might keep man from the greater world with the brilliance of a great light".

The idea of a personal God is a great stumbling block for many contemporary persons, who approach Jung. The one-sidedness of the overwhelming mass of Judeo-Christian-Islamic religion, with its rigid interpretation of the concept of the monotheistic deity ruling man and his world, has created an abiding suspicion in many minds against the very idea of "God." The disgust of numerous highly intelligent and creative persons in our culture with the Semitic god-concept has led these same people into a condition where they have become suspicious of and antagonistic toward religion in all its recognizable forms. As against these attitudes, Jung assumed a most unusual position. Jung held that there is no such thing as a really irreligious person, that the professed atheist is simply one who does not acknowledge an important realm of his or her unconscious. Those who are consciously irreligious have strong unconscious concerns with religious matters, since the unconscious inevitably stands in a compensatory relationship to the conscious. The confirmed doubter in his unconscious is more of a believer than he likes to admit; a conscious agnostic attitude evokes responses of a truly Gnostic character from the unconscious. Heresy hunters and fanatical fighters against evil are usually persons whose unconscious harbors great doubts and antagonisms against their accepted creed. Similarly, dreams and fantasies of the atheist usually reveal religious images and transcendental manifestations. Yet with all of these views Jung combined once again an attitude which may be described as profoundly Gnostic in the classical sense. Jung said in essence that human beings have a religious need, but that this need is not for religious *belief* but rather for religious *experience*. Religious experience is a psychic event which tends toward the integration of the soul, and thus represents the functioning of the psyche as a whole. Religion is the acknowledgment of the higher realities that consciousness fails to recognize, and if carried to its full psychological fruition, it brings about the inner unity and wholeness of the human being. This objective—which Jung's spiritual forebears in the early Christian centuries called *Gnosis*—is never accomplished by beliefs in ideas but only by realization in the form of experience.

It is evident from these considerations that when Jung spoke of God in a positive sense he did not speak of an idea. Jung's God was not thought, believed in or contrived, nor apprehended or explained by ideas: his God was experienced. Only what man experiences of the divine is alive: what he believes about it is dead.

In lieu of a God to believe in, Jung presented us with an existential reality we may experience. He called this reality the *God-image (imago Dei)* and at times also the *God-symbol*. Like the Gnostics of old, Jung rejected the "god of faith" as a metaphorical and intellectual representation of God, and chose the reality of an image or symbol of abiding psychological vitality. Instead of the much-abused concept of faith, Jung advocated the use of the power of the imagination as a means to *Gnosis*, or the knowledge of God. Imagination, the great magical faculty extolled by Paracelsus, Albertus Magnus and numerous representatives of the alternative-reality tradition, was viewed by Jung as an actualization of the contents of the unconscious. The individual who uses the power of the imagination participates in the life of the images (fantasies) of the unconscious, but at the same time continues to employ certain conscious controls. The active imagination, or active participation in imagination, requires that the content of the unconscious brought into the light be taken absolutely seriously, while at the same time realizing that the images made to rise in this fashion are not true in the conventional sense of truth but are symbolic expressions of the underlying movements of the psyche. In magic, alchemy and related Gnostic disciplines, the concept of *imaginatio* has always served as the most important key to the success of esoteric workings. The symbolism employed in alchemy has been amply documented psychologically by Jung himself.

An analogous symbolic process was utilized in the practice of ceremonial magic—a symbolic system of transformation which the Middle Ages inherited from the theurgists and goetic practitioners of classical antiquity and which ultimately goes back to ancient shamanistic origins. The magician, standing in a clearly drawn circle of protection, evokes or invokes spiritual entities into an area of manifestation outside the circle and converses with them in accordance with definite formulae. The circle stands for the protection of consciousness, which will not permit the ego to become overwhelmed by the forces of the unconscious made to appear in the area of manifestation by way of the magical imagination. Unlike trance conditions, in magical evocations and invocations the magician never relinquishes contact with consciousness and utilizes the available controls of the conscious will. Never is the mind of the magician permitted to fall under the spell of the manifesting spirits, but maintaining his own conscious sovereignty, he discourses from a position of conscious power with the entities he has conjured. Such exercises of the imagination, archaic though they may appear from a contemporary point of view, have been known to widen the personality, reduce the dominating force of the unconscious, and to bring about generally beneficial modifications of the ego. Alchemical and magical operations are some of the clearest examples of the systematized projections of psychic content; they are powerful psychic happenings whereby the imagination activates and projects important aspects of the psyche. It must be remembered that ceremonial magic once included the practice of *theurgy*, which translates as the working of divinities, or the bringing into manifestation of the gods. Theurgists, such as Iamblichus, Proclus and many others, were wont to make the gods of their religions appear before their eyes in visible form by way of their trained magical imagination. When Jung brought forward the terms *god-image* and *God-symbol*, he was following once again in the footsteps of the ageless magico-mystical tradition, to which he gave modern psychological formulations.

According to Jung, all persons are in reality theurgists of sorts, for they all make God-images for themselves through their imagination. The God-image thus created is not the result of perceiving or contacting someone or something external to the human being, but rather it may be said to be the expression of a psychic fact, the imaginative formulation of a spiritual actuality which the mind has to exteriorize in order to grasp. The conventional-minded religionist or occultist would, of course, revolt against this view. Jung has been repeatedly accused by persons in both of these camps of the charge of "psychologism." Yet, the fair-minded among his critics were ever bound to admit that his point of view held undeniable practical advantages in existential and empirical terms. In order to dispel some of the more justified misgivings, we may mention at least two important factors. First, we must be aware that Jung does not imply that the God-image arising in the psyche is the creation of personal whim. Such an image comes into being in a realm far beyond the caprice of any individual or even any human collectivity. God-images are not made, they become. The second consideration is that Jung did not intend to limit the extent of any spiritual principle by declaring it *psychic*. When he called the God-image a *psychic fact,* he was not saying that it is *merely* or only psychic. When he was asked whether with his alleged psychologisms he has deified the psyche, he very gravely replied that he had done no such thing, but that the creator himself had deified it. It is not to be supposed that the conscious, or even the unconscious, of the individual creates God; it may be stated, however, that certain suprapersonal functions of the psyche are creating the God-image. Whenever people consciously contrive to create God-images for others to follow, they are, in fact, guilty of the worst sort of idolatry. In contemporary times such graven images tend to appear more often than not in secular and often political guise. Some examples are the welfare of the race and nation (as in German National Socialism or the interests of the proletariat, the achievement of the classless society (in Marxism). The true God-image—as distinct from such substitute God-images—is never the outcome of a conscious act of will. Humans can experience the God-image; they cannot determine the form in which it will manifest or the course it may take.

What, or who, is God from the point of view of Jung? The Seventh Sermon defines God as a star which glimmers in immeasurable distance above, but nevertheless represents the individual's goal, guidance, repose and even the destination of his journey after physical death. In his scientific writings Jung has represented this same God or God-image as an autonomous complex of great strength and intensity which is ultimately the expression of the intensity and strength of life itself. The power of this God-image is far greater than that of the conscious, personal will, for it, unlike the will, partakes of the objective psyche or collective unconscious, which has access to the boundless collective resources of being. As the Seventh Sermon states: "This is his world, his Pleroma, his divinity." Rooted in the fullness of being, within the objective psyche, the God-image partakes of what conventional religion has so often defined as omnipotence. It is here that the next passage of the Sermon assumes a significant meaning: "To this One, man ought to pray. Such a prayer increases the light of the star. Such a prayer builds a bridge over death. It increases the life of the microcosm; when the outer world grows cold, this star still shines." It is an undeniable truism of contemporary life that the more individuals rely on themselves as egos, instead of on a power that transcends their personal selfhood, the more they are condemned to misery and alienation. No human ego is strong enough, wise enough and good enough to live life by its own lights alone. The reality of God, not as an idea but as an experience, represents the most potent solution to the predicament brought about by the insufficiency of the human ego. These are curious words to be written in the wake of the declaration that God is an autonomous complex. Few persons today take literally the metaphor that God is in heaven, but even fewer contemplate that God might be in the soul. Jung, quite logically, said just that, but virtually in the same breath he also affirmed that in experiencing God the human being partakes of the divine creative power. Rightfully may one ask, how can this be?

The answer to the apparent dilemma lies in the contention that psychic or soul reality is indeed real. We need to disabuse ourselves of the fateful notion, implanted into our culture primarily by non-Gnostic Christianity, that everything psychic is "merely" psychic and therefore inferior. Whatever exists in the psyche *exists,* and this psychic existence is just as real as physical reality. This being the case, the God-image is no less potent for existing within us rather than outside us. The more we trust it, rely on it, submit to its wisdom—while maintaining our conscious judgment, which rightly has been called God-given—the more we will partake of the effortless creativity of the objective psyche. "My yoke is easy, and my burden light," speaks the God-image in the soul. When the human ego is capable of relinquishing its self-conscious arrogance—the curse of the archons, as the ancient Gnostics might have called it—the splendor of the suprapersonal resources of the God-image begin to irradiate its sphere of activity. A self-conscious creativity is not creativity at all, while a creativity of self-surrender partakes of the spark of the ultimate fullness of all being. The arrogance of the alienated ego resents reliance on the God-image and continues to harp on its own so-called creativity and personal artistic or similar calling. Nevertheless, if the creative power is to manifest according to its eternally ordained patterns, the lesser must become a junior partner to the greater, and man must learn how to humble himself before that existence which has been called God. It is of the self-consciousness of the ego that it was written in the New Testament: "It is a fearful thing to fall into the hands of the living God."

The matter of prayer, as expressed in the previously quoted passage from the Seventh Sermon, brings this issue into even clearer focus. As the human ego depends on God for creativity, so God, the paradigm of being, or the God-image, depends on the ego for its nourishment in the form of trust, confidence and the acceptance of archetypal intentionality. God's dependence on man, and man's dependence on God are necessary corollaries. "Such a prayer increases the light of the star," says our Sermon. In one of his early works, *Psychological Types,* Jung quoted with much approval the noted mystical verses of Angelus Silesius, which reflect the same psychological reality as the one expressed in the Sermon:

> I know that without me
> God can no moment live;
> Were I to die, then He
> no longer could survive.
>
> I am as great as God,
> And He is small like me;
> He cannot be above
> Nor I below Him be.
>
> In me God is a fire
> And I in Him its glow;
> In common is our life,
> Apart we cannot grow.
>
> He is God and man to me,
> To Him I am both indeed;
> His thirst I satisfy,
> He helps me in my need.
>
> God is such as He is,
> I am what I must be;
> If you know one, in truth
> You know both Him and me.
>
> I am the vine, which He
> Doth plant and cherish most;
> The fruit which grows from me
> Is God, the Holy Ghost.[44]

While the doctrine of man's dependence on God has been stated with great frequency in religious preachments and teachings, the necessary corollary, i.e. God's dependence on the human soul, has been far less frequently expressed. This idea has been called the relativity of God, and in it Jung has revived important Gnostic motifs, as well as linked his own realizations with those of several representatives of the alternative reality tradition. The light of the divine star is increased by the prayer of the human being precisely because this star is not outside him but resides within him. The doctrine of the relativity of God rests, not on theological belief or philosophical speculation, but on experience. It goes almost without saying that the kind of prayer alluded to in the Seventh Sermon is not the usual human petition to God for favors. Mystical religion in the West, in accordance with the ancient Gnosis, has always recognized a form of prayer that was far beyond the mere asking of God for benefits. This view has ever held that prayer in its purest form is the human soul's delight in its experience of a full communion with Deity itself. Rather than asking anything of God, such a prayer is the soul's joyous giving of itself wholly and unreservedly to God. It is the breaking down of the last barriers between its separate existence and the allness of the Godhead—the finding of its total unity with the inmost self of all. Jung once defined God as a mighty activity within one's own soul, which, unlike the absolute God who exists beyond all human experience, is a matter of immediate and vital concern at all times. Ralph Waldo Emerson, the American Transcendentalist philosopher, put it with unique directness when he wrote: "Man is weak to the extent that he looks outside himself for help. It is only as he throws himself unhesitatingly upon the God within himself that he learns his own power and works miracles. It is only when he throws overboard all other props and leans solely upon the God in him that he uncovers his real powers and finds the springs of success." These statements embody a very important principle, namely that what one does not use one will lose. This adage is well illustrated in the Gospels, in the parable of the talents. While the secularized contemporary person trusts only in his or her own conscious ego and the devout soul is praying to an outside power for help, the creative energies resident within both are atrophying. The cultivation of the relation between the outer ego and the indwelling capabilities of the objective psyche constitute the true *gnosis kardias,* science of the soul. The yearning of the ego to awaken and to enjoy communion with this divine immanence is the real prayer that increases the luminosity of the God-image, poetically represented as a star in the Sermon.

The Seventh Sermon makes two references to Abraxas also, which are interspersed, as it were, with the main theme. One of these statements reads: "In this world man is Abraxas, who gives birth to and devours his own world." At a later point in the Sermon we read: "There is nothing that can separate man from his own God, if man can only turn his gaze away from the fiery spectacle of Abraxas." Abraxas, as noted earlier in our commentaries, is the fiery force which acts as the primeval union of the opposites at the foundation of psychic life. As Abraxas appears in classical Gnosticism as a cosmic ruler, placed into the seventh of the heavenly mansions, so the Abraxas symbol in the Sermons is that creative life of the psyche which forms and transforms the personal cosmos of the individual. It would appear that Jung throughout his works has shown us two functions of the spiritual nature of man, or, as he sometimes called it, of the "spirit." These are the power to create and the power to experience meaning. The former is what might be called the Abraxas power, if we are to utilize the terminology employed in the Sermons. The Abraxas power then in all likelihood is that part of the unconscious which has not yet attained to consciousness. In contrast with this, the power to experience meaning might be considered to be in that portion of the unconscious which is above consciousness. Jung purposely never used such terms as *subconscious* and *superconscious*, for he did not wish to attach a valuation to the idea of the unconscious. In his view the unconscious is as much below as it is above consciousness, and no value judgment should be attached to any of these attempted descriptions. At the same time a distinction should be made between the creative force which has not yet reached consciousness, which forever strives to break through into conscious awareness, and the element of meaning which is above consciousness, or is superior to it. It must be admitted that with all this, creativity remains somewhat of an enigma, even in Jung's teachings. About the only certainty that emerges from his various statements is that creativity is always in some manner connected with and dependent upon the unconscious, although the kind of connection and degree of dependence may vary.

Jungian textbooks frequently use an image to illustrate the nature of the individual's consciousness, that of an island emerging from the unconscious as if from an ocean that surrounds it. In the light of our present considerations, we might suggest this image might be viewed in such a way that the rising of the island from the ocean might be ascribed to two forces. The upward movement of the island is first caused by the force of Abraxas, which drives the landmass upward from below, and secondly by a gravitational force which draws from above, that of the shining star of divine meaning as symbolized in the God-image. The former gives natural energy or raw psychological force, while the second bestows guidance, confidence and ultimate significance. Thus, speaking figuratively, we might see the human being functioning between the natural ground of his being which has not yet attained consciousness and the celestial crown of his being which is already above consciousness. These two poles of the psyche (which remind one of the two extremities of the Kabbalistic Tree of Life, i.e. Malkuth, the lowest *sephira* and Kether, the highest) both affect consciousness, but in different ways; one creates and re-creates, the other sanctifies with meaning. Perhaps they might be called the naturalistic psyche and the spiritual psyche, which are interdependent yet different in quality. The subpersonal and the suprapersonal, nature and supernature, are destined to achieve a cooperative union, but this union can only be effected when they are not in a state of rivalry with each other. In one of his statements, Jung referred to a danger whereby spirit might turn man against life in a state of extreme sublimation of the psyche—an infatuation which would sacrifice all life to spirit, or would, in our terms, sacrifice Abraxas to the star:

> Life is the criterion of the spirit's truth. A spirit that carries man beyond the bare possibility of life and seeks fulfillment only in itself is a false spirit.... Life and spirit are two forces or necessities, and man is placed between them. Spirit endows his life with meaning and the possibility of large developments. But life is indispensable to spirit, for the truth of the spirit is nothing if it cannot live.[45]

At the other extreme, and encountered with perhaps far greater frequency, we find the possibility against which the Seventh Sermon warns us, namely, that the fiery spectacle of

Abraxas diverts the attention of the psyche from the starlight of meaning and spiritual guidance. The fiery spectacle mentioned can take many forms, all of which are in the nature of a danger to the meaning of the soul. The creative power of Abraxas is resident in innumerable pursuits and facets of activity and living, each of which can become an influence diverting the psyche from the vision of the star. Not only the ordinary features of so-called worldliness, materialism, sensuality, attachment to personalistic and egotistical motives and endeavors, but many more subtle influences can be counted in this category. We shall give one of the manifestations of the fiery spectacle a somewhat more extensive treatment because of the deceptive subtlety of this particular trap, which, just because of these qualities, is the subject of some ill-founded criticism directed against Jung. This is the widely held attitude of a certain spiritually false optimism. In a sense, this false optimism is rooted in the Western religious heritage with its Semitic background, which in a rather primitive manner extols the virtues of physical life and the joys of a world which it regards as God's and therefore good. Jung pointed out the importance of life, too, but in a much more total way, as consciousness and as the opportunity for the acquisition of additional meaning and transformation.

Like the Gnostics of old before him, so Jung also was accused of being gloomy and pessimistic in his outlook. Perhaps the best illustration of his attitude is found in the dream of a woman patient, mentioned earlier, who saw herself submerged in a pit filled with a dangerous substance and who then perceived Jung pushing her right down into the pit with the words, "Not out but through!" It has been reported that whenever Jung discussed this particular dream in public or before friends, he showed visible enjoyment, delighting in the fact that such a clear recognition of his essential attitude should have emerged from the dream of his patient. To Jung, life has always two movements: one upward, the other downward. To the Pollyanna optimism of the spiritual adolescents, there is only one direction or motion, and this is up. Whether we look to the so-called "born again" Christianity with its once-popular slogan "one way," or to the nineteenth-and early twentiety-century New Thought schools with their near-obsession with the concept of evolution and the power of positive thinking, this false optimism seems to be prominently represented. It is to be doubted whether genuine spiritual growth is possible under such circumstances. Suffering accepted, darkness recognized and sorrow understood are great assets to the authentic life of the spirit. Composure, serenity, and authentic psychic strength all arise from the recognition and acceptance of the reality of evil and darkness and not from their denial due to false optimism. Heedless cheerfulness, on the other hand, almost inevitably changes eventually into sorrow and discontent, for it denies the reality of one important aspect of life. His last amanuensis, Aniela Jaffe, writes of Jung in this regard:

> Jung followed the downward movement of life if it was in keeping with the intrinsic truth of the moment. Yet he could experience joy whenever it came his way as few were able to, and wholeheartedly joined in the joy of others. Only when one got to know him better, over the years, did one discover that he...was never without the canker of a secret care, for he knew the play of life's pendulum, the inevitable compensation of "high" by "low." Have you "suffered a success?" he would ask at a suitable moment, half mocking, half amused. He saw where it would end.[46]

Continuing her reminiscences about this side of the personality of Jung, Aniela Jaffe continues:

> Any kind of "joyful Christianity" or sentimental prettification exasperated Jung to the limit. Never shall I forget his outburst of scorn and anger over a card announcing the birth of a child, garnished with the customary embellishments. The sorrows of life, the wretchedness of the times, were alive and present for him every moment as realities that had to be endured. This open-eyed alertness he expected also of others.[47]

It is precisely this "open-eyed alertness" that has been anathema to those, who, as the Gnostics might have expressed it, are under the spell of the demiurge. For is it not to the advantage of these intermediate powers—who, like malicious cosmic-psychological complexes, vampirize the misplaced optimism and enthusiasm of souls—that the harsh realities of being should be igorned? Has it not ever been the custom of the demiurge, so asks the Gnostic, to confine humans in a fool's paradise where childish naivete masquerades as childlike innocence and confidence?

It is therefore absolutely understandable why the Seventh Sermon considers it necessary that man should turn his gaze away from the fiery spectacle of Abraxas in order not to be separated from the guidance of the indwelling star. All sorts of objections may be raised against this view, but none will stand up to the valid scrutiny of an informed comparison with the utterances of the seers and wise men of history. The Buddha—who declared that the child is wise when it weeps upon its entry into the world—the Gnostics, the Neo-Platonists, the greatest of Christian mystics and many more, all knew that the naturalistic psyche, although it may serve to supply the creative energy of life, must not be allowed to usurp the meaning-bestowing function and the guiding action of the spirit.

The contrast between the human ego and the spiritual God-image is poetically brought to our attention by Jung in the final portion of the Seventh Sermon: "Man here, God there. Weakness and insignificance here, eternal creative power there. Here is but darkness and damp cold. There all is sunshine." God as a psychological fact is not the same as God as an adjunct of the ego. Whether theologically defined or psychologically intimated, God is both near and far from us at the same time. *"Nah ist und schwer zu fassen der Gott,"* near but difficult to grasp is God, said the German poet Hölderlin. Although within the reach of our own spiritual experience, the God-image, along with other numinous powers of the psyche, belongs to that mysterious category of being which we may experience but with which we may not directly identify ourselves save at very great peril. The experience of the indwelling Godhead, therefore, is a process whose significance transcends personality and all the purposes of the ego. As Jung very clearly stated in his most Gnostic book *Answer to Job*, from these recognitions it is but a short step to the view that in man God is in fact accomplishing his own transformation. The vicissitudes of life, the anguish of alienation, the sorrows and the joys of the transformative journey are in the last resort nothing less that the manifestations of the growth of God. The pattern of the emerging of Deity is impressed upon the mandala of our own lives, and the ways in which we move within this, our own magic circle, are in turn meaningful and useful for the accomplishment of wholeness on the part of God. Our human experience is related to what is going on in God; our weakness is also God's weakness and our victories tend to bring the imperfect Godhead closer to its own Pleroma, or ultimate fullness of Being. While the final portion of the Seventh Sermon appears to affirm the self separating man and God, in other works, including *Answer to Job*, the interrelatedness of the two are indicated. To Jung, God is never a theological or philosophical postulate, but a psychological reality; not an essence, but an experience. Thus it is only natural that this God may be experienced as remote and at the same time be also intimately involved both as subject and object in human transformation. Once again, we are dealing with the principle of the opposites which converge in the experience of the psyche.

In his book *Aion* Jung gave a psychological paraphrase of a statement written originally by St. Ignatius Loyola, founder of the Jesuit Order. The Jungian version of the statement is as follows:

> Man's consciousness was created to the end that it may (1) recognize its descent from a higher unity; (2) pay due and careful regard to this source; (3) execute its commands intelligently and responsibly; and (4) thereby afford the psyche as a whole the optimum degree of life and development.[48]

In this statement is summed up what in certain ways might be considered the quintessence of the relationship of the human psyche and the starlike God-image that overshadows it. Recognizing our descent from and dependence upon a higher unity we are aware of the star which, like the legendary star of Bethlehem, shines down upon our own nascent divinity. All the other steps of the process of individuation, as outlined in the above statement, follow from this recognition. The star which is described as man's God and goal is the bright radiance of the divine soul or God-image shining in the innermost recesses of individuating human minds and rising with the individuated ego, as it comes forth, from the dark night of its immersion in aeonial unconsciousness and incomprehension. High above the damp and dark cold of alienation and of personalistic concerns shines the guiding star of human life. To it goes our long journey, perhaps not only after death but during our lives as well. Out of our travails and our searching, we come, in the end, to a vision where the dynamic simplicity of ultimate meaning naturally unites the lowest with the highest, and where all human knowledge is replaced with *Gnosis*. Nothing remains for us but to marvel at the sublime. Everything is meaningful; everything is miraculously right in its own meaning; and this rightness is as tenderly comforting as the smallest lightbeam of the most distant star of the heavens, yet as powerful as the thundering chariot of Abraxas himself.

If we can experience a measure of this rightness which flows from the essence of ultimate meaning, we will gradually come to a life of trust and deep confidence in the wisdom of psychic events and purposes occurring beyond consciousness. We will find that our pilgrimage through the spaces of mind and spirit is taking us to the fullness of being and to the realization that in darkness and in light, in joy and in sorrow, in sunshine and in damp cold, still all is well. And as in celebration of this essential rightness where both heaven and earth unite in joyous recognition, the soul's wordless voice rises to exclaim:

> O star, Who shinest, serene, in the crystal ether of heaven
> Who like a fish swimmest, bright, in an ocean of peace,
> Let me journey, serene, and swift, pressing breast against windstorm
> Guided, and nourished and blessed with the gift of Thyself.[49]

Epilogue

The Once and Future Gnosis

Contemplating the mysterious panorama of the *Seven Sermons*, one is reminded of a saying of the philosopher Bacon: "Animus ad amplitudinem Mysteriorum pro modulo suo dilatetur; non Mysteria ad angustias animi constringantur." (Let the mind, so far as it can, be open to the fullness of the mysteries; let not the mysteries be constrained to fit the narrower confines of the mind.) It is, perhaps, more than befitting that Jung should close the *Sermons* with an incomprehensible anagram, never to be deciphered by any reader. It may well be that this was his way of conveying a quality of mysterious infinitude, of a curiously suggestive open-endedness to this treatise. No matter how open our minds may fancy themselves to be to the mysteries contained in the *Sermons*, these same mysteries can never be contained by the confines of the conscious mind. Like all genuine manifestations of the *Gnosis*, the contents of the *Sermons* may be likened to the ocean, wherein a child can cool his feet in the shallows, while at the same time bold navigators may attempt to explore its expanse, and skilled deep-sea divers may plunge into its watery depth in search of sunken treasure.

Contrary to the assertions of many orthodox critics, Gnosticism was never guilty of seeking to subject the mystery to the comprehension of the human ego, and of diverting the transcendental power of the greater for the service and aggrandizement of the lesser. The Gnosis of old was always a *Gnosis kardias*, a knowledge of the heart, rather than the ego-knowledge of the head. Similarly, Jung's present-day approach to the Gnosis was never content with anything short of a knowledge of the heart when it came to the "mysterium tremendum et fascinans" (the awesome and bewitching mystery) of the unconscious. Not for him the simplistic, conscious approach of the growth psychologies, the humanistic and holistic trends which in more recent times so frequently avail themselves of Jung's name and of his concepts. These inhabitants of the spiritual halfway houses toward Gnosis overemphasize personalistic feelings and the expansion of consciousness, inward turned to what Goethe would have called the realm of the mothers, away from the practical realities of the dull, everyday world. Some of this school claim that the way to enlightenment consists in holding dialogues with the archetypes, fantasy figures of the objective psyche, surrounding yourself with the personified projections of your mind in the form of "higher selves" and "inner guides." Not so, says the voice of the once and future Gnosis, for this is precisely what your mother, Sophia, did long ago. Sophia, so Valentinus informs us, in her hubris lusted for the impossible task of personally comprehending the fathomless Abyss. Thus she fell into the dark anguish and pain, imprisoned by the elements of earth, water, fire, and air, which arose as projected manifestations of her grief, fear, bewilderment, and ignorance, and she gave birth to monstrous children of arrogance, who became rulers and lords of limitation of her very consciousness. The personal mind is no fit vehicle for the forces of the vast and mighty mysteries of eternity. To adopt a facile attitude toward the dreadful darkness of the depths of being can yield no satisfactory result. It would be both fatal and regrettable if present-day psychology committed the ancient error of philosophy and attempted to trivialize the ineffable greatness. Similarly, the "new age" optimism and superficiality of those who reduce the dark mysteries of Jung's Gnosis to the shallow level of their own limitations are apt to make people into the victims of the very unconscious they tend to treat so lightly. Those who naively wish to use the archetypes for their personalistic ends will be made subject to their cruel tyranny.

The *Seven Sermons to the Dead* serves as a true example of the Gnostic principle which declares that the mysteries cannot be made to fit the limited scope of the personal mind. The secret of the *Sermons* is not in the least diminished by the kind of exegesis we have attempted in the foregoing. Nay, it may even be said that such attempts can only deepen the mystery and render the secret more profound. One of Jung's most creative disciples, Marie-Louise von Franz, pointed out (in her splendid work, *C.G. Jung: His Myth in Our Time*) that Jung recognized himself as being deeply related to the figure of Merlin, the archetypal magician of the Arthurian and Grail mythos. In the French versions of the Grail Saga as referred to by Jung, Merlin dictated to his guardian, the priest Blaise, the story of the Holy Grail, and while so doing he instructed the scribe: "The Apostles write nothing concerning Our Lord that they have not seen or heard for themselves; thou too must write nothing about me except what thou hast heard from me. *And because I am dark and always be, let the book also be dark and mysterious in those places where I will not show myself.*"[50] The inscrutable profundity of the Sermons is thus by implication revealed, according to Merlin's example, to be none other than the dark mystery of Jung himself.

Who or what Jung truly was may indeed remain a secret forever. He was a figure not unlike the magical and alchemical god Mercury, who appears in the old texts as embodied in wind, ocean, in the flight of the eagle, and in heroic humanity as a mobile, shape-shifting spirit pervading all things. Like Taliesin, the Welsh magician and bard who joined Merlin in his forest-hideway, Jung could have exclaimed also:

> I am the wind that blows upon the sea;
> I am the ocean wave;
> I am the murmur of the surges;
> I am seven battalions;
> I am a strong bull;
> I am an eagle on a rock;
> I am a ray of the sun;
> I am the most beautiful of herbs;
> I am a courageous wild boar;
> I am a salmon in the water;
> I am a lake upon the plain;
> I am a cunning artist;
> I am a gigantic, sword-wielding champion;
> I can shift my shape like a god.[51]

Duplicating in some ways Taliesin's poetry, Jung himself exclaimed when describing his life at Bollingen: "At times I feel as if I am spread out over the landscape and inside things, and am myself living in every tree, in the plashing of the waves, in the clouds and the animals that come and go, in the procession of the seasons...Here...in space for the spaceless kingdom of...the psyche's hinterland."[52]

This mystery, the psyche's hinterland, is Jung's true kingdom, and it is also the kingdom where the *Seven Sermons to the Dead* originate and where their true meaning will ever repose in the shadows. Like Merlin's celebrated cry, Jung's Gnostic voice will continue to be heard in the great forests of the mind of humanity, echoing from rock to rock and from tree to tree. The words he wrote about his mythological hero, Merlin, remain true when applied to himself and to his Gnosis:

> Men still hear his cries, so the legend runs, but they cannot understand or interpret them. ...Parsifal is a Christian hero, and Merlin...is his dark brother. In the twelfth century, when the legend arose, there were as yet no premises by which his intrinsic meaning could be understood. Hence he ended in exile, and hence "le cri de Merlin" which still sounded from the forest after his death.... His story is not yet finished, and he still walks abroad. It might be said that the secret of Merlin was carried on by alchemy, primarily in the figure of Mercurius. Then Merlin was taken up again in my psychology of the unconscious and—remains uncomprehended to this day![53]

The available corpus of Jung's contribution to the spirit of our culture is here for all to see. His writings are unique. They speak louder than any exposition or commentary of lesser minds, declaring wisdom, sanity, and a balanced and creative approach to human life. At the same time, like all mystic and Gnostic scriptures, they conceal vastly more than they reveal. The cry of Merlin issues forth from them, and the growing, transforming soul discovers and understands in this cry only what it is able to grasp as the result of its own interior growth. Unchanged by time, unaffected by criticism, unsoiled by the mud flung at it by the rationalist's fury or by the dogmatism of the orthodox, Jung's ideas stand today, as they did when first uttered by him, like majestic and ever unmovable rocks in a stormy sea.

He confronted Freudian reductionism, with its dreary preoccupation with infantile functions and sexual repression. He challenged political ideologies of both left and right which arrogated to themselves permission to dwarf the individual within the Behemoth structures of state and government. His teachings brought the light of imagination, the renewing power of creativity, of romance and existential courage and joy to numberless weary and heart-hungry men and women seeking meaning. The impact of his message burst the constricting shell of the theologies which had lost their own former Gnosis, showed as lifeless the empty wranglings of academic philosophers, enmeshed in fruitless cerebrations over logical equations and linguistic analysis, and counterbalanced the triumphal march of soulless materialism disguised as science. Still, with all of this and much more to his outer credit, Jung continues to be involved in an inward mystery from which only his Merlin-like cry echoes forth in eerie cadences.

It has always been thus. When we observe within a historical perspective those whom the world calls great, we find two principal categories of persons. The first includes individuals who were regarded as great in their own lifetimes, but whose stature tends to steadily diminish after their death. This temporary greatness may be said to result from the fact that such persons lived and acted chiefly from the level of their conscious or temporal selves, and once this self passed out of sight, their greatness was destined to vanish along with it. On the other hand, those in the other category of human greatness seem to be placed ahead of us in time, as it were, rather than in the past. There have always been outstanding persons whose greatness became increasingly clear with the passage of time; whose stature increased after their physical passing from history. Though time has confined them to exile in the magic forest of death, as the enchantress Morgan did to Merlin, the utterance of their word from the shadows becomes perhaps mightier than it had been when proceeding from the daylight. The truly great spirits loom larger on the scene of history after the passing of the years than in their own lifetimes. This is exactly what has happened and is happening to Carl Gustav Jung. Not only do his books appear increasingly on the shelves and in the hands of the creative elite of the world; not only are the words which he introduced into the contemporary idiom of Western languages now part of the vocabulary of countless people in our culture; but in addition to these—and many other clear facts testifying to the depth and extent of his impact—there is a mysterious, indefinable greatness of the man which is sensed only by those whom the ancient Gnostics would have called *pneumatikoi*, men and women of the spirit. Laurens van der Post, one of Jung's most pneumatic biographers, exclaims with almost helpless amazement: "But what this greatness consists of is almost impossible to define. I myself cannot attempt to do so. . . . Even if I could, I do not believe I would."[54]

It is impossible from the present writer's point of view to regard this indefinable greatness of Jung in any other than Gnostic terms. The ineffable greatness of the Pleroma, the fullness of being, may be seen clearly present in souls such as Jung, who in a considerable measure restored that very fullness within themselves. The aeon of this world has become the Pleroma for such persons, as the Gnostic gospels have declared. That is why Jung must be regarded without doubt as the herald and pioneer of a new Gnosis and Gnosticism, which, in spite of its contemporary character, is yet organically connected to the Gnosis and Gnosticism of old. Jung was a cultured and educated man in the nineteenth century European academic sense. His background, education, and training all prepared him to become a physician and scholar within the bounds of the intellectual traditions of the differentiated and extraverted attitudes of consciousness which have characterized the scientific and philosophical disciplines of the West for centuries (indeed, in a manner of speaking, ever since the so-called Golden Age of Greek thought). In spite of this, Jung turned the most significant focus of his inquiry unto the spirit of the Alexandrian or Hellenistic phase of the ancient world. In contravention of the prevailing fashions and disciplines of Western intellectuals, he saw in the teachings of Gnosticism, Hermeticism and kindred arcane disciplines the forerunners and ancestors of his psychology.

It may be difficult to recall at the present time how nineteenth- and early twentieth-century Western thought tended to denigrate, not only Gnosticism, but the entire Hellenistic period of the spiritual history of antiquity. Mainstream scholarship

looked to classical Greek philosophy and science, as expressed
by Socrates, Plato and Aristotle, as the source and inspiration of
Western culture. It was generally accepted by the intellectual
world that the Gnosis of the Hellenistic period was a
phenomenon of decadence which contrasted sharply and
unfavorably with the intellectual knowledge sought by the
representatives of the earlier Greek spirit. Western intellectuals
for centuries had shown a decided preference for what they
called the clarity of the Golden Age of Greek philosophy over
the search for mystery and distrust for extraverted rationality
shown by Gnostics, Hermeticists and the like. The philosophers,
so students were taught in our universities, were to be com-
mended for overcoming and transmuting fantasy and myth by
exact logical conceptions and scientific thought, and the involvement of the Hellenistic spirit with imagination, myth, and ritual
was regarded as a reversion and retrogression symptomatic of a
disintegration of the healthy-mindedness of the classical
world—connected no doubt with the much-touted slogan of the
"decline and fall" of Rome and the ancient world in general.

As against this view, Jung recognized that in these despised
and supposedly decadent manifestations of spirituality could be
found transformative insights and inspirational wisdom which
are psychologically far more valuable than the logical and
rational clarity of Aristotle. Not that Jung ever renounced the
philosophical and scientific heritage of Western thought. Far
from it! He regarded this heritage as a rightful achievement of
the differentiated and extraverted ego of Western man which
should not be allowed to vanish. At the same time, he recognized
that man, whether Western or any other, does not live by the
solid fare of the differentiated ego alone, but that he must
address himself to the unconscious mystery within as well. The
Hellenistic period of the history of late antiquity was, according
to Jung, precisely such a phase of the development of the culture
when this internal task became once again imperative and
demanded urgent recognition. The Gnostics and their fellows
responded to this request of the psyche, even as Jung felt that he
must respond to a very similar emergency arising in the psyche
of the contemporary world. In his noted treatise *Modern Man in
Search of a Soul*, Jung analyzed and, with prophetic insight,

foretold the rebirth of the ancient Gnosis and of Gnosticism in our era:

> We must admit the fact, however difficult it is for us to understand, that something which previous ages have discarded should suddenly come to our attention. ...We can compare it only to the flowering of Gnostic thought in the first and second centuries after Christ. *The spiritual currents of the present have, in fact, a deep affinity with Gnosticism.* [Italics ours.] There is even a Gnostic church in France today, and I know of two schools in Germany which openly declare themselves Gnostic. The modern movement which is numerically most impressive is undoubtedly Theosophy, together with its continental sister, Anthroposophy; these are pure Gnosticism in Hindu dress. Compared with these movements the interest in scientific psychology is negligible. What is striking about Gnostic systems is that they are based exclusively upon the manifestations of the unconscious, and that their moral teachings do not baulk at the shadow-side of life. ... I do not believe that I am going too far when I say that modern man, in contrast to his nineteenth-century brother, turns his attention to the psyche with very great expectations; and that he does so without reference to any traditional creed, but rather in the Gnostic sense of religious experience. ... The modern man abhors dogmatic postulates taken on faith and the religions based upon them. He holds them valid only in so far as their knowledge-content seems to accord with his own experience of the deeps of psychic life.[55]

Jung could perceive several decades ago that something "previous ages have discarded" is with us once again—the Gnosis. The stone that the builders rejected becomes the cornerstone of the building; in the great economy of the spirit, rejection does not involve loss. It is thus that our humanity may justly reach in our days for a radically and cruelly rejected element of Western culture, which after years and years of persecution, underground existence, and neglect emerges into plain view once more. It could be argued, and indeed has been argued, that the need for a rediscovery of this nature has never been greater than today. It has been said ad infinitum (and at times ad nauseam) that there is a great crisis in our world today that brings all of us very close indeed to the brink of vast and unprecedented disasters. Depending on their predispositions and prejudices, different people perceive this peril from radically different directions. The menace of nuclear weapons, im-balances introduced into the ecology of nature, the overpopula-tion of the earth, the lengthening shadow of totalitarian regimes bent upon world conquest and world revolution—these factors and many more are held up as the causes of global disaster. While many of these predictions can rightfully be de-emphasized as manifestations of mankind's ever-present doomsday syn-drome, there are some elements evident in our situation which should be regarded with a degree of seriousness.

When observing the contemporary world with that attitude which the ancient Romans regarded so highly, which they called "sine ira et studio" (without hostility or interest), we find that all of the serious ills of culture seem to be related to psychological concerns, which in turn are joined to human behavior or action. It is neither politics, nor the economy, nor ecology, nor the sources of physical energy such as oil, coal, or nuclear fission that are failing us so disastrously, but our con-duct and the ethics which motivate our conduct. It is not our political acumen, our economic efficiency, or our understanding of nature that is at the back of our woes, but rather an ethical crisis, which in turn affects these areas of concern along with others. The relevance of Jung's role, as well as of the rediscovered Gnosis which he mentioned so often, can be discovered precisely in this most urgent area of ethics, or the motivation of behavior.

Beginning with Plato and Socratic philosophy, it has been a generally valid principle in Western culture that ethics are based on some form of metaphysics. The meaning of human acts and the worth of life has ever been involved in the larger question of the nature of the world and the meaning of man. Since the third and fourth centuries A.D., the metaphysical struc-ture that dominated Western culture was the belief in an an-thropomorphic, that is, man-shaped God, who acted as the one and only lawgiver and judge (as well as the policeman and execu-tioner) of the universe. Upon the law given by this deity, much of the morality of the ensuing fifteen-hundred-odd years was based. God was in his heaven and all was well with the world, as long as his commandments were adequately observed by his children, who could expect to be treated in a kindly and loving fashion by their Heavenly Father only as long as they did not displease him by disobeying. With the passage of time, this anthropomorphically ruled universe became less and less credible to the thinking elite of humanity. The first serious assault on Jehova's hegemony came from the most abstract of the physical sciences: astronomy. Kepler, Copernicus and Galileo brought forth a serious challenge to the medieval world-picture at the time of the Renaissance. Their discoveries were prevented from producing far-reaching effects by the vigilance of the Inquisition and by the inability of science to absorb them adequately; but the process of the gradual destruction of Jehova's world could only be slowed down, it could not be prevented. Thus, with the coming of Isaac Newton, a now irreparable blow was struck against the old world-image, which transformed the model of the universe from one ruled personally by a great heavenly man, to another, resembling a self-regulating and self-propelled machine. Newton established the existence of an automated universe, which neither needed nor possessed a personal directing agent. A few hundred years later, Charles Darwin came to inflict an even more serious wound on the old anthropomorphic model of reality when he demonstrated that not only the macrocosm of stars and solar systems, but the microcosm of living organisms was also self-regulating, and that living creatures needed a personal divine creator even less than celestial bodies in space. From a divinely directed cosmos, the world became an automatically directed machine; anthropomorphism was replaced by mechanomorphism.

While the venerable divine greybeard of Palestine can be safely said to have suffered some potentially deadly wounds during the seventeenth, eighteenth and nineteenth centuries, his death and burial did not occur until our very own twentieth century. Freud and the modern depth psychologists became the administering agents of what might be called the final coup-de-grace to anthropomorphism, when they convinced large numbers of persons that the soul or mind of man shows no more evidence of and demonstrates no greater need for the existence of a personal god than astronomy or biology. The history of Western thought shows that Newton banished Jehova from nature; Darwin banished him from life; Freud drove him from the last fortress, the human psyche. The Newtonian world-image displaced the theology of revelation and made room for the natural theology of the Enlightenment. Freud in turn drove out remaining vestiges of theology, preparing the way for the death-of-god theology. In the eighteenth and nineteenth centuries it was still possible for thinkers to assume that the destruction of the old-time religion would in some mysteriously illogical way leave the old-time morality untouched; that the demise of Jehova would not herald the demise of Jehova's law. The psychological revolution, which burst upon our culture with Freud's publication of his epochal book on the interpretation of dreams in the year 1900, has effectively destroyed this naive hope. Kant could still hold to the belief that "the moral law within" would give man direction, even though the personal god, author of the commandments, has been banished from the universe. Naive nineteenth-century thinkers could still say: "A man can believe the universe is blind and life aimless and yet behave as nobly and as cheerfully as any saint." After Freud such notions became less and less tenable and effective. Conscience, the categorical imperative of Kant, the inexplicable moral obligation assumed to be inherent at least in civilized humanity—all these mighty shiboleths have been unmasked by the iconoclast of Vienna as the result of conditioning imposed on the young for the convenience of their elders. As Freud explained in his noted study *Totem and Tabu*, ever since primitive times the power-elite has inculcated restrictions into the minds of the young and the powerless, which were calculated to keep them from those pleasures which the old and the mighty wished to enjoy without youthful or proletarian rivalry.

It is, of course, true that other leaders of modern psychology, notably C.G. Jung, have drawn different conclusions from the data offered by the depths and heights of the human psyche, and have been kinder to both the mythos of religion and to the rationale of morality. Yet, the Freudian rationalist argument proved more effective, and led to the virtual destruction of the remaining underpinnings of the old morality of the old-time religion.

The unshackling of consciousness in Western culture from the anthropomorphically based morality has so far proceeded fairly slowly. It has taken nearly three hundred years for a more-or-less consistent picture of the failure and defeat of the old morality to be worked out. Even today—or perhaps one should say, especially today—there are large numbers of persons who carry on elaborate crusades designed to bring this dead morality back to life. Recent history has experienced two great liberating periods when the conclusions derived from the above-noted data were freely drawn by large numbers of persons: the periods we refer to are the 1920s and the early portion of the 1930s; and the later 1960s and early 1970s.

One may observe that these periods were not only noted for their liberating influence but also for their self-indulgence and compulsive non-conformism. Such indeed is the law of the workings of the psyche; the opposites always co-exist and complement each other. As the *Sermons* rightly say: "To every blessing of God the Sun, the Devil adds his curse." The excesses accompanying progress and liberation should not rob us of the appreciation of those moments in history in which consciousness receives new opportunities for growth. Long after the fleeting intemperance and compulsive fervor of the newly unshackled minds have passed into oblivion, the enduring achievements of these historical turning points will still be apparent.

Following both of these periods of liberated consciousness were times of relative retrogression and reaction, wherein the previous gains seemed well-nigh to have vanished. The era of the flapper was succeeded in Europe by the frightful tyrannies of Nazism and Fascism, while in America the upheavals of depression and war led to the inane period of the 1950s, characterized less by neo-puritanism than by sheer unconscious trivial-mindedness. It is not unreasonable to conclude that the age of the hippie will now be followed by a period of aggressive reaction, highlighted by counter-evolutionary forces. Still, these are but temporary developments which of necessity are destined to yield to the sweep of the *Zeitgeist*. The old morality is dead while no new morality can be said to have emerged, and the agony of the culture thus continues.* Jung himself referred to our age in his work *The Undiscovered Self* as a period that the ancient

---

*For a detailed analysis of the moral crisis of our era the reader is referred to the singularly insightful and prophetic trilogy by the late Gerald Heard, *Morals Since Nineteenhundred, Pain, Sex and Time,* and *The Third Morality.* Heard named the old morality of anthropomorphic religiosity the first, the present transitory condition the second, and the forthcoming spiritualized and conscious ethical orientation the third morality.

Greeks would have called *kairos*, the right time, wherein the metamorphosis of the gods takes place. He referred to the momentous transformation in the soul of humanity at this time and pinpointed this phenomenon as a change within the unconscious of man. He then went on to say:

> As at the beginning of the Christian Era, so again today we are faced with the problem of the moral backwardness which has failed to keep pace with our scientific, technical and social developments. So much is at stake and so much depends on the psychological constitution of modern man. Is he capable of resisting the temptation to use his power for the purpose of staging a world conflagration? Is he conscious of the path he is treading, and what the conclusions are that must be drawn from the present world situation and his own psychic situation? Does he know that he is on the point of losing the life-preserving myth of the inner man which Christianity has treasured up for him? Does he realize what lies in store should this catastrophe ever befall him? Is he even capable at all of realizing this would be a catastrophe? And finally, does the individual know that *he* is the makeweight that tips the scales?
>
> Happiness and contentment, equability of soul and meaningfulness of life—these can be experienced only by the individual and not by a State, which, on the one hand, is nothing but a convention of independent individuals and, on the other, continually threatens to paralyze and suppress the individual...The social and political circumstances of the time are certainly of considerable significance, but their importance for the weal or woe of the individual has been boundlessly overestimated in so far as they are taken for the sole deciding factors. In this respect all our social goals commit the error of overlooking the psychology of the person for whom they were intended and—very often—of promoting only his illusions...
>
> I am neither spurred on by excessive optimism nor in love with high ideals, but am merely concerned with the fate of the individual human being—that infinitesimal unit on whom a world depends, and in whom, if we read the meaning of the Christian message aright, even God seeks his goal![56]

The world in this latter quarter of the twentieth century does not appear to be a particularly promising place. Life styles and mores which were heretofore accepted as normative have receded into an at least partial limbo in many lives, while the vociferous few desperately labor for their restoration. Messianic prophecies and movements abound, ranging from expectations of the return of Christ to the enthusiasm for the political advent of Marx, or the fiercely simplistic tyranny of religious fundamentalism. As always before in history, these developments appear to be primarily projections of the individual human being's need for psychic redemption and meaning. The fragmented souls of men and women cry out in agony and a great pall of collective soul-weariness blankets the land. As William Butler Yeats expressed it in his celebrated poem, "The Second Coming": "The center will not hold...the best lack all conviction, while the worst are full of passionate intensity."

Still, it appears that it would be erroneous to conclude that the progress of the spiritual history of humanity could be arrested by such passing phenomena. It is more than likely that what we are experiencing today is none other than the prolonged death-agony of the old morality combined with the birth pangs of the new. It has been noted that when caged animals are set free, often time is needed before they realize their newly recovered power. Similarly, moral emancipation takes getting used to, and the periods required for such an adjustment might extend over hundreds of years. A new life, a new morality, a new world "slouches towards Bethlehem to be born." Will it be a better world, a more worthy setting wherein the jewel of the human spirit might repose and shine with increased brilliance? What, if anything, may we do to advance such a possibility? In his own unique way Jung gave us the answer: "To the constantly reiterated question 'What can I do?' I know no other answer except 'Become what you have always been,' namely, the wholeness which we have lost in the midst of our civilized, conscious existence, a wholeness which we always were without knowing it."[57]

Today, just as in the second or third centuries, humanity's greatest need is that attainment to wholeness or fullness of being which comes to the soul in the form of Gnosis. Religious and moral fervor, faith in God or in political ideologies, advocacy of harsh law and rigid order, apocalyptic messianic enthusiasm—not only are these imperfect solutions to our problems, but in reality they are no solutions at all. As long as vast numbers of individuals expect all problems to be solved and all ills to be remedied outside themselves, they will be beset by inhumanity upon inhumanity, holocaust upon holocaust. We are not faced with a problem we can solve, but with a predicament from which we need to extricate ourselves; a predicament of *a-gnosis*, of a lack of intimate, personal and firsthand knowing of our authentic nature.

The once and future Gnosis is with us again. Men and women walk the earth who are willing to assume the burden of consciousness, and with it to take upon themselves the equally heavy burden of freedom. They are now as ever, the salt of the earth, and the leaven whereby the level of expression of the world's spirit will be altered. Jung spoke of the task of these new Gnostics, the contemporary heroes of consciousness when he wrote:

> The effect on *all* individuals, which one would like to see realized, may not set in for hundreds of years, for the spiritual transformation of mankind follows the slow tread of the centuries and cannot be hurried or held up by any rational process of reflection, let alone brought to fruition in one generation. What does lie within our reach, however, is the change in individuals who have, or create, an opportunity to influence others of like mind in their circle of acquaintance. I do not mean persuading or preaching—I am thinking, rather, of the well-known fact that anyone who has insight into his own action, and has thus found access to the unconscious, involuntarily exercises an influence on his environment. The deepening and broadening of his consciousness produce the kind of effect which the primitives call "mana." It is an unintentional influence on the unconscious of others, a sort of unconscious prestige, and its effect lasts only so long as it is not disturbed by conscious intention.[58]

Such then is the task: to become what we have always been and to gently and wisely assist others to do likewise. This is a Gnostic task, in close accord with and in direct continuation of the Gnosis of nearly two thousand years ago. The *Gospel of Truth*, inspired by Valentinus, declared centuries ago: "The day from on high has no night....Say in your heart that it is you who are this perfect day....That it is in you that this light, which does not fail dwells....Speak of the truth with those who seek it, and of the Gnosis with those who in their error have committed sins. You who are the children of the understanding heart....Joy to the man who has discovered himself, and awakened and blessed is he who openeth the minds of the blind.'' Jung, the man of the understanding heart of our age, has made the declaration again.

Laurens van der Post reported that shortly before his death, Jung had a dream. In his dream he saw ''high up on a high place'' a boulder in the full sun. Carved into it were the words: ''Take this as a sign of the wholeness you have achieved and the singleness you have become.'' Perhaps the archetypal gods thus presented the aged Gnostic, the old knower of the things that are, with a final token of their regard and affection. Many decades earlier, when he descended into the underworld and dialogued with its denizens in their own kingdom, these same archetypal gods presented him with the mysterious treatise which came to be called the *Seven Sermons to the Dead*. Veiled in hoary allegories illustrated by images and symbols of awesome power, they enshrined the seeds of the major portion of his world-transforming opus. From it, as from the boulder or the tree where the spirit of Merlin is concealed from mortal eyes, issues forth the utterance of the word of the once and future Gnosis, the cry of Merlin. To hear the cry and to heed its message is the appointed task of those who have ears to hear. The new Merlin, the twentieth century Basilides whom the world called Carl Gustav Jung, does not demand more of them, and he will accept no less.[58]

Appendix

Translator's Note

The above translation of the *Septem Sermones Ad Mortuos* was prepared from a privately printed German edition of this treatise, which was printed without copyright and without date, although presumably sometime in the early 1920s, and certainly prior to 1925.

As recounted in the Prologue of the present work, this German text was copied by hand by the author in 1949 and retained for private purposes of study in his possession.

When in 1962 Rascher Verlag in Zurich and Stuttgart published the first German edition of *Memories, Dreams, Reflections* edited by Aniela Jaffe, the same contained two separate appendices, both containing the somewhat amazing footnote, "Nur in der deutschen Ausgabe" (only in the German edition). The first appendix (p. 387) concerned the *Red Book* of Jung, and contained remarks made by Jung in and after 1959 regarding the still unpublished mysterious treatise. The last entry made by Jung in the *Red Book* and bearing the date 1959 is reproduced in this appendix. It contains, among others, his admission that he worked on the *Red Book* for sixteen years, a period of time far in excess of the one usually assumed.

The second appendix concerns the *Septem Sermones ad Mortuos* and begins with a statement by Aniela Jaffe, declaring that this writing of Jung's was printed by him privately in brochure form. The appendix then reproduced the full text of the Sermons (pp. 389-398). This text was found to be identical with the original text copied by the present writer in 1949.

The following is a summary of the publishing history of the Sermons:

First German Edition, privately printed, without date and copyright.

First English Edition, privately printed without copyright in 1925 by John M. Watkins, London. (Translated by H.G. Baynes)

Second English Edition, printed and published by Random House Inc. copyright 1961, 1962 and 1963.

Third English Edition, printed and published by Robinson & Watkins, Ltd. London, copyright 1967.

The first American edition of *Memories, Dreams and Reflections*, edited by Aniela Jaffe, translated by Richard and Clara Winston, published by Pantheon Books, New York in 1961, did not contain the text of the *Seven Sermons*, true to the statement made in the German edition.

A subsequent American edition, published by Vintage Books, (Alfred A. Knopf, Inc. and Random House, Inc.), copyright 1961, 1962, and 1963, published *The Seven Sermons* under the heading, Appendix V (pp. 378-390).

Notes

1. Jacques Lacarriere, *The Gnostics*, p. 59.
2. Hippolytus, *Philosophumena. See also* G. R. S. Mead, *Fragments of a Faith Forgotten*, p. 259.
3. H. P. Blavatsky, *The Secret Doctrine*, vol. 1 (Adyar, Madras, India: Theosophical Publishing House, 1971), pp. 91-92.
4. Friedrich Nietsche, *Thus Spake Zarathustra*, 3rd part, Chapter 11.
5. C. G. Jung, *Civilization in Transition*, vol. 10 in *Collected Works*, Bollingen Series XX, trans. R. F. C. Hull (Princeton, N.J.: Princeton University Press, 1970), para. 567.
6. ____, *Psychology and Religion: West and East*, para. 292.
7. *The Gospel of Philip*, Logion 10.
8. Hermann Hesse, *Demian* (New York: Bantam Books, 1966), p. 76.
9. Ibid., p. 78.
10. Ibid., pp. 92-93.
11. Miguel Serrano, *C. G. Jung and Hermann Hesse: A Record of Two Friendships* (New York: Shocken Books, 1966), pp. 6-7.
12. Joseph Campbell, *The Hero with a Thousand Faces* (Cleveland and New York: The World Publishing Co., 1970), p. 391.
13. Jung, *Psychological Types*, vol. 6 in *Collected Works* (1977), para. 357.
14. Wing-Tsit Chan, trans., *Source Book in Chinese Philosophy* (Princeton, N.J.: Princeton University Press, 1969), p. 166.
15. Lacarriere, *The Gnostics*, pp. 74-76.
16. Jung, *Archetypes of the Collective Unconscious*, vol. 9i in *Collected Works* (1977), para. 217.
17. Dag Hammersjold, *Markings* (New York: Alfred A. Knopf, 1964), p. 169.
18. Jung, "Transformation Symbolism in the Mass," in *The Psychology Of Religion: West and East*, para. 391.

19. _____, *Psychology and Religion: West and East*, para. 206.

20. _____, *The Practice of Psychotherapy*, para. 390.

21. _____, *Psychology and Religion: West and East*, para. 433 and 435.

22. _____, *Freud and Psychoanalysis*, vol. 4 in *Collected Works* (1970), Introduction.

23. _____, *On Psychic Energy*, vol. 8 in *Collected Works* (1981), para. 345.

24. Johann W. Goethe, *Faust*, trans. Bayard Taylor (New York: Appleton-Century 1946), Part I, Act I.

25. Jung, *Aion*, para. 24.

26. Ibid., para. 14

27. Jung, *Mysterium Coniunctionis*, para. 226.

28. _____, "Marriage as a Psychological Relationship," in *The Development of Personality*, vol. 17 in *Collected Works* (1954), para. 338.

29. Johann W. Goethe, *Faust*, trans. Louis Macneice (New York: Oxford University Press, 1951), Part II, Concluding stanza.

30. *The Gospel According to Thomas*, Logion 45.

31. Jung, *Alchemical Studies*, vol. 13 in Collected Works (1976), para. 40.

32. _____, *The Psychology of the Transference*, vol. 16 in Collected Works (1954), pp. 54-55.

33. Miguel Serrano, *The Serpent of Paradise* (London: Rider & Co., 1963), p. 15.

34. Ibid., p. 17.

35. *The Gospel According to Thomas*, Logion 79.

36. Jung, *Psychology of Transference*, pp. 24-25.

37. _____, *Psychology and Alchemy*, para. 245.

38. _____, *The Undiscovered Self* (New York: Mentor Books, 1957), p. 23.

39. Aniela Jaffé, *From the Life and Work of C. G. Jung*, trans. R. F. C. Hull (New York: Harper & Row, 1971), p. 20.

40. Ibid., pp. 37-38.

41. Wolfgang Pauli, "Naturwissenschaftliche und erkenntnis-theoretische Aspekte der Ideen vom Unbewussten," *Dialectica* (vol. VI, 1950), pp. 300-1.

42. Jung, *Aion*, para. 412.

43. See Jung, "On the Nature of the Psyche," *The Structure and Dynamics of the Psyche*, vol. 8 in *Collected Works* (1981), para. 418.

44. Jung, "The Relativity of the Idea of God in Meister Eckhart," *Psychological Types*, Chapter V, 4 (b).

45. _____, "Spiritual Problems of the Present," *Contributions to Analytical Psychology* (London: Beilliere, Tindall & Cox, 1920), p. 400.

46. Jaffé, *Life and Work of Jung*, p. 104.

47. Ibid., p. 104.

48. Jung, *Aion*, para. 253.

49. Original verse by the author, inspired by a sonnet by Frederick Baron Corvo.

50. As quoted in Marie-Louise Von Franz, *C. G. Jung: His Myth in Our Time*, p. 276.

51. Ibid., p. 281.

52. Jung, *Memories, Dreams, Reflections*, pp. 225-26.

53. Ibid., pp. 228 and 216.

54. Laurens Van der Post, *Jung and the Story of Our Time*, p. 4.

55. Jung, *Modern Man in Search of a Soul* (New York: Harcourt, Brace & World, 1960), pp. 238-39.

56. Jung, *Undiscovered Self*, pp. 123-25.

57. ____, *Civilization in Transition*, para. 722.

58. ____, Undiscovered Self, pp. 120-21.

Quintessential Gnostic Glossary

Abraxas (barbarous word) Name given by Basilides and after him by other Gnostics to a mythological figure associated with the union of the opposites.

Achamoth (Heb.) Sophia in her lower, or inadequate form.

Anthropos (Gr.) The Man. A heavenly prototype of humanity, created by true divinity.

Archon (Gr.) Ruler. An inferior cosmic being ruling over and imposing limitations on the human soul.

Barbarous words. Words not originating in any known language, usually consisting of vowels and frequently used in Gnostic scriptures as formulae of power.

Barbelo (Heb.) A representation of the Divine Feminine in her perfect aspect.

Carpocratian. Follower of Carpocrates. This school is associated by most authors with the concept of reincarnation and with strongly libertarian tendencies.

Demiurge. (Gr.) The fashioner of the lower world; himself of limited intelligence and imperfect.

Gospel (*Evaggelion*; Gr.) In Gnostic usage any scripture designed to advance the enlightenment, or Gnosis, of humanity.

Gnosis (Gr.) Spiritual knowledge, arrived at intuitively.

Ialdabaoth (barbarous word). One of the names of the Demiurge.

Kabbalah (Heb.) The once secret tradition of Judaism. Often called Jewish Gnosticism.

Logos (Gr.) The Word of the most high God. Often equated with Jesus.

Mandaeans (Aram.) The only indisputably direct successors of the Gnostics, still surviving in the Middle East.

Manichaeism (Per.) The Gnostic system first taught by Mani of Persia, and having survived until the twentieth century.

Norea (Heb.) Wife of Noah, mentioned in Gnostic scriptures.

Nous (Gr.) Platonic term for the higher mind; in Gnostic usage the first conscious emanation of the Supreme Deity.

Ogdoad (Gr.) The sacred eightfold principle, usually denoting the transcendence of the seven planetary spheres.

Ophite (Gr.) Gnostic school connected with the symbol of the divine serpent.

Pistis (Gr.) Faith, and Faithful. A quality of spiritual trust, often attributed to Sophia, who is called *Pistis Sophia*.

Saclas (Aram.) The fool. One of the names of the Demiurge.

Simonian (Heb.) The school attached to the figure of Simon Magus, according to tradition the first Gnostic teacher in history.

Sophia (Gr.) Wisdom. The name of the feminine principle involved in the manifestation and life of the cosmos and of man. She is the helper and inspirer of all Gnosis.

Valentinian (Lat.) The school of Gnostics attached to Valentinus. Known as the most Christian of all Gnostic schools.

Selected Bibliography

Primary Sources on Gnosticism

Foerster, Werner, ed. *Gnosis, a Selection of Gnostic Texts.* Translated by R. McL. Wilson. Oxford: Clarendon Press, vol. 1, 1972; vol. II, 1974.

Greenlees, Duncan, ed. *The Gospel of the Gnostics*, vol. 13, The World Gospel Series. Adyar, Madras, India: Theosophical Publishing House, 1958.

____. *The Gospel of the Prophet Mani*, vol. 12, The World Gospel Series. Adyar, Madras, India: Theosophical Publishing House, 1956.

Grant, R. M., ed. *Gnosticism, a Sourcebook of Heretical Writings.* New York: Harper & Row, 1961.

Mead, G. R. S., *Fragments of a Faith Forgotten.* New Hyde Park, N.Y.: University Books, n.d.

____. *Pistis Sophia: A Gnostic Miscellany.* Blauvelt, N.Y.: Multimedia Publishing Co., 1973.

Robinson, James M., ed. *The Nag Hammadi Library in English.* San Francisco: Harper & Row, 1977.

Studies of Gnosticism

Dart, John. *The Laughing Savior, the Discovery and Significance of the Nag Hammadi Gnostic Library.* New York: Harper & Row, 1976.

Jonas, Hans. *The Gnostic Religion, the Message of the Alien God and the Beginnings of Christianity.* Boston: Beacon Press, 1958.

Lacarriere, Jacques. *The Gnostics.* New York: E. P. Dutton, 1977.

Pagels, Elaine. *The Gnostic Gospels.* New York: Random House, 1979.

Quispel, Gilles. *Gnosis as Weltreligion: die Bedeutung de Gnosis in der Antike.* Zurich: Origo Verlag, 1972.

Studies in Christian Origins Related to Gnosticism

Kuhn, Alvin Boyd, *A Rebirth for Christianity*. Wheaton: Theosophical Publishing House, 1970.

Pfeiffer, Charles F. *The Dead Sea Scrolls and the Bible*. New York: Weathervane Books, 1969.

Smith Morton. *The Secret Gospel, the Discovery and Interpretation of the Secret Gospel According to Mark*. New York: Harper & Row, 1973.

Yadin, Yigael. *The Message of the Scrolls*. New York: Simon and Schuster, 1957.

Biographical and Autobiographical Works on C. G. Jung

Brome, Vincent. *Jung*. New York: Atheneum, 1978.

Hannah, Barbara. *Jung, His Life and Work, a Biographical Memoir*. New York: G. P. Putnam's Sons, 1976.

Jung, C. G. *Memories, Dreams, Reflections*. Edited by Aniela Jaffé. New York: Pantheon, 1961.

Van der Post, Laurens. *Jung and the Story of Our Time*. New York: Pantheon, 1975.

Von Franz, Marie-Louise. *C. G. Jung: His Myth in Our Time*. New York: G. P. Putnam's Sons, for the C. G. Jung Foundation for Analytical Psychology, 1975.

Works of C. G. Jung Dealing with Gnosticism

Gnostic interest runs through all of Jung's numerous writings. The following are some of the most important in this regard:

Jung, C. G. *Collected Works*, Bollingen Series XX. Translated by R. F. C. Hull. Princeton, N.J.: Princeton University Press.
Aion, vol. 9ii, 1970.
Mysterium Coniunctionis, vol. 14, 1970.
Psychology and Alchemy, vol. 12, 1968.
Psychology and Religion: West and East, vol 11, 1969.
The Symbolic Life, vol. 18, 1976.
Symbols of Transformation, vol. 5, 1967.

Index

More Quest books about Jungian psychology

And a Time to Die - *Mark Pelgrin*
  One man's search for a meaning to his life and to his
  approaching death.

The Choicemaker - *Dr. Elizabeth Howes and Dr. Sheila
Moon*
  Man was created for the purpose of making choices.
  A book about Jung, Jesus, and how to attain a
  "wholeness of being."

Storming Eastern Temples - *Dr. Lucindi Mooney*
  About Jungian psychology, Hinduism, the American
  Indian, and their many correspondences.

Available from:
The Theosophical Publishing House
306 West Geneva Road, Wheaton, Illinois
60187